The Secretary stated [that] [the] [la]undry woman at Bar[net] [h]ad left when he was [requested] [t]o procure another.

Miss Burdett Coutts having [k]indly offered to pay the passage [m]oney of Sixteen boys to Nova [S]cotia Resolved that the offer be [a]ccepted and that proper outfits [be] procured for the boys.

The following ~~candidates~~ cases [f]or admission into the Refuges [w]ere enquired into and ordered [to] be received viz Boys George [E]dwards Richard North John [S]mith Charles Gee Thomas Turner [W]illiam Ryan William Roberts [J]ohn Henry Priest Benjamin [E]dwards William Morden William [B]aker William Thomas Edward [P]oole John Holmes

Girls . Elizabeth Knight Sarah [T]redwell Martha Bunn

The Chance of a Lifetime

The Chance of a Lifetime

The Story of

The Shaftesbury Homes and Arethusa

by
Marion Bailey

Dianthus Publishing

This book is dedicated to

the children and young people

– past and present –

of the Shaftesbury Homes and Arethusa

Published by Dianthus Publishing Limited
The Pool House, Kemble, Cirencester, England. GL7 6AD
Tel: +44 (0)1285 770 239. Fax: +44 (0)1285 770 896

ISBN 0-946604-11-8

CONTENTS

My thanks are due to:

The Shaftesbury Homes and Arethusa's Head Office staff for their kindness and encouragement; the men and women who as children were helped by the Society and in their turn shared their memories with me; David Corcos for research and help, particularly with information about the ships; my family and friends for their help and support; Esher District Local History Society for information about Esher Place; and Twickenham Library for information about Fortescue House.

W hen I became President of the Shaftesbury Homes and Arethusa in 1987 I was
delighted to have the opportunity of supporting
the Society to which my philanthropic great-
great-grandfather Lord Shaftesbury devoted so
much of his life and a cause which, for over a
hundred and fifty years, has done so much to
improve the lives of a great many truly disadvantaged children and young people.

It was William Williams' experience during
his railway journey to the West Country which
compelled him to establish one of the very first
ragged schools and it was when Lord
Shaftesbury, as a boy at Harrow School, witnessed the rowdy antics at a pauper's funeral that
his eyes were opened to the appalling plight of
the poor and deprived classes of the day. The
two men became firm friends and their combined efforts to give deprived children a better

The Countess Mountbatten of Burma CBE, CD, JP, DL,
President of The Shaftesbury Homes and Arethusa

chance in life resulted in one of the largest and most effective children's charities of the day.

The Shaftesbury Homes and Arethusa has a glorious and fascinating history which has
been admirably recorded by Marion Bailey in this very interesting and entertaining book. But
the Society does not dwell on its history and, in taking due account of the traditional values
and standards encouraged in the past, it has courageously set itself on course to tackle the
problems of young people today in a thoroughly modern and relevant manner.

The present work of the Shaftesbury Homes and Arethusa is just as important as it was all
those years ago when William Williams started his ragged school in a hayloft over a cowshed
in one of the poorest districts of London. Although now very different in character with its
registered homes for children and young people in care, its houses for the young homeless in
London and Suffolk, its Arethusa Venture Centre near Rochester and the Arethusa Sail
Training Vessel, the Society provides a stable and secure upbringing to a great many disadvantaged young people and, above all, it gives them a sense of belonging and a wide variety
of opportunities which will help them grow up into happy and responsible citizens. I com-
mend the work of the Shaftesbury Homes and Arethusa to readers of this excellent book and
I hope that the example of unselfish dedication to underprivileged children and young people which has been handed down through the ages will continue to guide the Society long
into the future.

Mountbatten of Burma

Chapter 1
SETTING THE SCENE

In 1843 a young solicitor's clerk, William Williams, witnessed the miseries of children condemned through poverty to live as the dregs of society. He was determined to help them. With a few friends he formed a Society to open a school in the notorious St. Giles district of London hoping that, with a basic education, the poor children might have a chance to earn a decent living.

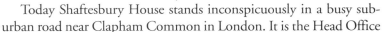

In the face of many difficulties and much hostility, the School was a success. William Williams and his friends persuaded others to help them; they raised enough money to open more schools and to build homes for those of their pupils who would otherwise have to live on the streets. By the time Williams retired in 1890, more than 13,000 children had been given a start in life that would otherwise have been denied them.

Many thousands of men and women living in this country and abroad have benefited from their time in the care of the Society which William Williams founded. Their many letters bear witness to the love and care they received – as well as the hard times they remember all too well.

William Williams
Founder and Secretary
1843-1891

Today Shaftesbury House stands inconspicuously in a busy suburban road near Clapham Common in London. It is the Head Office of The Shaftesbury Homes and Arethusa, a charity dedicated to helping children in need. Stored within Shaftesbury House is a collection of documents from the earliest years of the Society to the present day. Together they unfold the story of how the vision of William Williams for a better life for the poor and destitute grew into an organization which, after more than 150 years, still works with children and young people in need to help them develop their true potential as responsible men and women.

Early in the reign of Queen Victoria, not far from the fashionable West End of London, was the locality known as The Rookery in the parish of St. Giles-in-the-Fields. Although not many miles from the present Head Office, it was a world away in environment and atmosphere. Thronged with noisy, scavenging people, it bred disease, crime and despair. A contemporary account described the area and its inhabitants.

Shaftesbury House, Clapham,
Head Office of the Society since 1975

"The Rookery of St. Giles was long notorious for its filth and fever; its dreadful riots and immoral revels ..old rickety, misshapen, and most dirty dwellings.. crowded to suffocation with.. prizefighters, crossing-sweepers, beggars, costermongers, prostitutes, and thieves. Every room was full of such persons; every street teemed with them ..There swore, fought, drank, and died some of the vilest men and women known to the police." [1]

What hope was there for children in these circumstances?

"Their earliest looks fell upon scenes of violence, debauchery, and crime. Their fathers were profane and lawless; their mothers unchaste, drunken, and cruel; their playmates, boys and girls profoundly versed in vice. To such children life dawned without visions of moral beauty and life-worth. Born in the midst of dunghills, dirty streets, and homes reeking with filth, they knew nothing of cleanliness and order. Habituated to the companionship of cadgers, prostitutes, drunkards, and thieves, they grew wise in all the arts of the profligate and criminal."

The Rookery, St. Giles

An article, published in *The Quarterly Review*[2] gives more details about the locality where many of these children lived. The author was Lord Ashley, later to become the 7th Earl of Shaftesbury, who worked unstintingly for William Williams' Society almost from its foundation. Lord Ashley had visited many such areas to gain first-hand knowledge of life in the slums.

"Visit these regions in the summer, and you are overwhelmed by the exhalations; visit them in winter, and you are shocked by the spectacle of hundreds shivering in apparel that would be scanty in the tropics; many are all but naked; those that are clothed are grotesque."[3]

These districts were totally unfit for habitation, with:

".. alleys terminating in a cul-de-sac, long and narrow like a tobacco-pipe, where air and sunshine were never known. On one side rose walls several feet in height, blackened with damp and slime; on the other side stood the dwellings still more revolting, while the breadth

(1) The *Ragged School Union Magazine*, vol.1, 1849 *The St. Giles' Rookery and its Ragged Schools.*

(2) *The Quarterly Review* - Dec. 1846 - *The 2nd Annual Report of the Ragged School Union, established for the support of schools for the Destitute Poor.* London, 9th June 1846.

(3) Hodder, Vol. 2, p.161 and p.165

Lord Ashley (later 7th Earl of Shaftesbury) – elected MP for Woodstock in 1826

of the wet and bestrewed passage would by no means allow us the full expansion of our arms."

He wanted to enter one of the buildings but could not, because he found the smell more than he could stomach. The streets of the area were as filthy as the houses and the drains were foul:

"Flowing before each hovel, and within a few feet of it, a broad, black, uncovered drain, exhaling at every point the most unwholesome vapours. If there be not a drain, there is a stagnant pool: touch either with your stick; and the mephitic mass will yield up its poisonous gas like the coruscations of soda-water."

Inside the houses conditions were no better:

"The interior of the dwellings is in strict keeping: the smaller space of the apartments increasing of course the evils that prevail without – damp, darkness, dirt and foul air. Many are wholly destitute of furniture; many contain nothing except a table and a chair; some few have a common bed for all ages and both sexes; but a large proportion of the denizens of those regions lie on a heap of rags more nasty than the floor itself. Happy is the family that can boast of a single room to itself, and in that room a dry corner."

The children living in these conditions faced a bleak present and a bleaker future. Many roamed the streets:

"Everyone who walks the streets of the metropolis must daily observe several members of the tribe – bold and pert, and dirty as London sparrows, but pale, feeble, and sadly inferior to them in plumpness of outline. .. Squalid and half-naked groups, squat at the entrances of the narrow, foetid courts and alleys that lie concealed behind the deceptive frontages of our larger thoroughfares."

To those who knew only a reasonable standard of living, these children appeared savage and almost subhuman:

"Their matted hair, the disgusting filth that renders necessary a closer inspection before the flesh can be discerned between the rags which hang about it; and the barbarian freedom from all superintendence and restraint, fill the mind .. with perplexity and dismay."

A typical slum in the St. Giles area, 1897

Lord Ashley knew that 'few of our upper ranks have much practical knowledge of any class greatly removed from their own'. Many people, living in comfortable surroundings, did not even realise such people existed. To those who did, the Rookery and other similar places, must have seemed like fires raging beyond control – best left alone.

It was here in St. Giles in a hayloft, over a cowshed in Streatham Street that William Williams' first School offered the local children enough education to escape from a cycle of poverty and misery. From that School grew the Society which today is known as the Shaftesbury Homes and Arethusa.

From a picture of a destitute child, by Charles Compton RA

Contemporary drawing of an early Ragged School

Chapter 2
WILLIAM WILLIAMS AND HIS RAGGED SCHOOL

Before Williams' School and others like it, children such as those described in the previous chapter received little or no education. Although schools did exist which catered for poor children, none of them were suitable for the poorest of all, such as The Rookery dwellers. A national system of compulsory education available to all was many years distant and families which had to survive by begging were unlikely to appreciate the long term benefits of education. Parents who trained their children to beg so as to increase the family income would not want time wasted by schooling. It was almost impossible to persuade them even to send their children to the Sunday schools available at some local churches because they were likely to get more by begging on a Sunday than on any other day in the week since more people were out and about.

To remedy situations such as this, in towns and cities all over Britain, people with a social conscience started schools to cater for children for whom no other schooling was available. They taught those whose parents could not or would not afford the fees, however small, of other schools for working class children. The ragged schools, as these new schools were called, catered for those who did not have enough, or even any, suitable clothes for other schools. Boys and girls with no family or friends to care for them were warmly welcomed.

The teachers initially worked unpaid in their spare time. The schools were usually in the heart of slum areas and housed in cheaply rented and dilapidated buildings. Finances apart, anything more grandiose would have intimidated any prospective pupils. Education was of a severely practical kind with an emphasis on order, cleanliness and discipline. The curriculum was basic with religious instruction and the three Rs, together with practical subjects which would help pupils to find employment.

Many ragged schools started as a result of parish work or through the religious convictions of the teachers. In London many such teachers belonged to the London City Mission, an organization established by three friends in May 1835. Through the work of the London

Extract from William Williams' Day Book, August 1845

City Mission five ragged schools were established by 1840 in London and more were set up in the next few years. *The Times* in February 1843 carried an advertisement for one of them:

"Field Lane Sabbath School,

65 West Street, Saffron Hill.

The teachers are desirous of laying before the public a few facts connected with this school .. It was opened in 1841 for instructing, free of expense, those who from their poverty or ragged condition, are prevented from attending any place of religious instruction. The school is under the superintendence of the District Missionary of the London City Mission and is opened on Sundays and also on Thursday evening, when the average attendance is 70 (adults and children) .. Any lady or gentleman willing to assist as teachers will be cordially welcomed."[4]

Field Lane School was in an area noted for its violence and lawlessness:

"Disturbances which occurred here were of so desperate a character, that from 40 to 50 constables would be marched down with cutlasses, it being frequently impossible for officers to act in fewer numbers or unarmed."[5]

Charles Dickens visited the School in its early days. He found:

".. a low-roofed den, in a sickening atmosphere, in the midst of taint, and dirt and pestilence. .. the teachers knew little of their office; the pupils, with an evil sharpness, found them out, got the better of them, derided them, made blasphemous answers to Scriptural questions, sang, fought, danced, robbed each other .. the place was stormed and carried over and over again; the lights were blown out, the books strewn in the gutters, and the female scholars carried off triumphantly to their old wickedness." [6]

The school survived, however, in spite of its apparent weakness. Gradually it changed for the better. Commenting on a visit two years later, Dickens 'found it quiet and orderly, full, lighted with gas, well whitewashed, numerously attended and thoroughly established'.

A few weeks after the advertisement for the Field Lane School appeared in *The Times* the St Giles's Ragged School was established. Little is known for certain about the childhood of William Williams, the founder of the school. His family origins are obscure and details of his private life have become veiled by time. No biographer has written his life story and he left no personal memoirs. The stories of the thousands of children he helped, the words of his colleagues and friends and the Society's records provide the key to understanding the nature of the man.

He was born on 22nd September 1818, in the parish of St. Clement Danes in the Strand. His portrait shows a clear-eyed, kindly man, small and pigeon-chested with his shoulders incongruously close to his ears. This was the result of an accident when he was five years old.

The story of how it happened and the consequences was often told to the Society's children. He was playing in the street outside his home near the Strand, in London, with a group of friends when a cart loaded high with timber approached.

One of the boys leapt on the cart and scrambled as fast as he could to the topmost logs. Another followed him, then another and another. Soon the gang was leaping on and off the cart, dancing from one log to the next. The driver's attention was on his horses as they clattered and slipped over the cobbles. Suddenly, from the other side of the road a passer-by gave

(4) Quoted in *Lord Shaftesbury and Social-Industrial Progress*, by J. Wesley Bready, Chap. XII
(5) R.W. Vanderkiste, *Notes and Narratives of a Six-Years' Mission, Principally Among the Dens of London*. London, Nisbet 1854
(6) Hodder, Vol. 1, p.485

a roar of disapproval, to warn the boys of the danger of their game.

The driver looked back to see what had caused the shout – he gave a yell, and in a panic, the boys began to jump off the cart, but the load was unstable and the noise was agitating the horses. In the scramble which followed young William slipped, lost his footing and fell to the ground. He lay still, unable to move. He was carried home and his Mother called a doctor who diagnosed a broken spine.

Luckily, in spite of the doctor's worst fears, he recovered his health. He grew up small and slight; his Mother, believing he was delicate, did not expect him to survive to adult life but he never allowed the physical weakness resulting from his accident to interfere with his ambitions. At school he was quick to learn and made good progress. When the time came for him to leave, he found a job as a junior clerk in a solicitor's office where he was put in the care of a man who soon became his close personal friend.

This man (whose name was probably Morison – although we cannot know for certain) was deeply religious, and he belonged to a group of men working in their spare time among the poor of the district around St. Giles. Mr. Morison was very distressed that his new young clerk, who came from a secure and loving home, had never been baptised. His Christian concern for others made a lasting impression on William Williams and consequently on 13th May 1841, in the Parish Church of St. Clement Danes, he was baptised by John Owen, the local Curate.

Mr. Morison introduced Williams to his friends and soon he too was working as a Sunday School teacher in the district and helping with the working men's groups and other enterprises with which the friends were involved. All this was just as important to him as his job in the solicitor's office. The poor Rookery dwellers became part of his life.

A chance encounter, when he was still in his early twenties, started him on the course which led to the founding of the school for the Rookery children. He was travelling by train from Paddington to the West Country when he heard violent yelling and sounds of fighting in a carriage nearby. On going to investigate, he came across a group of young boys, starved, cold, dirty and miserable, chained together and destined for shipping to Australia as convicts.

Williams knew the cause of their plight was poverty which had led them to crime. He felt helpless in the face of such injustice and could hardly bear to think of the life that lay in store for them. By night and day, asleep or awake, the frightened faces of those convict boys were ever with him. He told his friends what he had seen. Again and again he described the incident. How could they help to prevent such tragedies recurring? They all knew from their work in St. Giles how easy it was for children to slip into a life of crime. The boys on the train were beyond their help but perhaps they could prevent others from suffering the same hardships. By starting a ragged school of their own, they might help other children lead a decent life and work for a secure future.

William Williams and his friends decided that they could afford to rent a cheap local room so they searched the neighbourhood until they found suitable accommodation in one of the back streets. It was a large dingy hayloft above a cowshed in the parish of St. Giles; far from luxury – but at least it was cheap and immediately available. The school building was not in an ideal environment:

"It presented no attractions to the sentimental and romantic. The school-house was a rude structure – infamous resorts stood before it – a large noxious yard extended behind it – and filth, noise, and crime were round about it."[7]

The group of friends cleaned the room, obtained a few benches, Bibles, spelling books and other essentials to start the School. The room could accommodate up to 150 and about 118 children were regularly attending by the time the School had been open for six months.

Williams organized his friends into a Committee to manage the School. The Committee's first Secretary was Mr. Morison; William Williams was the Superintendent of the Sunday School and became the Secretary of the Committee soon afterwards when Mr. Morison relinquished the post. At first they could afford only to open the School on Sundays. During the day it was for children and in the evening classes were held for adults. The first Annual Report of the School has not survived in its entirety but an extract, reprinted many years later, informed the public that:

"some benevolent persons among the working classes have united in opening a Sunday School in St. Giles's for ragged children. There are 23 teachers engaged in the School all of whom belong to the working class of the population."[8]

Of the first pupils:

"Fourteen are the children of costermongers, eight of persons who sweep crossings in the streets, and eleven of street-singers and beggars: fourteen of the children sell water-cresses, fourteen are without fathers or have been deserted; and the remainder chiefly get their living by selling fruit. The rest are children of common labourers, or persons of low character. Many of the children are obliged by selling water-cresses and other articles in the streets, to earn their breakfast before they can come to School".

One boy was singled out for special mention as being typical of many:

"A lad 14 years of age came to the School; he has neither father nor mother, and gets his living by holding horses and picking up garbage in the markets. He had no shirt, and nothing to cover him but a pair of tattered canvas trousers, and a piece of an old sack thrown over his shoulders."

A teacher visited the home of one of the girl pupils. Her father sold bones on the streets around the Rookery:

"Not an article of furniture was to be seen in the room, which evidently had not been swept for weeks; a heap of filthy straw in one corner served for a bed, an old herring barrel turned upside down for a table, an old saucepan, bottom upwards, was the seat of the mother, and a bag half full of old bones served as a seat for the father. These with a few articles of broken crockery, constituted the whole of their worldly goods."

The 23 voluntary teachers had a hard task before them working in the shabby schoolroom. Their pupils were quite ignorant of the very basics of civilised behaviour. Many times the police were called in to restore order and many times the school was ransacked and vandalised. The teachers toiled on in spite of set-backs and derision and gradually they noted improvements. Some of their pupils were helped to a better way of life and found jobs. This

(7) *The St. Giles' Rookery and its Ragged Schools.* Article in the *Ragged School Union Magazine,* 1849
(8) *The Ragged School Union Magazine,* Vol.1. 1849. *The St. Giles' Rookery and its Ragged Schools.* A facsimile of the first page was published in the *Logbook Magazine* of the National Refuges.

encouraged others to attend and persevere in their efforts.

By the end of 1844 much of the Rookery was demolished as part of a new building scheme for the area. The Committee at first was afraid that it would have fewer pupils as a result but:

"The former inhabitants of the Rookery have been scattered about the surrounding neighbourhoods of Drury Lane, Seven Dials, Short's Gardens etc., so that although a considerable number of the original scholars have left the School, a great influx of new ones have come .. indeed many applications for admission have been rejected, for want of a sufficient number of teachers to instruct them."

From the very beginning, as the teachers struggled to cope with their difficult pupils, they were supported by the firm belief that they were doing God's work.

"..while the Committee and teachers feel greatly encouraged in this good work and labour of love they humbly acknowledge the finger of God in all they do. It is not us, but God by us."

Chapter 3
LORD ASHLEY – SUPPORTER AND FRIEND

The difficulties facing St. Giles' School were not unique. Teachers in other ragged schools of London shared the same problems. Another solicitor's clerk, Mr. S. R. Starey, who like William Williams gave much of his time to the care and upbringing of ragged children, felt that more could be achieved by co-operation than by individual and isolated effort. Accordingly, in April 1844, he called a meeting for men and women working in the London ragged schools which was held at his rooms in Ampton Street, Gray's Inn Road.

Of the three who arrived for this gathering, Mr. Locke was a woollen-draper, Mr. Moulton was a second hand tools dealer and the third was a London City Missionary. Their experience was wide, but their influence was minimal. They each had to earn their living, so all their efforts for the local children were in their spare time. At the end of the meeting they passed a resolution:

"To give permanence, regularity, and vigour to existing Ragged Schools, and to promote the formation of new ones throughout the Metropolis, it is advisable to call a meeting of superintendents, teachers, and others interested in these schools, for this purpose."[9]

The four men energetically publicised the event. They urged their colleagues to come; they persuaded their friends and acquaintances. Within a month they held another meeting, this time in St. Giles' School. On this occasion about 40 teachers, school superintendents and other missionaries were present who between them represented 16 different schools. It was decided to set up a group which would help them all. In July 1844 they formally established the new organization which they called the Ragged School Union (RSU). The aims were to help the formation of new ragged schools, encourage established ones and to spread the work to other areas of the Country. The members of the organization would share their expertise on any subject to do with the running of the schools, and the Committee would raise funds to supplement the income of individual schools where necessary. Each school in the new Union would maintain its independence and have its own organizing committee.

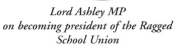

Lord Ashley MP
on becoming president of the Ragged
School Union

In the autumn of 1844 the Committee of the RSU asked the Rt. Hon. Lord Ashley MP to become its first President. Coming from a prominent family, with valuable connections, he was already well known for his work for the poor of inner cities. As a Member of

(9) C.J. Montague *Sixty Years in Waifdom*, 1904, p.167.

Parliament with government experience he had involved himself closely with attempts at social reform. From personal experience he understood what was involved in making changes and persuading people that change was necessary. He knew people with influence and power. He was the ideal person for the task.

What was even more important for the ragged school workers and their pupils was that he understood, from bitter personal experience, the effects of an unhappy and deprived childhood and he had practical knowledge of the lives of the destitute in inner cities.

He was born Anthony Ashley-Cooper at 24 Grosvenor Square on 28th April 1801, the fourth child and eldest son of nine children. His father, Cropley Ashley-Cooper, 6th Earl of Shaftesbury was an able statesman and a man of authority. He was widely acclaimed for his competence and honesty. His success in public affairs however was not reflected in a peaceful family life. His children saw little of their father and, when in his presence, they were frozen by his icy manner.

His wife, before her marriage, was Lady Anne Spencer, daughter of the fourth Duke of Marlborough. She had little interest in her children, being concerned mainly with fashionable people and the pleasures of high society. Lord Ashley, from his earliest childhood, felt unwanted by both his parents.

He started keeping a personal diary at the age of 24 and continued it throughout his long career, first as Lord Ashley and subsequently, on the death of his father, as the 7th Earl of Shaftesbury. In this diary he recorded events, meetings and decisions as well as his feelings, hopes and ambitions. "What a dreadful person our mother is!" he wrote in 1825, "Her whole pleasure is in finding fault."[10] About his father he wrote:

"As to friendship and affection between him and me, years of experience had sufficiently proved that outward civility and only civility is the utmost that can be looked for."[11]

Numerous accounts of his life have been written. Edwin Hodder, whose *Life and Work of the Seventh Earl of Shaftesbury, KG* (published in 1887), was the biographer to whom Lord Shaftesbury revealed many personal details. Hodder wrote:

"He placed at my disposal a mass of material, and .. was good enough to allow me for many months to be in frequent personal communication with him, when, pen in hand, I took down the record of his life as he narrated it. His memory to the very last was surprising, and as the scenes of his earlier life passed before him, he would recall facts and figures, dates and words with such accuracy, that although at his request I subsequently verified them, it was almost unnecessary to do so."[12]

Ashley's parents were frequently away from home for long periods and left their children, often cold and hungry, in the care of servants. The Sixth Earl was a firm believer in discipline. "I and my sisters," wrote Lord Shaftesbury in a note to Edwin Hodder "all three of them older than myself, were brought up with great severity, moral and physical, in respect of both mind and body; the opinion of our parents being that, to render a child obedient, it should be in a constant fear of its Father and Mother".[13]

One kind person helped Ashley in his early childhood; in later life he often referred to her as his best and closest friend. Her name was Anna Maria Millis. At Blenheim she had been

(10) The National Register of Archives, London, Shaftesbury (Broadlands) MSS SHA/PD/1, 18-23 Sept. 1825.
(11)Ibid. SHA/PD/1, 16 Nov. 1825.
(12) Hodder, Vol.1, Preface p.V.
(13)Hodder, Vol.1, p.51

St. Giles House, Dorset, hereditary seat of the Ashley family

the maid of his Mother who retained her in her new household when she married. She acted as Ashley's nurse, confidante and first teacher. The love, affection and closeness that he lacked from his parents he gained from her. Although not an educated woman she had the power of directness and conviction. She read him Bible stories, spoke to him about God and the Church and taught him how to pray.

In his adult life, when he was tired, worried or anxious he often used a special prayer of hers. We do not know the words, but he once remarked that the memory of his old nurse and that particular prayer never failed to comfort him. Ashley never forgot her, and never forgot the lessons she taught him. Towards the end of his life he wrote:

"She was an affectionate, pious woman. She taught me many things, directing my thoughts to highest subjects; and I can even now call to my mind many sentences of prayer she made me repeat at her knees. To her, I trace under God, my first impressions."[14]

On his eighth birthday when he was already away at school, Maria Millis sent him a poem she had written especially for him signed `from your affectionate friend A.M.M.' It wished him well on this earth and in the next. Shortly after this she died and in her will she left him her watch and seal. He wore this and no other to the end of his days saying that it was the gift of his best and first friend.

Ashley was sent, at the age of seven, to Manor House School in Chiswick. If he had looked forward to going there as a relief from the icy indifference of his parents, Ashley's disappointment must have been severe. He could never forget his time at that School:

"Nothing could have surpassed it for filth, bullying, neglect and hard treatment of every sort; nor had it in any respect any one compensating advantage, except, perhaps, it may have given me an early horror of oppression and cruelty."[15]

He stayed at Manor House for five years. His life greatly improved when he was sent from there at the age of twelve to Harrow and lived with other pupils in the house of Dr. Butler, the Headmaster. He made friends and revelled in his deliverance from his previous school in which civilised behaviour and the love of learning were notable only for their absence.

While he was at Harrow, aged about 14 or 15, he witnessed an incident which determined the course of his life. When he was an old man he told a friend, the son of his former Headmaster, that it was on the very day this incident occurred that he decided what his life's work would be.

(14) Hodder, Vol.1, pp 50-51.
(15) Hodder, Vol.1, p.51

He was walking down Harrow Hill, during time free from lessons, when he heard yelling, scuffling and loud laughter in a side-street. Strident celebrations were in progress. A throng of down-and-outs, all weaving unsteadily to and fro, singing and dancing, was making its way down the street. Ashley, nervous and uncomfortable, stayed rooted to the spot shrinking away from the rowdy scene. As he waited for the party to pass, his nervousness turned to disgust as he realised that this was no ordinary party. It was a funeral.

The link with Harrow School continues: Harrow boys formed the choir at the Society's 150th Anniversary Thanksgiving Service attended by The Queen Mother at St. Giles-in-the-Fields in February 1993

A cheap, roughly made coffin was being hauled unceremoniously to the cemetery by a drunken band. As the mourners hiccoughed and belched on their way, one of the coffin bearers tripped, lost his balance and staggered forward. The whole group stumbled one against the other, falling like dominoes. The coffin slipped from their shoulders, the lid fell off and the corpse tumbled out onto the ground. The hilarity of the mourners left poor Ashley feeling sick with shame.

The ideals he had learned from Maria Millis came immediately to his mind and he contrasted them most painfully with the degradation he had just witnessed. He instantly resolved that, when he was an adult, he would devote all his energies to helping the poorest and most despised of the nation's citizens.

At the age of 15 Ashley was removed from school and sent by his father to a clergyman in Derbyshire who was to act as his private tutor. As no instruction took place, he perceived that the true reason he was sent there was to be out of the way. From Derbyshire, he went up to Oxford where, in 1822, he gained a first class degree in Classics. After university, Ashley spent much time staying at the homes of friends; he toured Europe, visiting France, Switzerland, Italy and Austria. Although this was a common practice among young men of his class at the time, in his case, the chief reason was that his father positively refused to have him permanently resident in either the family house in London or the country home in Wimborne St. Giles, Dorset.

"Here are the consequences of a Mother's dereliction of her children" Ashley confided in a letter to the mother of a friend: "Your feelings are so vivid, so maternal, and so arduous towards your offspring, that you almost doubt my assertion that such unnatural, such deeply horrid examples are found in a human and a Christian soul." [16]

---

(16) Finlayson, p.13 (quoting the Castle Howard Archives, Carlisle MSS, 1st Ser. Book 67, 9th Oct. 1821)

The Sixth Earl had intended that his son should have a military career, but this was totally alien to Ashley's temperament and character. Friends, acting on his behalf, managed to persuade his father to allow him to enter Parliament. Accordingly, in 1826, he was elected member for Woodstock in Oxfordshire. At last he was able to start the work he had been planning since, as a schoolboy, he had seen the poor man's funeral party in Harrow.

Despite his own unhappy childhood he was anxious to be married and have a family and in June 1830 he married Lady Emily `Minny' Cowper. They were devoted to each other and, within a loving and peaceful home, she provided the support and security he so earnestly desired.

He travelled the country visiting farms, factories, mines, and mills – anywhere where poor workers were employed. Often his wife accompanied him. He spoke to rich and poor, employers and workers and he made many friends in all sections of the community. Even when on holiday he found time to make such visits; his purpose in doing so was to collect accurate information to help his efforts to allow the poorest citizens their rightful dignity and a decent standard of living.

In February 1843 he made a long speech in the House of Commons on the living conditions of the working classes and their need for education. He had thoroughly researched the subject and he presented information and statistics relating to towns in all parts of the country. He quoted the words of many people with detailed knowledge of the working classes and their problems, including destitute boys and girls and their parents. "We owe to the poor of our land a weighty debt" he said. To his mind moral training and religious teaching for young children were essential:

"The early ages are of incalculable value; an idle reprobate of 14 is almost irreclaimable; every year of delay abstracts from us thousands of useful fellow citizens; nay, rather, it adds them to the ranks of viciousness, of misery and of disorder."

No one after that could be in any doubt about his knowledge, or about his commitment to helping the poorest people in the land.

Shortly after making his speech, he read the advertisement for the Field Lane Ragged School and immediately contacted the teachers. He told Edwin Hodder later `I never read an advertisement with keener pleasure. It answered exactly what I had been looking and hoping for. I could not regard it as other than a direct answer to my frequent prayer.' [17]

In November 1844 he agreed to become President of the Ragged School Union. `I shall be happy to aid you to the full extent of my power' he stated in his letter of acceptance `... it will give me much pleasure to see you and hear your report. We may, I think, do much for these poor children.'

Subsequently he met many teachers from ragged schools and was immensely impressed by the work they were doing. One of his first contacts was William Williams who had by then started the St. Giles' Rookery School. The two men had much in common and became good friends. They worked together on behalf of ragged school children for more than 40 years.

Just before Christmas 1843, the Committee of the St. Giles' Ragged School presented its first Report on progress. This explained why they had started the School, what had been achieved, and their hopes for the future. Each subsequent year they printed copies of their Annual Report containing information on pupil numbers and attendance and comments by the teachers. Printed lists of supporters and results of appeals were shown along with requests for money and other help. From 1847 regular annual public meetings were held to report on progress and fund raising.

From its small beginning, the School grew rapidly. A class for men and older boys was introduced. It met twice a week in the evenings with an average attendance of about 40. The absolute necessity for such a class may be seen from a comment in the first Report:

"At a meeting recently held in St. Giles by the City Missionary, there were 17 adults present and some children. Out of 13 adults who remained for a short time after the meeting was over, only one could read and that very badly; four also knew their letters. When it was intimated that a class for adults would be opened, 11 gave in their names with many thanks requesting to be admitted to the class. The adult class has since been opened and so great is the desire for instruction that there are now on the books no less than 89 adults whose ages vary from 14 to 52 years."

The Report for 1844 gave the number of men on the school register since the opening as 186. Although many of them were eager to learn, others were troublesome pupils:

".. being the offspring of the most ignorant and depraved of the population. Having been nurtured amidst scenes of misery, vice and iniquity, they have imbibed the vicious habits and propensities of their parents and associates."

In June 1845 William Williams, as the Superintendent of the Sunday School, started a School Logbook. It gave details of voluntary teachers' attendance rotas, pupil numbers, information about the homes and families of the pupils, jobs they found after leaving school, the weekly Bible text and difficulties with discipline. The first entry stated:

"In reviewing the many opportunities I

The front page of the Society's first Annual Report in 1843 have had during the past two years of visiting the children of this School I cannot but reflect with the sincerest pleasure on the earnestness with which they have always listened to my addresses .."

By March 1846 the School had expanded. Classes for men and boys were held on Tuesday and Thursday evenings from 8 until 10 o'clock; women and girls came to school on Monday and Friday evenings from 7 until 9 o'clock. There was a separate sewing class on Wednesday evenings. On Sundays the School was open all day.

Classes were crowded. All the pupils were poor; some close to starvation. To help those who did not have any money at all for food or school clothes or who needed respectable clothes to go for a job, William Williams started a special Emergency Fund which he administered separately from the rest of the School's finances.

An old pupil returned to the School in May 1846 and his story was recorded in the Logbook:

"Thomas Regan aged 18 had attended the school for two years; he had no relations; was in a very destitute condition, having scarcely any clothing and was also frequently in a starving condition. As his conduct was generally good, he was recommended to the Marine Society and obtained a situation in the Merchant Service. Today he called, equipped in a new suit of clothing; there was such an alteration in his appearance that I scarcely knew him; he had come to town that morning, and said he could not rest satisfied until he had seen

A page from William Williams' Log Book

me; he then, with much gratitude, thanked me for my kindness – said he liked the sea and produced a certificate for good conduct from his Captain which had procured him a berth on board a man-of-war. He said he was sure if he had remained in St. Giles's he would probably have been transported, and although he had a month's leave of absence, yet he determined not to stop more than two days, as he knew what St. Giles was, and the temptations he might be under; adding 'Mr, I hope, if I continue to go on as hitherto, to become a bright man yet. Many and many is the time I have thought of you, and what I have heard in your School when on my night watch.' "

The classes for women and girls were very popular. The teacher organized a Provident Fund for the pupils. The amount they saved was returned to them at Christmas with one penny interest added to each shilling put by. The lessons were so successful and the pupils made such progress that several of the older girls found jobs as servants – an impossible dream before they came to the School. This encouraged new young girls to apply for admission even faster than older pupils left.

As soon it could be afforded, the Committee hired a paid teacher to take charge of the boys' Night School and in 1846 a second teacher was employed to work with the men and boys. This doubled the number of pupils immediately but demand for places continued to grow and, on some occasions, as many were sent away as were admitted because of teacher shortages.

Every time pupils were turned away an opportunity was lost, so the Committee was constantly looking for more teachers, and larger, more suitable premises. William Williams did most of the searching. He tramped the streets, inspected rooms and buildings, talked to clergy and church goers about his School, followed up every hint of help, wrote letters to people who could perhaps be of use to him through their money, knowledge, contacts, skills or accommodation.

The school rooms had to be in the streets and alleys where the pupils lived and worked. They had to be cheap and accessible, not grand or superior. It was hard to find anywhere suitable because much of the St. Giles' parish and surrounding area was being demolished to make way for smart new shops, factories and houses. Whole new streets were being built. These now form part of the area around New Oxford Street.

Although Williams was continually enquiring, landlords did not welcome such unsavoury tenants as the pupils of ragged schools. In 1848 the School was forced to share premises, on a temporary basis, with another – the Irish Free School in George Street, St. Giles. The Committee felt that, if suitable premises could not be found, it would have to abandon its work in the St. Giles district altogether.

To avoid this, at the end of 1850, St. Giles' School merged with two other ragged schools experiencing similar difficulties. The combined society was called "The St. Giles and St George Bloomsbury Ragged Schools". One of the schools with which it merged was in Neal's Yard, St. Giles, and the other in Abbey Place, Little Coram Street, near Russell Square. Both schools had been founded about two years previously. Neal's Yard had a bad reputation.

".. entered by obscure ways, it suits the necessities of lewd, turbulent, dishonest persons.

It contains an assemblage of stables, carts, and barrows, dunghills, and pools of filthy water; old workshops and dark lofts; ruinous lodging dens and dirty rooms, inhabited by coster-mongers, bad women, and daring thieves, such as make it a moral nuisance."

The Annual Report for 1850-51 stated that schools were being carried on in three places. At Great St. Andrew's Street in Seven Dials, there was a girls' Night School with a paid mistress, a girls' Sunday School with two paid and several voluntary teachers and a girls' sewing class. Neal's Yard School, 'in a very dirty stable yard in the lowest part of the Seven Dials', was for boys. It was open every morning from Monday to Friday. Abbey Place School was in a stable yard in Little Coram Street; an area 'where the poor congregate in large numbers'.

Small schools, rented buildings, temporary locations were only partial solutions. The Committee decided to look for a large centrally situated property which could be purchased as a permanent home for the Society's various schools. It made a public appeal for funds towards the costs.

In 1852 the Committee's prayers were answered. The 'freehold carcass of a large building' at the corner of George Street and Broad Street was available. Supporters were delighted to learn that:

"The building is admirably adapted for the operations of the Committee. It was built for a Gin Palace, and it is capable of being made the Model Ragged School of London if the subscribers and friends will only come forward and enable them to open it free from debt."

The premises seemed ideal, being spacious with four floors and a basement. There was ample space for separate schoolrooms for boys, girls and infants. There were also rooms which could be used as dormitories for up to 100 children. The price was £1,800 with an extra £800 needed for alterations. The special purchase fund already contained £750 and friends had promised a further £300, leaving a balance of £1,550. The Committee bought the building (sometimes referred to as being in Broad Street and sometimes as in George Street), taking out a mortgage for part of the sum.

A grand opening ceremony took place on 23rd June 1852 when 300 pupils celebrated with a feast of roast beef and plum pudding. Lord Shaftesbury took the chair at a public meeting the same evening to help raise money to clear the debt. Under one roof, the Society could now provide day classes, night classes, industrial (i.e. employment) training for boys and girls, a day class for infants and Sunday schools.

The Committee was at last in a position to offer a home to those pupils who had no families of their own and nowhere to live, children such as the two of whom the schoolmaster at Neal's Yard had stated as being 'nuisances in the School and the neighbourhood on account of their mischievous and thieving propensities. Neither of them is provided for; both are left to steal or starve as they may'.

Since William Williams and his friends had first started work in the Rookery they had always hoped that a time might come when they could afford to offer a home (or 'refuge', as it was then called) to homeless children. Now, at last, with the purchase of this large building their dream was realised. Initially, they had only sufficient funds to enable them to accept four boys and five girls. It was a small but tremendously significant start. `The rooms occupied for dormitories are large and well ventilated. Each child has a separate bed and is provided with three wholesome meals a day.'

This building was large enough for the Committee to expand its industrial training for boys and girls. This was a most important aspect of the work. It encouraged the children to persevere at school as a way of escape from their present poverty. Girls were trained in `every kind of household work such as cooking, washing, ironing, scouring, needlework, so as to fit them for service.' The boys' training included carpentry, wood chopping, horsehair-picking, and shoemaking. The object was not merely to train the boys for a particular craft or trade `.. but to train their minds so that they may not only feel it to be their duty to work for their daily bread but take pleasure in doing so.'

The teachers and Committee reviewing nearly ten years' hard work were justly proud of what had been achieved. It had not been easy. The children who they were trying to help were the sons and daughters of the least fortunate members of society. Order, calm and respect for authority did not come naturally to them. The chosen method of maintaining order had been the same since the Society was founded. `It has only been by a rigorous but at the same time kind discipline that anything like a moral control has been obtained over them.'

One of the first teachers at the school, John Pullin, admitted how difficult the classes were when he wrote in the School Logbook:

"Thirty-five boys present, the majority of whom would no doubt have been attentive but for the misconduct of a few who ought to be suspended if not dismissed. One was detected by a policeman in the act of throwing a very large stone."

Elsewhere in the Logbook, an unsigned entry reads:

"Mr. Williams' class very attentive and remarkably well-behaved – with the exception of one boy – the other classes not so attentive – about eight were turned out – at close they were tolerably attentive."

The teenage boys who attended were particularly difficult, as they had spent far longer than the younger children on the streets learning dubious ways of survival. The teacher in charge of their classes commented that when he started working with them:

"It was no uncommon thing for the windows to be broken and the building in which we met to be covered with mud, while the persons of the teachers were assailed with missiles and their ears pained with language of the most disgusting character."

Finding paid staff who were able to cope with the working conditions was hard, but organizing a large group of competent voluntary helpers was just as difficult. Williams persuaded everybody he could to help and, in the early notebooks, among the regular teachers are recorded the names "Miss Williams and Miss E. Williams" – perhaps members of his own family.

He persuaded influential people to visit the School and encouraged others who might be willing to help. The Committee's first President, the Hon. and Rev. Montague Villiers, the Rector of St. George's, Bloomsbury, did not visit the School until two years after it had opened. The Logbook records that:

"He went from class to class making enquiry into the personal history of the children .. they behaved admirably. There were 37 present. He heard the scholars repeat one or two of the sonnets they had learned by heart as also the Text of the week. He addressed them from Matthew Chapter 5 verse 6 `Blessed are they which do hunger and thirst after righteousness'."

He stayed about an hour and a half and was so impressed with what he saw that he apologised for not having been sooner and promised to come regularly in the future. As he left he said that he `never felt more in the path of duty than on that evening'.

His experience was not unique. Other people saw what was being achieved in these difficult surroundings and some were so moved that they offered their help. Seven little girls from the School attended a local chapel and greatly impressed a lady of the congregation by their excellent behaviour. She came to visit the School and volunteered her services as a teacher immediately.

In the early years money was a constant worry and, right from the start, the Committee had found it hard to make provision for the growing numbers. William Williams however had a gift for attracting the right kind of publicity and when The Dowager Queen Adelaide heard of his efforts, as early as 1844, she sent a donation of £5; yet, in spite of this, subscriptions and donations that year totalled only £160.

The following year the total was down to barely £100. In 1846-7 subscriptions and donations rose to about £160 again from the two hundred or so donors and subscribers. The contributions ranged from half-a-crown upwards apart from a 7d contribution from "two little girls belonging to the School". Gradually the donations increased and by 1852 when the building in George Street was bought, the list of subscribers and donors was twice as long as it had been in 1844 and the accounts showed receipts in excess of £2,140.

In spite of all the difficulties and set-backs of those early days there was a growing feeling of confidence and optimism `The days of darkness are now passing away' wrote one of the teachers `and the light of truth is made to shine where it never appeared before'. On another occasion a schoolmaster wrote that `now, though our numbers have so much increased, the youths assemble and retire in a quiet and orderly manner, and we have not heard any offensive language for several months'.

A visitor to one of the girls' classes remarked on how neat and tidy they looked, which she felt was `in a great measure to be attributed to the benefits of the Clothing Club, into which many of them pay their half-pence and farthings, and thus obtain some comfortable garments.'

Early in 1853 the Committee, alarmed at the number of boys roaming the streets by day with nowhere to sleep at night, opened up the Neal's Yard premises as a `night refuge'. At first, 21 boys were given a bed for the night and a small piece of bread morning and evening. They had to fend for themselves during the day. The Committee however was soon convinced that they should offer more since `the boys have no honest means of obtaining the food necessary for their support during the day. Accordingly the lads have since been furnished with food and clothing, as well as lodging.'

Their time at Neal's Yard was a test of their desire to improve themselves. If they showed they were eager to learn and willing to be taught they were moved to George Street when space became available. 'The sleeping accommodations are far superior in George Street to Neal's Yard and the lads at the latter house look forward with great delight to the time when they shall be received into the former.'

The refuge work, as well as the ragged school operations, was always considered very important and, in 1853, the Annual Report included for the first time "Refuge for Destitute Children" in the Society's title. The refuges assumed more and more importance as the years went on. The Society's full title in 1854 was "St. Giles and St. George, Bloomsbury, Refuge for Destitute Children and Ragged and Industrial Schools".

The work continued to expand and, in the 1854 Report, the Committee proclaimed that at George Street its operations were 'on a grand scale'. It now ran:-

- An Infants' School with average attendance between 63 and 86 according to the season.
- A Girls' School, open every week-day morning and afternoon and four evenings per week with 70 to 80 girls between 6 and 14 attending.
- A Boys' School, open the same hours, with an average 85 attending during the day and 50 to 60 at the night classes.
- A Sunday School open 3 times each Sunday and conducted by between 30 and 40 voluntary teachers.
- Refuges for boys and girls.

The Annual Report gave statistics of children admitted to the refuges. Since July 1852, 127 boys had been admitted (55 of them within the previous twelve months) and 84 girls (37 within the previous twelve months).

"Of the 211 boys and girls admitted, 61 applied of their own accord, 34 were sent from other ragged schools, 45 were admitted on application of friends, 23 brought by Missionaries and Scripture Readers, 19 found in the streets in a state of destitution by members of the Committee and Superintendent, 9 sent by magistrates from police courts, and 6 sent by chaplains of prisons on their discharge."

This chapter has given an outline of the development of the various schools, the industrial training and the refuges for boys and girls. The following chapter, covering approximately the same time span, reviews how the Society educated girls and the way this part of the work developed.

Chapter 5
EDUCATING THE GIRLS AND HELPING THEIR PARENTS

The first pupils at the Rookery school included five girls in the same class as the boys but, as soon as numbers allowed and they had enough money, the Committee increased the number of classes so that the boys and girls could be educated separately. The times and days of the classes were different but, apart from the practical subjects, there was little difference in what they were taught.

In 1844 the class for young women had 124 on the books with an average attendance of 47. When they joined the School:

44	did not know the alphabet
47	could not read
26	could read, but not write
7	could read well and write a little

A few months later their teacher reported that:

"Many of these can now read tolerably well, 24 are learning to write on slates and in copybooks, and most of the others are making a rapid progress in their several classes."

Although the material circumstances of the women attending were as bad as the men's, they were less difficult pupils:

"..quiet in their demeanour, teachable in their disposition, and regular in their attendance, the teachers find no difficulty in at once establishing order amongst them. Most of those attending obtain their livelihood by selling watercresses and other articles about the streets, sweeping crossings, begging etc. So great is their poverty, the teachers are often grieved to find that while they are instructing the mind, the body is suffering from extreme want."

One of the first pupils at the School was a girl of seventeen. She was an orphan who had been living on her own for three years after her father died. She was one of a despised class of women who made and mended clothes for the Army but, as she could not earn enough to live by this alone, she tried selling watercress in the streets. So many others were already doing the same that even with two jobs she was not managing.

The girl regularly attended the School and one evening the teacher noticed she looked very ill and pale. She asked what was troubling her and discovered that she had not been well enough to go out to sell and her stock of watercress had gone bad. She had no money to buy any more and so had not eaten for two days.

The teacher gave her some bread at once and some money from the Special Reserve Fund to buy a fresh stock of watercress but she was by then too weak to make the effort and in a few days was dangerously ill.

Some friends from the School carried her to hospital. A doctor examined her but would not admit her for treatment as he said there was nothing wrong with her apart from starvation and exposure. Her friends were just as poor as she was; their last resort was to take her to the infirmary of the local workhouse where two doctors declared that she was unlikely to survive more than a day or two. Luckily their gloomy forecast was proved wrong; to the delight of her friends and teacher she gradually got better.

As soon as she was strong enough, she went straight back to school and rejoined the sewing class. She attended as often as she could and soon afterwards, with the help of her teacher, found a job as a skilled needlewoman, with shorter hours and much better pay than when she was working on army uniforms.

Sewing was one of the most popular subjects as it was a skill the girls could use to make money and improve their living conditions. The teachers' reports show just how basic the lessons were. Before any sewing could be taught, the girls had to learn how to wash and keep themselves clean so the school provided washing facilities and all the girls had to make themselves presentable before they went to any lessons. This rule was strictly observed but could not have been totally effective because the hovels in which they lived swarmed with rats and mice and were alive with fleas. The girls were dirty and often covered in lice and consequently the teachers had to be particularly careful about their own hygiene. One of the first teachers told the Committee that she had, on occasion, to burn the clothes she went to school in so as to keep her own home clean and free from infestation.

One pupil, a girl of 15 who was healthy and strong, ran away from her stepmother and the man who was living with her. They had been abusing her regularly. She was a determined girl with a mind of her own. She would rather die on the street, she said, than put up with the kind of life her stepmother was living and the cruelties she had been inflicting on her.

The poor girl went filthy to school, barely covered in a few rags and slept where she could at night. When she was ready for employment her teacher got her a suitable set of clothes and arranged an interview with a woman who ran a laundry. She willingly offered the girl a job, but was appalled at the state she was in.

"Her mistress found it absolutely necessary to send her out on the following day to get her hair cut off. She was found in such a state that no hairdresser would undertake the office."

The long-suffering teacher somehow managed to cope with this additional set-back and, when at last the girl returned to the laundry clean and shorn, she got on well and her employer was very pleased with her.

As soon as the girls were clean enough to begin their sewing, they were taught how to hold a needle and then the basic stitches. When they had made sufficient progress, they went on to learn how to make and repair all their own clothes. This skill was put to practical use when a girl in the sewing class was admitted to hospital. After a preliminary examination the doctor told her to go home because she did not have anything decent to wear during her stay. When the teacher heard about this she told the class and asked if any of them would volunteer to make the things the girl needed:

"They all with one accord exclaimed `I will, I will'. One of the Committee entered the school while they were thus occupied; he found 28 girls present, and as many as could be employed were busily engaged on the required garments, one on a sleeve, another on a collar .."

The teachers often made appeals for old clothes or material which their pupils could work with, because `the only needlework which can be procured for those in the sewing class, is altering and repairing the old garments thus sent'. Sometimes well-wishers offered new clothes, but this was not so acceptable as it was not the most efficient use of material. The Committee suggested 'to those friends who have sent new articles of clothing, that it would be of great advantage to the class if the materials were supplied unmade.' When the clothes were made they were given to the pupils.

Progress was always slow due to the irregular attendance of the pupils and the constantly changing school population but in 1850 the girls' teacher reported that:

"It gives me great pleasure to inform you, that the Sewing Class is going on very nicely, and those children who have attended the most regularly have made decided progress. Some of the children are beginning to learn knitting, which is taught them as an encouragement for regular attendance. We are sometimes interrupted by newcomers, but by degrees we see them improve. I should feel most happy if any friends would visit this class and see some of these poor outcasts of society, who not long ago were scarcely clothed, but now appear clean and tidy."

The girls came as and when they could. Illness, starvation, and cruelty kept many of them from attending regularly. Sometimes the schoolroom was full but on occasions it was nearly empty.

Although the girls were better behaved than the boys, they were not angels. Sometimes fights broke out in class. The teachers, if driven to it, would expel girls for bad behaviour, although only as a last resort. The threat of this action was often enough to make the girls change their ways because they realised they were throwing away any hope of a job. It was lonely without school friends and sometimes a girl would beg for one last chance to return and behave herself.

In 1852 the girls' teacher at Great St. Andrew's Street noted a gradual improvement:

"For the first six or eight months the School was opened they were most unkind and malicious, fighting with each other on their way home. Now, I am happy to say I hardly ever hear of a quarrel between them, and when there is, they come and appeal to me. Upon visiting the parents, they often say they cannot tell what makes their girl so fond of school, for they cannot get them to stay at home when they want them."

Mrs. Edmond, who was in charge of the Girls' Refuge in 1855, admitted that at times the tasks facing the teachers seemed insurmountable, yet overall she saw a steady improvement in the pupils and in their hopes and prospects. She wrote in her report to the Committee:

"Many of the girls are taken from the lowest scenes of misery and vice, and all are destitute, and if they were not with us they would be either in the streets or in prison. There is a marked improvement in the general conduct of the inmates of the Refuge. It is very seldom that I now have to punish for the use of bad language or any improper conduct. They are more like a family than a school, and it has been my constant aim to bring about this very desirable feeling."

The girls' classes were under the control of an acting Ladies' Committee whose task it was to see that the girls received enough basic education and thorough practical training to help them lead decent lives when they left the School:

"The girls are now daily taught (in addition to that religious and secular instruction which is common to the whole School) to make and mend articles of clothing, to hem, sew, stitch, darn, and in fact every useful application of the needle; they are also set to clean, sweep, dust and scour the schoolroom and school furniture, and to well cleanse themselves with soap and water."

The girls' teacher at Neal's Yard explained that the aims of the practical lessons were "to afford employment and material for instruction in that industrial occupation, which will at the same time, furnish the readiest means of making the term 'ragged' inapplicable to the child after its entrance within our walls."

A warning was published in one of the yearly reports following a special request for old clothes for the sewing classes. A lady living in the neighbourhood had some old clothes but when she visited the School it was closed. She spoke to a boy who was playing nearby who told her that he was a pupil at the School. She asked him to let his teacher know that she had a lot of old clothes at home which she would happily give for the sewing class, provided some-one would collect them. Shortly after this, a polite, well mannered boy called at her house and said he had come to collect the clothes for the School; the servant who opened the door, acting according to instructions, handed over a large sack and the boy went away. Neither he nor the clothes were seen again.

So successful were the girls' classes that their mothers begged for something similar for themselves and so, in November 1852, a Mothers' Club was inaugurated. It was the one evening in the week when the women could spend two hours in decent surroundings. They took their sewing and sat quietly while the teacher read aloud. At the close of the meeting, the teacher read an extract from the Bible and explained it to them. They all said a prayer and then went home. There were 74 names on the register and 54 attended regularly.

The class had other benefits – a money club as an encouragement to save, a small loan library of books for those who could read and, above all, the sympathy and help of their teacher. Once a quarter they had a 'tea meeting' and on one of these occasions Miss Gurney who ran the classes was presented with a 'handsome work box' for which the class members had saved. It was inscribed:

"Presented to Miss Jemima G. Gurney by the members of the Mothers' class, meeting in George Street, St. Giles, as a small token of their gratitude for her exertions to promote their temporal and spiritual welfare. 1st January 1856".

William Williams was present and made a speech thanking Miss Gurney on behalf of the women for all she was doing for them. The women were quick to see the advantages of work-ing together and with the encouragement of Miss Gurney they started a clothing club for the sale and exchange of second-hand and re-made clothes. Every year they had a club outing and treat in the country; Richmond was a favourite place.

When the women decided that their husbands were in need of improvement, they begged the teachers to set up a fathers' class in the school at Broad Street. The first meeting was in March 1856. Only five men enrolled on that night but the numbers quickly increased. Mr. Harvey who ran the class reported:

"A reading room has been opened for the use of the men, and newspapers and periodicals provided for their use. The average attendance is about 16 each evening. The reading-room is open from 8 till 9, and there is a lecture or conversation from 9 till 10, at which hour the meeting breaks up."

Mr. Harvey organized a tea meeting and invited the fathers of all the children in the School. More than a hundred men attended that night. The outcome of this meeting was that they agreed to organize themselves into a working men's club for the purpose of establishing a benefit fund:

—To afford relief to the members in sickness of 10/- a week for 12 weeks, and then 5/- a week for another 12 weeks, if the sickness continue.

—Each member to receive on the death of his wife £3; and the wife, on her husband's death to receive £7.

Every man who joined the Club paid two shillings as an entrance fee, and thereafter a weekly contribution of four pence.

The men enjoyed the weekly lectures which were one of the Club's activities. The average number of men present for these occasions in 1856 was 125 and there were similar numbers in subsequent years. The topics for the lectures covered a wide area, for instance – `Soap and Its Uses', `A Trial at Law', `Ballad Histories', `Biographies of Men of Science', `Gleanings from the Vegetable World', `The Contested Election', and `Rough Notes of a Steam Voyage from Hungerford to the Tower'.

Yet in spite of the overall progress, all was not well. Mr. Harries, the master in charge of the Boys' Refuge at George Street, resigned in the autumn of 1854. The main reason was that for many months he had been anxious about the dormitory arrangements in the Refuge. It was essential, he felt, for the boys' and girls' refuges to be in separate buildings. He was a loyal, trusted worker and the Committee accepted his view and started to look for suitable premises but without success. Regretfully they were forced to accept his resignation. The search for separate boys' accommodation continued but this proved difficult and it was not till May the following year that William Williams found suitable premises in Arthur Street, St. Giles. Here the boys could sleep and have their industrial training but they still had to go to George Street for their other lessons. Mr. James Wood and his wife were in charge of the new premises with a joint salary of £100 a year plus coal and lighting.

"The removal of the Boys' Refuge from these premises" wrote Mrs. Edmond, "has greatly added to the efficiency of this department of labour, and relieved the Matron of much anxiety, as the girls can now perform their various household duties without the necessity of that continued watchfulness which was required when both Refuges were under the same roof."

The girls' education was further enhanced when a member of the Committee provided the money for a Library at the Refuge:

"The formation of the Library is of great use to our girls; many of them are very fond of reading, and are now enabled to do so. Through the kindness of Mr. C. T. Ware we now have a library of upwards of 100 books suited to the capacities of the girls, and I hope and pray that great advantages may be derived therefrom."

The importance of separate accommodation for boys and girls became clear in the autumn of 1859 when, despite the best efforts of their teachers, a major crisis arose. The reports and meeting minutes do not tell us specifically what happened but at the Committee Meeting in November it was resolved:

".. that Mr. Wood and Mrs. Edmond have each a fortnight's leave of absence in consequence of the great anxiety and increased labour they have had in connection with the awakening that has recently taken place among the children under their charges and that a gratuity of £5 be given to each of them to pay their expenses."

Their annual holiday period had in effect been doubled that year because of what had occurred. House hunting was clearly now an urgent matter. A move was already being considered even before the events which impressed upon the Committee the need for action:

"For the last two or three years the Committee has been impressed with the importance of having another house a short distance from town, where the girls most ready for service might be transferred, and where they could be more effectually trained in household work than it was possible to do in the Broad Street house."

In May 1860 40 senior girls from the Refuge were moved to the safer environment of a house in Acton, five miles out of London. The new Home was "in every way adapted for the work, so much so that no outlay was required to alter the building, and the only expense incurred was for bedsteads, bedding, and furniture, and some whitewashing, painting etc." It was opened with a public meeting on 3rd July by the Earl of Shaftesbury. Subscribers were informed that:

"All the washing for the Boys' Refuge and the Girls' Refuge in Broad Street, as well as that for the Acton House is done by the girls at this country home. There are all the children in the Refuges to wash for every week, and the bed clothes, towels, etc. to keep clean. The girls are all received into the Refuge in Broad Street, and afterwards drafted to the Acton House."

Mrs. Edmond was in charge of the two girls' refuges and travelled frequently between them. The extra work and travelling involved took its toll and after a time her health began to suffer:

"Up to June last, both these houses were superintended by Mrs. Edmond, but the work and anxiety connected with this oversight at length proved too much for her strength, and in July last it was arranged that she should remove to the Home at Acton, to superintend the girls there, and that a new Matron should be engaged for the Town House."

Mrs. Edmond continued at Acton until 1863. In March of that year, members of the Committee were dismayed to receive her letter of resignation. Her reasons for this step are not recorded. She came to the next meeting at which they hoped to persuade her to change her mind. She told them that she had been thinking of resigning for the past six months as she was no longer happy in her job and, if she were not happy, she could not be useful.

William Williams acted quickly. Before the month was out he had recruited a new Matron but, equally quickly, she wrote that she had changed her mind. An assistant teacher at the Acton home took charge, on a temporary basis, but the Committee decided she was too young and inexperienced to be offered the post on a permanent basis. If it was difficult to find suitable candidates, it was even more difficult to retain them. Trouble over repairs and the lease forced the girls to move in 1866 from Acton to temporary premises in Kilburn. In October 1866 the Committee appointed Miss Frost as Matron of the Kilburn Home at £35 per annum. She was an experienced school teacher and for the past two years had been deputy matron at a training college.

Shortly after that, the Committee found a suitable property for a permanent girls' refuge in Ealing. It was "a large, substantial and old fashioned residence with about 2 acres of garden and kitchen ground". Miss Frost, the staff and the girls moved in at the end of July 1867.

The Girls' Refuges at Ealing and Broad Street were run on similar lines:

"The girls in both refuges are provided with a plain but useful education, based upon sound Christian and evangelical principles; they are also clothed, lodged, and provided with three meals a day. Domestic service being the ultimate object for which these girls are educated and trained, they are of course taught to do all kinds of household work, such as washing, cooking, cleaning, etc. Their own clothes are also made and repaired by the inmates. The shirts for the boys are likewise made by the girls. The girls in the Broad Street Refuge wash a portion of their own clothes, but the greater part, together with the washing for the Boys' Refuge, is done by the girls at Ealing. This is found to be most useful in the training of the girls and a great saving to the funds of the Institution. The average number of articles washed by the girls at Ealing every week is 100 dozen, which if valued would amount to £6.5s. at least, or about £325 a year.. They attend church twice on Sunday and are present night and morning at family worship. On Sunday afternoons voluntary teachers attend and impart Bible instruction, which is much prized by the girls who take delight in learning hymns, and portions of Scripture."

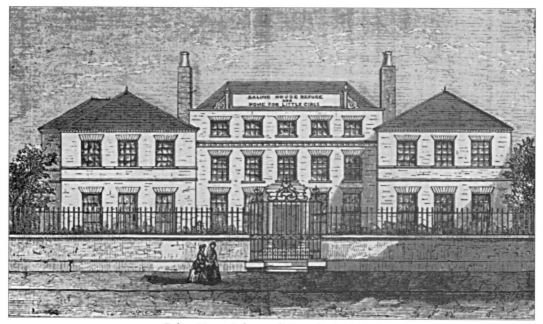

Ealing House Refuge and Home for Little Girls

Chapter 6

WILLIAM WILLIAMS, LORD ASHLEY AND EMIGRATION

It is now necessary to go back a few years to review the Society's overall development and the work of William Williams and Lord Ashley, soon to become the 7th Earl of Shaftesbury.

The need for suitable accommodation, so that the older girls could be separated from the boys in the Refuge, was only one of the concerns facing the Committee at that time. The Annual Report for 1853 put it bluntly:

"Salaries of the teachers have to be paid, and about 60 boys and girls to be provided with three meals each a day, besides clothes and other incidental expenses. The anxiety of the Committee is not be wondered at, especially at a time when bread and all other articles of food are so dear. It is utterly impossible that, without timely assistance, the Committee can provide food and clothes for all the orphans and the destitute children now under their charge."

Money was so short in 1855 that the Committee was seriously considering whether to close the Boys' Refuge. Mr. Ware, (the gentleman who had donated the library books to the Girls' Refuge, as described in the previous chapter) recounted what happened:

"Mr. Williams, whose hopefulness never failed, and myself were the only persons of the Committee who stood out for continuing the boys' branch. As we two were unwilling to yield, it was decided to hold a special meeting of the Committee at Mr. Villiers' rectory to settle the matter. At this meeting it was decided to make one more effort to retain the Boys' Refuge. A special donation of £100 was obtained from the Ragged School Union, a similar donation was given by Mrs. Robert Ware. A collection of more than £75 was raised at Belgrave Chapel after a sermon by Mr. Villiers and Mr. and Mrs. Villiers consented to arrange a fancy sale for our funds. The sale was most successful and realized between £500 and £600. By these means our wants were for the time supplied and the boys' branch was saved."

The following year William Williams presented the Committee with eight new proposals for increasing funds, which were immediately implemented. His ideas were successful and when in February 1860 he applied to the Reformatory and Refuge Union for a grant towards the cost of running the refuges, his application was turned down on the grounds that the Society's finances were now so sound that no grant was necessary. When the Dowager Countess of Haddington died the following summer she bequeathed the sum of £1,000 to the Boys' Refuge. For the time being, at least, finance was not such a major worry.

Another constant concern for the Committee was finding and retaining paid staff; it was like an obstinate ulcer which refused to heal – always painful and always there. The problem was left to William Williams to deal with. It was he who had to find suitable teachers for the Committee to interview and obtain references for short-listed candidates, often visiting them at work and talking to their head teachers and supervisors.

It was to William Williams too that the staff poured out their complaints – about the children, the buildings, the job and each other. He listened and often visited the classes to see for himself the difficulties teachers were experiencing. When staff proved unsatisfactory it was his job to recommend their dismissal to the Committee. All this and more he dealt with. He found suitable premises for the schools and refuges, organized the rent or purchase, arranged mortgages and insurance. He engaged architects, surveyors and builders and kept a check on the adaptation and all subsequent maintenance of the Society's establishments.

No problem was so daunting that he could not cope, no task however small was beneath his notice. The building in George Street needed a supply of fresh water; he prevailed on the New River Company to provide it without charge. The children required medical attention; he persuaded a local doctor to treat them and supply medicines free. A gas fitter did not carry out his work according to contract; William Williams spoke to the man and arranged for him to put matters right. As well as all this, he still found time for his teaching at the Sunday Schools. By now he had a wife to consider as well as his responsibilities to the Society. He was still employed in a solicitor's firm, but was often away from his Office during working hours on business connected with the schools and refuges. Even assuming that all the legal affairs for the Society were handled by his Employers, it must have demanded considerable restraint on their part to allow him so much freedom.

It was obvious that he could not continue in this way for much longer. His colleagues on the Committee recognised this and decided to appoint a full-time assistant to take over as much of the routine work from him as possible. They realised that to find the right person would take time, so they did what they always did on such occasions – they asked William Williams to find and interview a suitable person for them to appoint. Accordingly, in June 1857, William Chappell became `Assistant to the Secretary` at a salary of £50 per annum. The effect of the appointment was double-edged; whilst it freed William Williams from the simpler day to day tasks, he immediately undertook more and more new work, thus his over-all situation was but little improved.

In spite of the best efforts of his assistant, he still could not reconcile the demands of his employers with the needs of the Society, so he took a characteristically courageous step. He resigned his position at the Solicitor's Office in the hope of finding enough private work to support himself and his family. Unfortunately this plan was not as successful as he hoped because he spent so much time working for the Society. He was forced to dig more and more deeply into his savings.

At this point, his friends on the Committee were finally goaded into taking what they had known for a long time was the necessary action. For the first time since the Society's foundation, they acted without consulting Williams and offered him a permanent, full-time, salaried position. In the words of their letter of 24th May 1858:

"We have felt the heavy and accumulating labours which now devolve upon you must necessarily occupy your time and thoughts to such a degree as to be scarcely compatible with other regular and continuous employment. We are aware that you have recently taken a step involving a considerable sacrifice to yourself in order to secure the time required for this work which you have so much at heart.."

They wondered at first if he might feel hurt at being considered as an employee rather than a friend, so they assured him that this salaried employment, if he were to accept, would not affect the great affection they felt for him. All 17 members of the Committee signed the letter. For a month he thought about the consequences and then asked them to postpone taking such a step at least for another six months as he felt that 'the Committee were scarcely in a position to engage a paid Secretary'.

They were determined, however, that he should accept their offer and accept it quickly. Fortunately for them he did but negotiating a suitable salary was difficult. After some bargaining, he reluctantly agreed to accept a salary of £150 per annum, which was less than the Committee had originally offered. It was also considerably less than he had been earning at the Solicitor's Office, yet he refused to consider a higher sum. The Committee stipulated that this offer should not preclude him from undertaking any private work or other employment if he felt it was compatible with his duties as Secretary. The children at the schools and refuges, and the members of the Committee had every reason to be grateful that he accepted the offer. He was indeed one of the best friends the Society ever had.

Another was Lord Ashley. He had supported St. Giles' School from the beginning; entries in his diary dating back to the early years of the Society's history show his strong support for ragged schools and his efforts on their behalf:

"May 29th 1846 .. a splendid display of luxury and grandeur, yet unsatisfactory. The contrast so great to the places where I have passed so many hours lately, that I felt almost uneasy. The few pounds, too, that I want, and shall not obtain, for the establishment of ragged schools, seemed wasted in every dish. All this is very well, according to their wealth and station, now and then; but the crumbs which fall from their table are in scanty proportion to the number and abundance of their feasts." And on another occasion in the same year he wrote:[18]

"June 12 .. Busy in founding a ragged school; peculiar evils require peculiar remedies.. Alas! alas! I can set up a school which shall give education every evening to 280 children for £58 a year – hardly more than it costs to prosecute one criminal – and yet I can barely collect the sum!"[19]

He was not a wealthy man and the allowance his father made him was barely enough for his own and his family's needs. He could not afford to support the ragged schools out of his own pocket.

One of his main concerns was how to improve the children's prospects when their school days were finished. He believed, as did many others, that emigration was a practical and humane solution. In the Colonies workers were needed. At home it was not easy to find employers willing to offer work and a home to ragged school boys and girls. These children, coming from the harsh realities of the streets, had so little to lose. Although those emigrating to the Colonies often faced a harsh future, it was, Lord Ashley was convinced, the best chance for those who were healthy, strong and determined to make their way in the world. Emigration would at least offer hope where none had existed before.

The Society's Committee were of the same opinion. To find suitable work at home for the boys was particularly difficult.

"It may be asked, how the lads are disposed of after the Committee are satisfied they are fit for service? This is a difficult and anxious part of their work and there would probably be no great difficulty in obtaining situations for them as errand-boys and porters; but it is clear

(18) Hodder, Vol.2 p166.
(19) Hodder, Vol.2 p167.

that such boys, unless residing under the roof of their employers, would, from the want of a home, be obliged to find that home, if it can be so called, in common lodging-houses, and in all probability would sooner or later become a prey to the wicked and designing persons who frequent such places. The Committee are therefore of opinion that emigration to one of the British Colonies is the best means that can be adopted."

In the House of Commons on 6th June 1848 Lord Ashley proposed that:

".. means be annually provided for the voluntary emigration to some one of Her Majesty's colonies of a certain number of young persons of both sexes, who have been educated in the schools ordinarily called `ragged schools' in and about the Metropolis."[20]

His speech lasted over two hours. He had thoroughly researched the topic, interviewing police, magistrates, missionaries and teachers - anyone who had detailed knowledge or personal experience. He had spoken to the children, visited their schools, the hovels where they lived and the workhouses which they would do anything to avoid. The children who would benefit from the scheme, he told the House of Commons, were not:

".. chance vagrants, beggars, or pilferers, who by a little exercise of magisterial authority, might be extinguished or reformed. It has only of late been discovered that they constitute a numerous class. .. For the knowledge of these details we are mainly indebted to the London City Mission."[21]

The missionaries had established themselves in the Rookery area. Because they were invited, not coerced, the children trusted them, and so were persuaded to come to the ragged schools. According to Lord Ashley's research, more than 30,000 naked, filthy, lawless and deserted children were daily roaming the streets of London. He described their habits and dispositions, their pursuits, livelihoods and where they lived and slept. He had questioned 1,600 of them. From their stories he had compiled the following figures:

"162 confessed that they had been in prison not once nor twice - many of them several times; 116 had run away from their homes, the result, in many instances, of ill treatment; 170 slept in lodging-houses – nests of every abomination that the mind of man can conceive; 253 confessed that they lived altogether by begging; 216 had neither shoes nor stockings; 280 had no caps, hats, bonnets, or head covering; 101 had no linen; 219 never slept in beds – many had no recollection of having ever tasted that luxury; 68 were the children of convicts; 125 had step-mothers, to whom may be traced much of the misery that drives the children of the poor to the commission of crime; 306 had lost either one or both parents, a large proportion having lost both."[22]

His evidence was overwhelming:

"Many of them" he told the House "retire for the night, if they retire at all, to all manner of places – under dry arches of bridges and viaducts, under porticoes, sheds, and carts; to outhouses, in sawpits, on staircases, in the open air, and some in lodging-houses. Curious indeed, is their mode of life. I recollect the case of a boy who during the inclement season of last winter, passed the greater part of his nights in the iron roller of Regent's Park. He climbed every evening over the railings, and crept to his shelter, where he lay in comparative comfort. Human sympathy, however, prevails, even in the poorest condition; he invited a companion

(20) Hodder, Vol.2 p254.
(21) Hodder, Vol.2 p255.
(22) Hodder, Vol.2 pp255-256

less fortunate than himself, promising to `let him into a good thing'. He did so, and it proved a more friendly act than many a similar undertaking in railway shares."[23]

His speech had tremendous impact. Lord Ashley recorded in his diary that night `June 6 .. eleven o'clock. Just returned from House of Commons, having made motion on Ragged Schools and Emigration. Had much success ..'[24] and a few days later: `June 12 .. this `Ragged' motion has produced considerable effect; much is said everywhere. I received abundant letters, .. in high terms of approbation'.[25]

As a result of his efforts, the Government made a grant of £1500 that year towards the cost of emigration for ragged school children.

The school children had to `earn' the opportunity to emigrate. In order to qualify they had to attend school regularly for at least six months. Good health was essential. They had to be able to write a sentence from dictation, to work the four simple rules of arithmetic, to read fluently, to repeat the Lord's Prayer and the Ten Commandments and show they understood their meaning, and to answer a few easy questions on the life of Jesus. At least four months industrial training or skill in a handicraft or other practical occupation was required.

The Society's Report for 1848 comments on the effect of the grant and Lord Ashley's help. The first 22 pupils to emigrate under this Scheme left England at the end of the year. The Society supplied each of them with a complete new outfit and a Bible. The night before they left they had tea together in the schoolroom for the last time. A clergyman conducted a short service, and members of the Committee spoke to them about what lay ahead. The

A group of the Society's boys, bound for the Colonies

---

(23) Hodder, Vol.2 p256.
(24) Hodder, Vol.2 p258.
(25) Hodder, Vol.2 p258.

majority of them were unemployed 'but all expressed themselves extremely anxious to do anything they could to obtain an honest living'.

After 1848 the Government did not renew the grant for emigration, although Lord Ashley was anxious to continue the scheme. The Committee of St. Giles and St. George's schools sent each year as many children as they could afford from their own resources.

Lord Ashley became the 7th Earl of Shaftesbury in 1851 on the death of his father. He inherited large debts which he struggled to settle as fast as he could. The family estate in Dorset was in a poor condition and he soon found himself entangled in an expensive and worrying law suit to put matters right. He refused to allow these problems to distract him from what he regarded as his life's work – to devote himself to the cause of the poorest people in society, in particular children.

In 1857 the Committee had sufficient funds to send ten girls to Canada. Mrs. Edmond, who was then Matron of the Girls' Refuge, travelled with them to Quebec on the North American Steam Packet on 15th July. She stayed with the girls until she was satisfied they had all found suitable jobs and then returned to London. On 2nd November 1857 she attended the Committee meeting and:

"..gave a detailed account of her journey to Canada with the ten girls and stated where and with whom she had placed them. She mentioned the cordial way she had been received at every town she visited and added that she believed from the reception she had met with and the information she had gathered that there would be no difficulty in procuring good situations for any number of respectable English girls."

The Annual Report gives us more information:

"The demand for English servant girls was so great that had Mrs. Edmond had 200 girls with her she could easily have found good situations for them all. After placing the ten objects of her charge in respectable families in various parts of the colony and gaining all the information she could to guide the Committee in the future emigration of girls as well as boys, Mrs. Edmond, by the good providence of God returned to her duties after fulfilling the arduous mission entrusted to her, having been absent only six weeks and two days, during which time she travelled nearly 7000 miles."

The next year she again went to Canada with another group of girls. After she had found suitable jobs for them all, she visited girls and boys whom the Society had sent out the previous year. On her return to England she was able to tell the Committee that she was satisfied with what had been done for the children in Canada and with the progress they were making. They undoubtedly had to work hard and conditions were often tough, but she found no evidence of undue hardship.

Emigration in combination with basic education and industrial training was, the Society believed, a way of escape for some but not all of London's ragged children. William Williams and Lord Shaftesbury continued searching for ways to help other boys and girls for whom emigration was not appropriate.

Chapter 7
The St. Valentine's Night Supper

By the end of 1857, when the refuges had been open for almost six years, 492 children had been admitted. Many more still roamed the streets. The Committee could accommodate only a limited number of those it wanted to help but, as the table below shows (apart from 1855 when the Committee was almost forced to close the Boys' Refuge because of financial hardship) the number of admissions rose steadily:

Year	Number of Children Admitted	
1852	36 (boys and girls)	
1853	83 (boys and girls)	
1854	55 boys	37 girls
1855	nil boys	67 girls
1856	57 boys	36 girls
1857	76 boys	45 girls

Mr. Wood, the master in charge of the Boys' Refuge pointed out in his report for 1857 that the Society's refuges were not for criminals but:

".. experience proves that, at least nine out of every ten of boys taken in are as deeply sunk in progressive felony as those who have been branded as such by the law. But by their cleverness in their assumptions of innocence and their adroitness in escaping detection, they pass as innocent.

Boys received into this Institution are the homeless and destitute but, before they find their way into an Institution like this, they become merged into other classes, namely, the vagrant and the criminal – the common result of a street education.

But where have they learned to be so clever? I have no hesitation in saying the education of the streets and the low lodging-houses, where such boys constantly resort, is the prolific source of all that is cunning, daring and vicious.

A street education does not end here: it not only fosters crime, but encourages the very extreme of laziness, and produces in the minds of almost all an abhorrence to anything like continuous labour; and this proves the great stumbling-block to the boys themselves when taken in."

Mr. Wood did not believe education alone would transform his charges into respectable citizens; it would merely enable them to be better criminals

Main Entrance of the Refuge in Great Queen Street

unless it was linked with training in good habits. Nevertheless, the boys had made considerable progress in spite of their shortcomings; their earnings from the industrial classes amounted to:

Shoemaking for both refuges and sale	£112. 4. 3
Tailoring for the refuge	£ 89.10. 5
Carpentry for refuges, schools and sale	£ 77. 9. 8
Making mattresses	£ 11. 4. 9
Chopping and selling firewood	£ 88.10.11

Mr. Wood felt that the main benefits of this training, apart from learning how to earn a living were that:

"The boys who work most invariably become the cleanest in their persons and the most tidy in their dress. They know they can now do work which in the market will produce a certain

Young Carpenters at the Refuge

amount, and this makes them begin to feel that they are somebody, and that they are now independent of the circumstances under which they had previously fallen, and a feeling of self-respect is created in the mind."

The Boys' Refuge in Arthur Street was small and inconvenient; the Committee had always known that it was not ideal but they had little choice since accommodation had to be provided after the disturbances mentioned at the end of Chapter 5. After deciding that a move from Arthur Street was essential, members of the Committee inspected several buildings before leasing an old coach factory in Great Queen Street. The cost of repairs, alterations and equipment was £850. This entire sum was raised through a grant from the Ragged School Union, an Appeal by the Earl of Shaftesbury and funds received after publicity in The Times. The formal opening of the new premises was on 30th November 1857.

Mr. Wood was thankful to leave the old, cramped Arthur Street Refuge with its 'bad drains and stench' but he and the boys had to live and work in the new premises whilst repairs were being

Young Tailors learning their Trade

carried out. After the move was complete, he described the problems of moving to:

"..premises with all its dilapidations and filth to be grappled with. For many nights we had to sleep with the roof uncovered, the rain pouring down in torrents, actually making the position of the boys, as far as their beds was concerned, much worse than if they were in the dry arches or passage of some very poor lodging house, yet they never grumbled."

By the end of 1858, things were much better:

A Class of young Shoemakers

"..more room, better drainage, a play ground, swimming bath, and a dormitory well ventilated. .. When some of the boys were talking about it to their Sunday School teachers they called it their `Palace Home' ".

Year by year the numbers of children in the refuges fluctuated, depending on how many the Society could afford to take in:

Year	Children Admitted		Year	Children Admitted	
1858	75 boys	50 girls	1862	66 boys	43 girls
1859	105 boys	56 girls	1863	134 boys	71 girls
1860	74 boys	65 girls	1864	96 boys	62 girls
1861	75 boys	52 girls			

Mr. Wood had blamed street education and living in low lodging houses before they came to the refuge for the boys' criminal ways. These lodging houses were notorious. An article in The Quarterly Review described the conditions in them and quoted the remarks of the City Missionaries who visited the people using them:

Back of the extensive old Coach Factory located between Great Queen Street and Parker Street

"These houses are never cleaned or ventilated. They literally swarm with vermin. It is almost impossible to breathe. Missionaries are seized with vomiting or fainting upon entering them.

It is impossible to convey a just idea of their state. The quantities of vermin are amazing. I have entered a room and in a few minutes I have felt them dropping on to my hat from the ceiling

An industrious group of Boys in their 'Palace Home'

like peas.

Few of the adults ever wash either body or clothes. As for the children .."[26]

For someone without the ability to pay even for these lodgings, the workhouse casual wards were available. A series of three articles published in the Pall Mall Gazette in the middle of January 1866 painted a vivid picture of a night spent in the casual ward of Lambeth Workhouse. The writer, disguised as a down-and-out, presented himself in the evening at the workhouse to find out what happened.

The articles did not tell the Committee or the Earl of Shaftesbury anything they did not already know, but they dramatically informed the public about the dangers to young children who mixed with adults in such places.

The reporter described the compulsory supervised bath with the filthy water which was unchanged all evening, the biting cold, the overcrowding, the damp, the crust of foul bread allocated to him (which he could not force himself to eat). He wrote of the inadequate and dirty straw mattresses, the nauseous smell of the smoke from the inmates' pipes, the swearing, obscenities and the fighting that went on most of the night.

The most poignant part of the story, as far as the refuges were concerned, was the description of a young boy who arrived at the workhouse late at night. He knew many of the men by name and displayed for them various small items he had stolen during the day, boasting that he would quickly sell them the next morning. It was obvious he intended to continue making a precarious living in this way. The men accepted, encouraged and praised him. He was no stranger to theft and his thieving skills were such that he had so far escaped detection – just such a boy as Mr. Wood had described earlier.

The Pall Mall Gazette writer went on to explain the morning routine where the men had to wash themselves and then reclaim their clothes which had been removed for safekeeping the night before. The children had to wait till the end. He watched `four poor little wretches, some with their rugs trailing about their shoulders and some quite bare' as they came shivering over the stones and across the bleak yard. They hung around in the freezing workhouse yard with the adults until they received their bread ration and a basin of gruel. Before they were sent on their way everyone had to pay for their night's stay with hard labour of some kind. The reporter himself had to work with others grinding corn. He noted how the men

(26) The Quarterly Review, Vol. 82, p.142. Dec. 1847

did nothing until forced to do so by the supervisors, and then did as little as possible or merely pretended to work. The children did the same.

In 1866, the year the Pall Mall Gazette printed these articles, the Earl of Shaftesbury became the Patron of the Society, an acknowledgment of his deep interest and long-standing commitment to its cause. From the time he became the Patron, the work grew rapidly under his guidance. He established the Society's position as a national organization with a reputation for high standards and substantial achievement.

His first actions as Patron were designed to expand the work of the

Matron fitting a boy with clothes

refuges and remove many more children from the streets and give them a training for employment. He discussed his ideas for the future with William Williams. Both men were particularly anxious not to destroy the independence of the street boys. They wanted to help those who were loathe to ask for help. Lord Shaftesbury told the subscribers:

"After some talk upon the subject we determined to ascertain the natural history of London lads if I may so speak. .. After some conversation, we determined to announce a `treat' to be given on an appointed night. The treat was intended for the various classes who eventually came – the ragged, the outcast and the homeless."

As a result of the Pall Mall Gazette articles and other reports in the press on similar topics, the public were more sympathetic to appeals for help and Lord Shaftesbury believed the moment had come when the Society should expand beyond the small local area where it had opened its first school and where most of the work still continued. Those boys who came to the `treat' would be offered a chance of a fresh start by moving out of London and training for life at sea. Any applicants who were unsuited to this would be given the opportunity to train for other work. If the plan succeeded, it would be possible to remove many boys from the streets of London and the evils of the lodging houses and workhouse casual wards. Lord Shaftesbury asked the supervisors of some London casual wards and night refuges to pass on a message to any boy under the age of 16 who stayed overnight on their premises. He invited the boys to a Supper at the Refuge in George Street on St. Valentine's Night (14th February) 1866.

Many boys suspected a trap and were too frightened to accept. Not used to kindness or invitations of any kind, they were gripped by fear of the unknown. What lay behind this mysterious invitation? Would they be dragged off into an institution where iron discipline and stern regimentation would force them into a life of drudgery?

To others, a free hot meal in the depths of the winter seemed too good to miss. Around 200 boys managed to defy the jeers and taunts of their more cautious companions and plucked up enough courage to accept. On the night of the Supper, a bitter wind was blowing as the boys crept along the murky alleys, their bare feet stumbling in the darkness. Hardly a glimmer of light lit the boys' path that winter evening as they scurried fearfully through the mean back streets.

At the Refuge all the windows were ablaze with light; cheerful voices and loud laughter from within echoed around the dingy street outside. The boys crowded at the doorway hesitating before finally forcing themselves to cross the threshold. At the entrance to the large schoolroom stood William Williams and his helpers to welcome them. According to the 1866 Report `the scene reminded one of the command in the parable "Go out quickly into the streets and lanes of the city and bring in hither the poor, and the lame and the halt and the blind" '.

A roaring fire blazed at one end of the room. The shabby visitors stared in astonishment. Trestle tables arranged closely in rows with benches at their sides filled the whole area. 200 boys, neatly dressed and healthy in appearance were already seated. The newcomers were taken to the tables and shown where to sit. The large school room, normally orderly and quiet, was now a strange sight. It was packed end to end with excited, chattering boys. The skinny, barefoot newcomers scuffled and pushed in their eagerness and anxiety.

The Committee and their helpers bustled to and from the tables and the kitchens with

The supper for homeless boys at the George Street refuge on St. Valentine's night in 1866

bowls and dishes piled high with bread and steaming, succulent smelling roast beef. As fast as the food was served, so another empty dish came back to the kitchen for more.

There followed a second course of plum pudding; the boys ate till they could eat no more. The meal finished with coffee. The visitors, now looked distinctly relaxed and more comfortable. Lord Shaftesbury walked up and down the room:

".. conversing first with one and then with another so as to gain the hearts and confidence of the guests .. their behaviour was excellent, and the way in which they joined the inmates then in the Refuge in singing the Grace before and after supper, was most touching, and brought tears to the eyes of many who were present."

Lord Shaftesbury asked them about their lives and their ambitions, how they managed to stay alive, where they slept when they did not go to the workhouses, what skills they had, what jobs they managed to find, how many of them had been to prison and how many times, how many had parents living, how many of them knew about Jesus and much more besides.

Then he approached the purpose of the evening. He called out for quiet, and spoke to the whole assembly, asking his guests:

"Now, boys, supposing that there were in the Thames a big ship, large enough to contain a thousand boys, would you like to be placed on board to be taught a trade or trained for the Navy and Merchant Service?"

They clapped and cheered, threw their caps into the air, roared their approval of the plan. `Do you think' Lord Shaftesbury continued `that another 200 boys out on the streets would say the same?' They assured him there would be any number of boys eager for such a chance. Lord Shaftesbury promised he would see about finding a ship for them. William Williams told them to present themselves at the refuge the following morning. He gave each boy four pence with instructions where to go for a decent night's lodging and then finally sent them on their way.

Chapter 8

THE CHICHESTER AND ARETHUSA TRAINING SHIPS

A few days later, Lord Shaftesbury approached the Lords of the Admiralty for their help in supplying the `big ship' he had spoken of to the boys after their meal on St. Valentine's night. The Scheme progressed so quickly after that and, although the Society's Committee members were somewhat bemused by the speed of events, they felt their efforts had been well justified. The Annual Report informed the subscribers that `of all the years this work has been going, the labours of the year 1866 have been the most arduous, and consequently the most successful'.

The Admiralty agreed to hand over to the Committee the frigate *HMS Chichester*, which was lying unused in a naval dockyard. No difficulties were put in the way of the scheme and the Committee was allowed to draw from the dockyard masts, sails and other stores required for completing and fitting out the ship to the value of £2,129.15.8d, the Committee undertaking to pay this amount at the end of nine months.

There were at the time other training ships on the Thames. At Woolwich, for example, was the *Cornwall* which served as a reformatory; the *Warspite* (established in 1756), was run by the Marine Society for destitute boys and those who had been apprenticed but had failed to follow their trades. At Greenhithe, another famous training ship was the *Worcester*, established in 1862 to train boys as future officers for the Merchant Navy. However, the *Chichester* was the first to be established since the turn of the century for the particular kind of boy that the Society cared for.

HMS Chichester – *the Society's first Training Ship, handed over by the Admiralty in 1866*

By the 1860s ironclads and steam were replacing wooden sailing ships – hence the Admiralty's readiness to make the *Chichester* available to the Society, albeit on terms which were far from generous.

The owner of dry docks in Poplar, Mr. Henry Green, agreed that his Company would do all the work needed to turn the *Chichester* into a training ship at cost price.

On 6th November Lord Shaftesbury wrote in his diary:

".. today to Poplar to see ship in preparation for our school. It has

Boys training on board the Chichester

been a dream of 15 years and more. We have dashed on and are ready for action. If the means are supplied, the result is as certain as the movement of the planets; but I tremble lest the zeal of my friend Williams, and my own, may not have plunged us into responsibilities beyond our strength."[27]

By early December, all the repairs and refitting had been completed and the inauguration ceremony took place on 18th December. It was a grand occasion. The *Chichester* was arrayed 'in her gayest bunting and an awning on which the flags of all nations were tastefully distributed, was erected over the whole length of the upper deck on which the ceremony of inauguration was held'.

Of the 170 boys then living in the London refuge, 50 had been chosen as suitable through health, character and aptitude to start training in the Ship under the command of an experienced Royal Navy Captain who would be responsible for their health and welfare. These boys would be educated and thoroughly trained for a seafaring life.

William Williams asked the party assembled for the inauguration ceremony to respond generously to appeals so that more poor boys could be helped in the same way. Lord Shaftesbury told the audience that, from his own experience, he knew the *Chichester* fulfilled a great need.

"Take the most naked, ragged, wretched children of the streets, breathe upon them the breath of life, and they become equal to the highest in the land. A year ago a large number were taken into the Refuge, and 70 or 80 added every week at haphazard. What was the result? Not a single act of insubordination was recorded."

He told the new boy sailors to come forward and they stood to attention before the large gathering 'the little blue jackets, attired in their new naval costume, presented a most interesting and picturesque appearance'.

A gift of £1,000 a few weeks later enabled another 50 boys from the Refuge to start in the Training Ship. Although it cost only £15 to keep a boy for a year on board, the full comple-

(27) Hodder, Vol. 3 p. 207

Seamanship Training on the River Thames

ment of 200 boys could not be made up until the following year due to a shortage of funds.

Only strong, healthy volunteers of good character were accepted:

"This Ship is not for criminal lads, but for those homeless and destitute ones not convicted of crime. The Committee sets its face firmly against turning the Ship into a house of correction for boys who they [i.e. the parents] cannot manage themselves."

A separate Training Ship's Committee was established and included several Naval Officers and men with shipping interests. A smaller Visiting Committee made at least twice-monthly inspection visits. Among the former Committee's members were William Munton Bullivant, founder of the training ship *Worcester* and Henry Green, of Messrs H. and R. Green, leading shipping agents. As well as the knowledge and experience such men brought to the running of the Ship, their assistance in obtaining necessary equipment and supplies either free or on favourable terms was invaluable to the Society which was in constant financial straits since 'not one farthing is contributed by the government'.

The Inauguration Ceremony for the Training Ship Chichester, *December 1866*

The Committee's first task was to appoint a Commanding Officer, who was to be known as the Captain Superintendent. They selected Captain A. H. Alston who had recently retired from the Royal Navy. He was a devout Christian and, by all accounts, a most efficient man – although, as it appeared later, he was stern and unyielding in his approach to discipline and somewhat inflexible in his relations with the Committee.

Morning Prayers aboard the Chichester

During 1867, the *Chichester*'s first full year of operation, 134 boys were admitted:

"The value of this outlet for boys received into the Refuge cannot be overstated. The eagerness that is manifested by the volunteers for the Ship is most surprising and yet it ought not to be so, for anyone at all familiar with the tastes and habits of these boys knows how very strongly they are influenced by the spirit of adventure and where can such spirits find better scope and a more congenial atmosphere than in a seafaring life?"

The daily routine of the boys in the *Chichester* was divided into three main areas:

- Seamanship training (compass and lead; knotting and splicing; sail making; knowledge of all running gear and parts of the ship; reefing and furling sails; rowing and steering).
- Formal education in the three Rs.
- Craft skills (cooking, carpentry and tailoring).

All the boys were taught swimming. Religious instruction, including time for private prayer and study, was another important part of the curriculum. The boys had morning and evening prayers each day. The Thames Church Mission and later the Missions to Seamen held regular Sunday services onboard and also prepared the boys for confirmation.

The first set of 19 rules and regulations of the Ship's Committee was promulgated in August 1867. Quarterly visits by a maximum of two friends were allowed `if any boy's conduct after he has been onboard the ship two months entitles him to the indulgence'. Sundays were to be strictly observed and `none but indispensable labour performed on that day and it must be the object of the Captain and the Officers in the religious observance of the day to make it happy as well as instructive'.

The initial staff complement of the *Chichester* was Captain Superintendent Alston at a salary of £350 per annum, a Chief Officer, Schoolmaster, two Seamen Instructors, a Cook and a Carpenter. The total monthly expenses for salary and wages was approximately £71. At first staff lived onboard and worked seven days a week. In later years cottages were bought or rented ashore to accommodate them and their families.

Captain Alston's first tasks were to arrange for the building of a landing stage on the banks of the Thames and a supply of drinking water. For the landing stage he commissioned a local

It is hardly surprising that the residents at first objected to this unsubtle form of advertisement

builder, Mr. Lockyer who, with the help of a work force made up of the boys onboard, completed the task in a matter of weeks for the sum of £50. Providing water was more of a problem because it was already evident that some local residents viewed the arrival of the *Chichester* with some dismay. Eventually Mr. Colyer, the owner of a sizeable estate, was persuaded to supply water from one of his wells for a fee of £5 per year. Captain Alston also obtained discarded hoses from the London Fire Brigade to bring the water onboard.

Initially the minimum age for boys to be accepted in the Ship was 12, but this was raised to 13 in 1869; the reason for raising the minimum age was that boys of 14 were not generally big enough to be acceptable to shipping employers. The maximum admission age was always 15. The time spent by boys on the Society's training ships varied considerably over the years: the Ship's Committee regarded two years as the ideal training time and one year the minimum. The length of stay was often determined by the strength or weakness of demand for the boys' services. The overriding object was always to place boys in the Royal Navy, Merchant Services or other suitable outlets.

As far as the Merchant Service was concerned, it was soon realised that the best way to obtain berths was to have boys available and ready as soon as a vacancy occurred in a particular ship. In 1868 a Mr. Scouler was employed as a shipping agent at a salary of £60 p.a. and based in the Society's property at 100 East India Dock Road. He was expected to have up to a dozen boys lodging with him until they could be found berths. Each day he would tour the docks with two or three lads in tow and visit every ship in an effort to place them. As he was paid a fixed sum annually rather than a bounty for each boy placed, as was often the case with other shipping agents, he invariably tried to find berths with reliable companies and reputable masters. Many of the boys spoke highly of Mr. Scouler in their letters to the Captain

Superintendent and he became a trusted friend to whom they would return at the end of each voyage or when seeking another berth.

Captain Alston resigned in April 1869. The Ship's Committee minutes record a series of disputes over the previous year between the Captain and the schoolmaster and also between the Captain and the Committee, whose authority Captain Alston clearly found unacceptable. These disputes culminated in a request by the Captain in June 1869 for the *Chichester* to be exchanged for a Line of Battle ship which 'would be much larger and afford ample space for classrooms, reading rooms and for suitable apartments' to enable him to live onboard with his wife and family. He claimed that since most of his time was spent away from home his management of the Ship was 'done with a divided heart' and added that 'half my heart is afloat and half on shore'.

The Captain's relations with William Williams deteriorated to the point where 'very intemperate' accusations were made in letters by the Captain to the Committee. Without consultation he promulgated a set of no less than 99 rules for the management of the Ship. A dispute over the construction of a poop to provide living quarters for the Captain and his family was only resolved by Mr. Henry Green supplying one, at his own expense, at a cost of £539. 5s. 4d.

By March 1969 however, Captain Alston had provoked an irreparable breach for:

"In answer to an enquiry as to when he intended to take up his residence onboard he replied that before doing so he wanted space allotted to him for a store room, a press room and a wine cellar in addition to the accommodation already allotted to him in the new poop and cabins on the main deck."

This request was promptly refused. At the next meeting of the Committee on 7th April 1869 no one was surprised to hear of Captain Alston's resignation which was accepted with alacrity. It was most unfortunate that, on his subsequent appointment to the Training Ship *Cumberland,* he took with him a small group of the best boys from *Chichester.* He also persuaded the schoolmaster, the carpenter, the tailor and two seaman instructors to resign shortly afterwards promising them an increase in salary.

From the 74 applicants to replace Captain Alston, the Committee appointed Captain Thurburn RN who impressed them with his 'calm and judicious mind'. He showed a 'patient loving spirit' and was 'in every respect eminently qualified for the important and arduous duties he has to discharge'.

Captain Thurburn firmly believed that the regime in the Training Ship offered great opportunities to the boys onboard. In 1869 he reported that:

"Three hundred and forty *Chichester* boys, including those who had made previous voyages as well as first voyage boys, sailed from England in the course of the year, or in other words were provided with ships through the instrumentality of the Institution, and about five per cent sailed twice in the above period. 209 returned, of whom 169 received Board of Trade Certificates marked 'very good' for ability and conduct, 12 'good' and 1 'bad'. 27 did not report themselves, probably having been discharged at some other port than London.

The long experience I have had amongst seamen .. confirms me in the opinion, that our boys, notwithstanding the homeless and destitute condition from which they have been taken, have proved themselves deserving the care, instruction and expense bestowed upon them."

Starting in June 1870 two examiners from the local Marine Board visited the Ship annually; they examined the boys in seamanship and also inspected the educational and craft work. Their reports were without exception very favourable. The first one concluded:

"The cheerful demeanour of the boys and the good condition of the Ship, their ready attention to orders, the quiet orderly discipline onboard combined with the perfect cleanliness of the Ship, tended to make our visit one of deep interest."

Not surprisingly, the early years of the Training Ship *Chichester* were not all easy. Each year a small number of desertions is recorded, often with the comment 'left not liking the restraint'. Usually absconders made a break when allowed ashore to play, only to be tracked down by the police and returned in due course. On one occasion a boy slipped away in one of the boats at night but found there were no oars. The tide took him downstream and returned him precisely alongside the *Chichester* the following morning.

The discipline and hygiene that prevailed onboard the *Chichester* kept fatalities and serious illness to a minimum but accidents occurred from time to time. One of the boys, Alfred Pillbeam, missed his footing when jumping from the starboard gangway to the chains where other boys were exercising with lead lines. He fell into the water and even though lifebuoys were hurled after him, and another lad dived to the rescue, by the time a boat had been lowered poor Pillbeam had sunk. Another casualty by drowning was Frederick Garrett who slipped whilst trying to board a boat to go ashore and, despite the Captain himself jumping overboard to try to save the boy, Garrett was swept away by the tide, sank and drowned. His body was found at Erith a week later.

The original cost specified by the Admiralty, for masts, sails, and other stores needed for completing and fitting up the *Chichester* caused a severe financial problem for the Committee. The agreement had been to pay within nine months. Efforts to have the Admiralty write off the money failed, so a policy of delay was adopted. A letter from the Admiralty was received in December 1869 requiring immediate payment, but 'it was thought advisable not to answer it'. Instead the Committee appealed in January 1870 to the Treasury for the debt to be written off, but in April 1871 the Admiralty gave warning of legal proceedings within one week 'if the claim for masts etc. was not paid'. William Williams replied that the Committee was not in a position to pay the claim and it therefore intended to get a Member of Parliament to move in the House of Commons that the amount of the claim be added to the Navy estimates so that it might be discharged from the Admiralty books.

Lord Shaftesbury, with a deputation from the Committee, met the First Lord of the Admiralty in July 1871 and 'it was arranged that the Committee should send to the Admiralty a statement as to the real value of the stores'. Admiral King Hall of the Committee then estimated that 'the stores, although charged to the Committee at £2,129, were not worth to the Nation more than £400 to £500'.

In November 1871 the Admiralty accepted the lower figure but 'Mr. Green was of the opinion that the matter had better stand over till the next meeting before an appeal be made to the newspapers for the £400.'

For some reason the claim then went into abeyance for over six years, till February 1878, when the Treasury Solicitor wrote demanding immediate payment of £400. By then, however, the Committee was clearly unimpressed by threats of legal action, for William Williams was instructed to 'write and offer the sum of £200 in discharge of the debt'. This offer was accepted in May 1878 and the sum then paid – eleven years after the debt of ten times that amount had been incurred.

In the period up to June 1874, more than 1300 boys were accepted for training onboard the *Chichester*. Of these, the overwhelming majority were placed in the Merchant Service, with the help of Mr. Scouler.

From the outset, the *Chichester* boys secured, with only the rarest exceptions, the enthusiastic approval of the Captains who engaged them. Many testimonials to the boys' good conduct, reliability and enterprise from their instructors, inspectors and later their employers were printed in the Annual Reports. The *Chichester* continued her service successfully and without major problems for over five years. There were usually 200 to 250 boys onboard – admissions depending on the rate at which those who had completed their training could be placed by the Shipping Agent. In good months he was able to send 20 or more boys to sea in merchant ships, with a few joining the Royal Navy. The boys 'are sent away well prepared to combat the world' Captain Thurburn reported in 1872, referring to the temptations that assailed young inexperienced boys 'in the forecastle of ships, where they have to encounter very often mixed crews of lawless and depraved men'.

So successful was the *Chichester*, that the Committee was encouraged to extend the work. At the Committee meeting on 7th May 1873:

"Some conversation took place with reference to the want of English seamen and as to the desirability of meeting that want either by the establishment of another ship for the reception of 200 more boys or exchanging the present ship for one capable of receiving 400 boys. The general opinion was in favour of a second ship."

Soon after this Lady Burdett-Coutts offered the Society £5,000 for the establishment and fitting out of a second ship. Lord Shaftesbury accordingly applied once more to the Admiralty for the loan of a ship and was offered the choice of three: the *Phaeton*, the *Severn* and the *Arethusa*. The Committee inspected all three and chose the *Arethusa* on the grounds of size and space onboard as she could accommodate some 250 boys together with staff and their wives. The *Arethusa* was the fourth Royal Naval ship of this name which derives from the water nymph Arethusa of Greek mythology who turned herself into a spring to escape the attentions of the river god Alpheus. The ship had been built at Pembroke and launched on 20th June 1849. During the Crimean War she took part in the bombardment of Odessa and in an attack on Sebastopol. She was the last British ship to go into action solely under sail but, in 1860, she was lengthened and fitted with screw propulsion. In May 1874 she was handed over to the Society and securely moored in her permanent position 50 yards astern of the *Chichester*. The official opening as a training ship took place on 3rd August with the

Earl of Shaftesbury and Baroness Burdett-Coutts in attendance.

No doubt the decision to increase the number of boys taken on board was influenced by Captain Thurburn's perception that 'the demand for boys is increasing and we need not feel at all doubtful of providing employment for a larger number'. Judging from past experience he felt 'confident that the demand will continue to increase'. This large expansion of the work brought heavy new financial demands. William Williams wrote that the vessel was 'like a walnut shell' and 'the trouble of fitting it up and complying with all the restrictions imposed can be better imagined than described'.

In July 1876 he reported the expenditure of £1,000 on fire precautions for the two ships, but noted that the Lords of the Admiralty did not 'give us the money to do what they order, nor do they even send us the material from the dockyard'.

The acquisition of a second ship meant an increase in staff. On Captain Thurburn's suggestion, the *Arethusa* and *Chichester* were fitted and equipped for complements of 300 and 200 boys respectively; the *Arethusa* was to be the Headquarters Ship and began her service with 200 boys on board while 100 remained onboard the *Chichester*.

Captain Thurburn transferred to the *Arethusa* and in September 1874 Captain Walter RN was appointed to command the *Chichester* at an initial salary of £200 per annum 'with coals, lights and apartments but no rations'.

HMS Arethusa, *the Society's second Training Ship, which came into service in 1874*

When the first boys had moved from London to the *Chichester* Training Ship, the Committee began searching for a large house in the country as a home for more of their refuge boys. The aim was to get as many children as possible away from the filthy London environment into the fresh air and healthier atmosphere of the country.

For 18 months the Committee sought to acquire a farm with 60 to 100 acres of land. They were uncertain whether to look for a property to purchase or rent – this depended on the asking price and the state of the Society's finances when something suitable was found.

Eventually, a farm came up for sale in the village of Bisley near Woking in Surrey. It had 88 acres of good, workable land, suitable for mixed farming. The price was £4725, to include all timber, some farm buildings, a few cottages and a small house. The land was very cheap and the area was healthy and invigorating. Unfortunately, there were no buildings on the farm large enough for what they had in mind. After consultations with their Architect and Surveyor the Committee decided to purchase the farm as it was and to appeal for funds to build a new Home and School for between 100 and 150 boys in the grounds.

They sent a letter to subscribers and friends in November 1867 giving details of the project and the farm which was 'just of that charac-

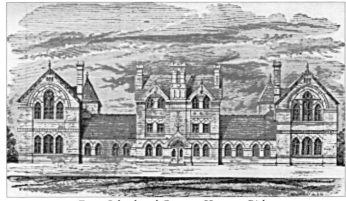

Farm School and Country Home at Bisley

ter which can with great advantage be worked by the boys. Suitable dormitories, workshops, a school-room and other conveniences must however be erected'. A Special Appeal was also launched for funds to purchase the property:

"This home is greatly needed in connection with what we have in mind for our boys, for very many come to us almost infants in age but with constitutions frail, weak, and shattered, owing to the sufferings and privations through which they have passed. They are too young and feeble to go onboard the ship, and it is distressing to keep such delicate ones in the London refuge. We have many such feeble ones with us just now."

Fortunately for the Society, in 1867, a grant of £350 was made by the Lord Mayor of London from a gift of £2,500 sent by the Sultan of Turkey for distribution amongst the poor of London. The Times and many other newspapers, both national and local, carried advertisements for the Society's Appeal for funds. By the end of the year donations from the public had not reached £500 but the Secretary had by then spent more than £1,500 on the Project. However, Miss Gordon, a long term supporter of the Society, sent a cheque for £500 and this, with other sums received, encouraged the Committee to proceed.

As soon as the purchase had been completed, 35 small, delicate boys were moved into the farmhouse at Bisley so that they could benefit immediately from the country air. Mr. Wood, the master in charge of the London Refuge was appointed as the first Superintendent and travelled with them. Shortly afterwards builders started work on the new Farm School.

Week by week during the first year, boys from the London Refuge, 25 at a time, went to Bisley for a week's holiday. They played in the fields, went for country walks and learnt something of country life. They had to camp in one of the barns, sleeping in the straw, but to children who were used to the rough life of London slums, this was no hardship. The Committee noted with satisfaction that .. 'they returned to the Refuge in Great Queen Street vastly benefited by their week's holiday in the country'.

On 23rd December Lord Shaftesbury came to the farm with other London visitors and, in the presence of the children, their teachers and local people declared the Bisley Farm School open.

By the end of 1868 the School was in full swing with 100 boys in residence. They worked on the farm, learned carpentry, tailoring, shoemaking or bread-making according to their abilities. Everything they learned was put to practical use. Produce from the Farm supplied the needs of the pupils and their teachers and any surplus was sold. In the trade lessons, the boys would help with the making of their own outfits and footwear or would make and repair furniture for the Home. Any surplus here was also sold although the Committee did not intend the Farm School to be primarily a profit making operation. The plan was 'to grow vegetables, fruit, and other light crops, breed pigs, poultry, keep cows, etc.' so as to provide healthy outdoor occupation for as many boys as possible, and to teach them good habits of work and discipline.

Apart from boys with poor health or weak constitutions others were sent to the Farm School if the Committee decided that London was unsuitable for them:

".. owing to the unhappy and vicious friends with whom they were associated in early life. To these lads the discipline and training they will receive at the farm before they emigrate will be most useful, as the knowledge they will there acquire will make them more serviceable on reaching the colonies, and so secure them constant employment, and likewise better pay."

Teaching at the Farm School covered a wide and varied syllabus:

"It must not be thought that at our Country Farm the boys are trained to be young farmers, although, no doubt, many will find employment in agricultural pursuits. We give them industrial, moral and religious training, and our hope is that ultimately they will be found faithfully doing their duty in that state of life into which it has pleased God to call them."

Not all the boys sent to the farm appreciated life away from town. If they did not settle, they were sent back to the London Refuge, as were the boys from the *Chichester* who did not want to continue training onboard. In 1869 17 were readmitted to the London refuge from the Farm and the Ship.

Music was always an important part of the school curriculum in all the Society's establishments. The Farm School was no exception. All the boys learned to sing in a choir and by

*Music was always an important part of school life; the School Band flourished
and many boys went on to join regimental bands*

1869 the school started its own brass band; the bill for musical instruments that year came to £45. 8s. 0d. In subsequent years, the Society frequently appealed for additional musical instruments for the boys.

By 1871 some of the more able Farm School pupils were learning telegraphy. As a result, when they left Bisley, it was easy for them to find jobs with the postal service or in other businesses. The master in charge reported that when the telegraph class had been in operation for little more than a year they had already 'sent out two very promising youths into the service of one of our Dock Companies, at the salary of £30 a year each, with the prospect of a yearly increase'. Boys were encouraged to work hard and behave themselves. Those who did were able to join the telegraph class if their work was up to standard.

Harvest Festival was celebrated for the first time in grand style at the Farm School in late October 1871. The Earl of Onslow, the local Lord of the Manor, was the guest of honour. He brought a large party with him including two Members of Parliament. The Society's General Committee was there in force together with friends of the boys, many local people and Society supporters.

It was a chilly day in late autumn. The day started with a service conducted by the local Rector in a large tent in the school grounds. The boys impressed everyone with their cheerful, vigorous singing. A celebration lunch followed and included roast pork, which had been produced on the Farm. After lunch everyone went to the large school room for the prize giving; there were many awards – medals and books, prizes for good conduct and application to work. Anthony Waterer, who owned a nursery at Knapp Hill nearby, was a member of the Farm School sub-committee. He donated six silver medals, to be awarded biennially for special achievement and progress. He was a good and loyal friend to the boys at Bisley and for many years after his death in 1896, his son continued the family support for the School.

At the time of this first Harvest Festival there was already a 'magnificent collection of shrubs' in the School grounds – a gift from Anthony Waterer. There were two special awards; one to a boy chosen by secret ballot among all the pupils at the School, and the second to a boy who showed particular aptitude and effort in the telegraphy class. The winner of the telegraphy award, although not yet 14, had got a job with a London business at £30 per annum.

Speeches followed at the end of the ceremony; Lord Onslow praised the work of the School and the efforts of the boys. With an eye to publicity and fund raising he emphasised to his audience how little it cost to save a destitute child from misery and offer him the chance of leading a decent life after he left school. William Williams appealed for help in kind as well as cash. The School needed an asphalt playground; sheep, pigs, and cows would make very acceptable gifts as the Farm was well stocked with roots and other food for farm animals. After tea, the ceremonies were brought to a close by the School Choir which led the company in a selection of songs. One of the visitors spoke to the telegraphy award winner who told him how he came to be in the Society's care. He had no idea who his father was, but he vividly remembered his early life travelling round the country with his mother who sold pins, needles and other haberdashery items. They never had a home but slept rough or in cheap lodgings. When the boy was nine his mother died of fever; he managed to make a living as a road crossing sweeper or by shoe blacking or running errands. A woman had pity on him, took him to William Williams and made a donation towards his upkeep at Bisley.

By 1872 two boys from the telegraphy class were working in the West India Docks. Their uniform was provided free of charge and they were earning an annual salary of £36, while a third boy, who had only recently started work, was earning £30.

When the time came to leave school, many of the boys aspired to join the Services, some of them hoping to become bandsmen. In 1872, 12 leavers from the Farm School were drafted into regimental bands. The following year a newspaper report of the Society's Annual Prize Day praised the musical training at Bisley:

"Very noticeable amongst this large family of once homeless and destitute were 13 lads, representing Her Majesty's land forces, who have been drafted into various regimental bands – foot and cavalry. They had received a preliminary musical training in the band of the Farm under its excellent and painstaking bandmaster, Mr. Digweed, and are now not only a credit to the noble institution which has opened to them an honourable and respectable career, but to the regiments whom they represent."[28]

Notwithstanding the best efforts of the Society and other worthy organisations and individuals, the streets of London were still home to vast numbers of ragged children and there seemed no prospect of their number diminishing. The Committee therefore decided to build another Home in the grounds of the Farm School. It opened in the autumn of 1873 and was

(28) The London *Mirror*, Jan. 4, 1873.

named Shaftesbury School; by the end of the year 57 boys were in residence.

Visitors were always welcome. In December 1873 a Mr. H.E. Page visited the two homes at Bisley with a party of friends. They arrived by train at Brookwood station. He afterwards wrote:

"It is a pleasant country, with its sweeps of heath and scattered clusters of houses half hidden among clumps of trees. Bisley, we were told at Brookwood, lay a couple of miles off (rather long miles, we thought them). Bisley is hardly a village – the population of the whole parish, prior to the settling of the Home, having been only some 350."

Mr. Page observed a typical school working day at the two schools. In the Farm School he went to all the class rooms and the new granary for which all the woodwork had been done by the boys and their master. He saw the kitchen, bakehouse and wash-house. He noted the spacious, airy dormitories which could each accommodate 50 boys. He saw the new 'fruit-walk' which had recently been laid out in the hope of boosting income in the future. He asked the Superintendent whether he had any trouble with the boys.

'Boys will be boys' Mr. Wood replied 'and sometimes they may play a trick, and neglect or forget a bit of duty; but on the whole, no gentleman's children could be more biddable, willing or grateful.'

The visitors stood in the playground to watch:

".. a little regiment in corduroys and blue blouses being drilled. There they marched, wheeled, and counter-marched at the double in most excellent order, and having done their due in this way under the active band and drill master, they set themselves to gymnastics. In the cattle yard, another detachment were busy loading the carts, and behind that a third were at it in the hayricks, and further in a field a couple had care of the cows grazing, while a fifth little group, who then had their play-hour, or may have been of a sickly tendency, were at play – one of their number bestriding a donkey, who to his honour seemed in no way refractory."

At the end of the afternoon they went back into the school building to listen to the band which was practising in the schoolroom. Mr. Page felt that 'the whole aspect of the place told of hearty enjoyment' and 'the music was such as would not have discredited any ordinary regimental band.'

The Treasurer's Cash Account for the year 1873 gives details about receipts from the Farm School Account:

SALE OF FARM PRODUCE
(exclusive of £558.5s.0d. used for the boys)

Barley, Potatoes, Carrots etc.	£223.14. 4.
Garden Produce	£ 50. 6. 6.
Pigs	£ 94.19. 3.
Butter, Bread, Pork, etc.	£ 72.17.11.
107 Sheep	£343.18. 8.
Cow	£ 8. 0. 0.
Coals	£ 3.10. 6.
TOTAL	£797. 7. 2.

The payments for that year recorded in the Farm School Maintenance Account amounted to £2146.4s.7d.

Shortly after Christmas, William Williams received a letter from one of the Committee members, Mr. Charles Hoare, describing his surprise visit with a friend to the two Bisley schools:

"Dec 27 1873

Fleet Street

Dear Mr. Williams

We arrived at the Farm home at about 12 o'clock and in less than 2 minutes after ringing the bell Mr. Wood made his appearance. Mr. Hubbard introduced me to him and explained that we had come down to Bisley without giving him any notice to see how things were managed in their normal state.

So without more ado we commenced our tour of inspection: of course there is no good in minutely describing to you how we found the boys employed, as you know it all so well; you will be glad to know however that we went everywhere over the buildings and farm and found the discipline, order, and conduct of the boys admirable.

It being only two days before Christmas, the large room where the meals are served was in a great state of confusion when we went in at about 12.15, undergoing a grand process of decoration, all the boys who were not otherwise engaged being cheerfully and happily busy. The work was done so orderly and quietly that there were some boys doing their lessons in the same room. One boy I saw was

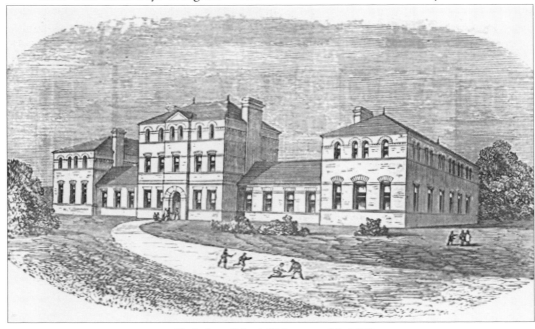

Shaftesbury School, Bisley, opened in 1873

writing a copy. I just looked over it and the writing would not have disgraced a clerk in a house of business.

From there we went upstairs. I was particularly struck with the cleanliness and tidiness of the dormitories, the beds looked clean, comfortable and warm. We then went to the Tailors' shop where we were told the boys were working extra hours as they had just received an order for 120 capes, which had to be executed by January 2nd. Here too there seemed to be admirable discipline and order, and although the boys were kept hard at work my recollection of their appearance is that the 'tout ensemble' was busy and bright.

We next paid a visit to the offices – wash house, bake house, larder, scullery and kitchen etc. where there was a very savoury smell of dinner. The boy cook was just giving a last stir to the soup which was to be the dinner of the day. There was now just time to see the farm buildings and outhouses before the boys' dinner. The arrangements here were equal to those in the house, which is saying a great deal, everything being orderly and well arranged.

We now returned to the large room, which was all upside-down when we first went in with Christmas preparations. During our absence on the tour of inspection, great progress had been made with the decorations, all the confusion too had disappeared, and the boys were seated and enjoying their dinner of thick good soup. I can speak for the soup being good as I ate the great part of a large basinfull myself at luncheon. The only improvement in the domestic arrangements I can suggest is in the matter of the WCs. When I saw them they were not quite clean and the foot water was standing in them: this was partly owing I believe, to the pumping gear of the well being out of order and undergoing repair. I should like to see these places all removed and in their place simple earth closets substituted.

We then proceeded to the other house, which we went over; it was all quite satisfactory as far as I could judge from a rather hurried visit.

In conclusion I think the subscribers might well be congratulated in the possession of so valuable a servant as Mr. Wood. He appears to maintain by a firm and Christian temper a thoroughly good discipline and tone throughout the establishment".

Chapter 10
EDUCATION REFORM AND NEW ENDEAVOURS

It had taken less than 30 years for the school above a back street cowshed to develop into a nationally known and respected Society controlling several schools and homes. This success was achieved against a background of general public apathy and criticism.

By June 1862, however, the Committee announced with confidence that:

"Happily for ragged schools their day of opposition is over. The blessed and beneficial results produced by them to the children educated therein, and to society at large, are admitted and acknowledged on all sides, and so long as care is taken to confine them to the class for whom they were intended, there is but little doubt that they will always have the sympathy and support of all who have the welfare of the poor at heart."

Public sympathy for ragged schools was in a large measure due to Lord Shaftesbury's commitment and support. He never faltered in his firm belief that, as long as there were ragged children living in the gutters, there should be suitable schools available for them and for them exclusively. To his mind, the ragged schools offered the best possible chance for deprived, neglected and unwanted children to succeed. It was wrong and unrealistic, he felt, to expect that such children could cope in the other schools available:

"You must keep your ragged schools down to one mark; .. you must keep them in the mire and the gutter, so long as the mire and the gutter exist. So long as this class exists, you must keep the schools adapted to their wants, their feelings, their tastes, and their level. I feel that my business lies in the gutter, and I have not the least intention to get out of it." [29]

Paradoxically, the success of his efforts to win recognition for what these schools had achieved was one of the factors leading to their gradual demise. He ensured that Parliament and the public were aware of the ragged children's plight. His sympathy for them created a corresponding measure of public sympathy. The need for a national system of education was, in the main, accepted and W.E. Forster's educational reforms were a consequence. Once the Education Act of 1870, which made elementary education available to all, was passed, the ragged schools lost ground and gradually were superseded.

There was general agreement on the need to educate all the nation's children, but inevitably there were differences of opinion as to what was suitable, how to provide it and who should be the providers. For some, Church schools providing religious instruction according to Church of England doctrine were the answer. Others wanted to see more Non-Conformist schools available. Yet others wanted a completely secular type of education.

The political manoeuvring of the various groups while the matter was being debated ensured that when the Act was passed it was a compromise. It pleased neither those who saw religious instruction as crucial to education nor those who wanted religion excluded.

According to the Act, School Boards were to be elected. Their task was to fill the gaps in education provided by the voluntary societies. Board School education would provide no sectarian religious teaching. Voluntary societies were given six months to ensure their schools were up to the required standard; after that they would be assessed and district Board Schools set up as necessary.

---

(29) Hodder, Vol. 2, p.410

A Ragged School orphan in about 1870

In Church schools religious education was to be optional and placed at the beginning or end of the day so that parents could withdraw their children if they so wanted. School Boards were given the power to make attendance compulsory if they wished and they could determine fees to a maximum of 9d. per week.

While these changes were taking place, and from then on, Lord Shaftesbury never missed an opportunity to praise the achievements of the ragged schools and the work of the refuges. In May 1876 he spoke at the Society's Annual Meeting. After he had presented the prizes he spoke of one particular boy:

"That lad who stood before you just now was fatherless and motherless and, but for such an Institution as this, what would have become of him? We have taken the children under a grand protective system, and have done this before they were tainted with crime, and have started them on the race of life.

Now, I ask you what can the School Board do like unto this? When will the School Board ever show the same parental influence which we have exerted over these children, and thousands besides them who have through our care been placed in honourable occupation, in trade, and in domestic life? We have sought to relieve the state of a burden and to train them up for the safety and honour of the country.

When they come down to destroy the schools we have set up, and over which we have so jealously and carefully watched, we feel that we must speak, and say that they at least are not the persons to speak of an inefficiency.

Look and judge what has been done. Look at the thousands that have been sent into service. Look at the *Chichester* and *Arethusa*. Have we not sent onboard those vessels no less than 2,000 lads who might have turned into a curse and a pestilence, but have through our influence been turned into magnificent fellows?"

On another occasion he said:

"So long as any ragged children remain in our land, so long must you have a ragged school system. How long the government of the country and the wiseacres of the country were before they came to the national system of education in 1870! Before that time I heard comments on the ragged school

Some 'Magnificent Fellows' in the Arethusa

system, but I invariably replied, 'I do not claim it to be perfect, but we are acting while you are deliberating; we are doing something while you are doing nothing.' " [30]

Yet his wide experience in public affairs told him that the ragged school system could not last much longer. In his diary[31] he described the ragged schools as 'a dying patient'. What he feared inevitably happened. It pained him very much when ragged school buildings which had been paid for by voluntary effort were handed over for use as the Board Schools in which no religious education was provided. 'All of this will greatly abridge my labours' he wrote in January 1872 'but it will half break my heart'.[32]

As their pupils found places at the new Board Schools paid for by Boards of Guardians, so gradually the ragged schools were forced to close. But adversity was the fertile soil in which these schools had taken root, and in adversity they flourished. One of their great strengths was flexibility. It is true they were a dying patient but their death was a slow one. It was more than 20 years after the passing of the Education Act that the Society's last remaining ragged school was forced to close.

In the meantime the Society, now known as 'The National Refuges for Homeless and Destitute Children', began to concentrate more resources and effort into its ships and the refuge work in London and the country. Poverty was still forcing many people to come to London looking for work. Young children still roamed the streets and learnt criminal ways.

Two members of the Society's Committee were particularly interested in helping street boys, many of whom tried to make a living selling newspapers and other items. John Fordham and William Hubbard wanted to provide a home for these boys. Unlike all their previous establishments, it would be neither a school nor a refuge. The leaflet advertising the venture stated:

"It is not expected that by these means the class of street boys will be entirely reformed or the City cleared of their ragged horde; for such an army as theirs there is only too constant a supply of recruits from overcrowded courts and alleys; but it is hoped that many boys may be raised up from their present doubtful calling, instead of being allowed to drift uncared for into a criminal life."

Enough money was raised for the Society's Newsboys' Home to open in 1871. The intention was 'to bring these boys under good influence without destroying that self-dependence which is their best characteristic, or exercising so much restraint as to frighten them from the Home altogether'.

The boys paid a small sum from whatever they earned during the day towards their lodgings and food. Mr. and Mrs. Barry were appointed as the first Superintendent and Matron. They made the boys welcome and encouraged them at the end of their day's work to enjoy them-

William Egerton Hubbard: Chairman and Treasurer 1868-1918, established the Society's Newsboys' Home at 80, Gray's Inn Road in 1871

(30) *Lord Shaftesbury and Social Industrial Progress*, by J. Wesley Bready, footnote p.169.
(31) The National Register of Archives, Shaftesbury (Broadlands) MSS, SHA/PD/9, 8 Mar. 1870
(32) Ibid., SHA/PD/10, 10 Jan. 1872

selves in the recreation room at the Home rather than roaming the streets and getting into mischief. Lord Shaftesbury visited the Home soon after it opened. 'What a rough, unwashed, uncombed lot!' he wrote afterwards 'but there is good material in them; and by God's blessing we can work it into shape'. (33)

By 1875 the name of the Home had been changed to the more appropriate 'Home for Working Boys', as it was by then catering not only for newsboys but also for other boys starting work in London who did not earn enough to pay for decent lodgings. Those who left the Society's refuges frequently transferred there when they started work.

A visitor described his impressions after an evening there in 1871:

"The average number of lodgers last week was 50. The boys were all orderly and quiet enough, some gathering round Mrs. Barry who was reading them a story. Others were playing draughts or dominoes. In one corner was a small boy doing tricks with a knotted handkerchief. Mr. Barry thinks those nimble fingers are sometimes used to no good purpose. At 10 o'clock the boys assembled for prayers - 5 minutes only, the boys are young and tired and had to work the next day. Then, they paid their money and went up to bed."

THE
NEWSBOYS HOME,
80, GRAY'S INN ROAD,
HOLBORN.

The Best Lodging in London, for Boys under 16 Years of Age.

CHARGES.

Bed .... 2d. per night, or 1s. per week.
Pint of Coffee or Tea .... 1d.
8oz. Loaf of Bread .... 1d.
Butter .... 1d.
Soap .... 1d.

HOT BATH AND WASH-HOUSE.

DRAUGHTS AND DOMINOES.

SAVING'S BANK AND NIGHT SCHOOL.

House Closes at 10 p.m., 9.30 p.m. on Sundays.

RULES.

Be Orderly. Use the Bath. Don't use bad Language.
Any Boy breaking the above Rules, or wilfully troublesome, will be turned out by the Superintendent, Mr. BARRY.
W. E. HUBBARD, Jun., *Treasurer.*
W. WILLIAMS, *Secretary.*

Printed by the Boys of the Door-step Brigade, 26, Eccleston Street East, S.W.

Handbill advertising the Newsboys' Home

Mr. and Mrs. Barry had to be careful about which boys they accepted into the Home, as one of their reports shows.

New arrival at the Home for Working Boys

"Two lads applied for lodging at the Home. One glance was sufficient to see that they were fresh from the country. They had an excellent story which they stuck to with great pertinacity. They were two brothers who had been cruelly treated at home, and so they had come to London to seek their fortunes."

The Matron was unconvinced, particularly as they had a large sum of money with them. After a few days they realised that London life was not living up to their expectations; wealth and fame had so far eluded them and their money was running out. At last they told Mrs. Barry the truth:

(33) The National Register of Archives, Shaftesbury (Broadlands) MSS, SHA/PD/9, 18 Mar. 1871

A Group of 'Working Boys'

"They had been reading some of the abominable trash which forms boys' literature nowadays, and seized with the idea of becoming heroes, they stole some money from their father's till and ran away from home. Very rebellious and full of loud talk they were when they found they would be sent back."

Mrs. Barry escorted them to the Railway Station and telegraphed to their parents, 50 miles from London, that the lost children were on their way home.

Miss Chipchase: 1866, Matron of Girls' Refuge, Broad Street, Bloomsbury; 1873-1911, Matron at Sudbury Hall School for Girls. The redoubtable Miss Chipchase retired after 45 years' service aged 75, and died in 1921 aged 86

It will be recalled that the older girls at the London Refuge had moved to Acton in 1860. This move was a great success; equally successful was the removal of many boys to Bisley and to the *Chichester.* In continuation of this process, in 1872, the Broad Street Refuge was closed and the girls, with their recently appointed Matron, Miss Chipchase, moved to Sudbury Hall in Sudbury, near Harrow. The new Home, which could accommodate 120 girls cost £3,200; it was a large house with nearly three acres of freehold land. The Committee informed the subscribers a few months after the move that 'the change that has taken place in the health of those who were formerly inmates of the Broad Street premises is most marvellous'.

Lord Shaftesbury, who had been the Society's Patron since 1866, became its President in 1874. Thereafter, for many years, he took the chair at every public meeting and worked with the Committee on all projects. The next new enterprise concerned the Boys' Refuge building in Great Queen Street. Although at the time it had been a vast improvement on their previous quarters, 'The Palace Home' as the boys called it, was palatial only in the boys' imagination. By 1878 it was dilapidated, dangerous and almost beyond repair. At first, the Committee proposed to have it demolished and rebuilt on the same site but legal difficulties arose which persuaded the Committee to look instead for a property out of town.

It was then that the Society acquired Fortescue House in Twickenham, a substantial mansion standing in its own grounds and close to the railway station at Strawberry Hill. It had been built in 1740; in the early

Fortescue House, Twickenham

years of the 19th century it was used as a school run by a Miss Dutton and Mary Shelley, the author of 'Frankenstein', is said to have been one of the pupils.[34] Prior to its purchase by the Society, it had been occupied for a few years by the Metropolitan and City Police Orphanage.

The price for the house 'with schoolroom, dining hall, playground and numerous outbuildings, $2\frac{1}{2}$ acres of Freehold land and $1\frac{1}{2}$ of Copyhold land' was £6,300, which the Committee considered represented sound value. Essential repairs, alterations and additions cost a further £1,300.

The old Refuge was closed, and a smaller building in Great Queen Street was leased for use as a reception home for children who applied to the Society for admission. When all necessary enquiries and formalities had been completed the children were transferred to one of the Society's other homes.

The boys and their masters moved in to Fortescue House as soon as everything was ready and the grand Opening Ceremony took place on Friday 25th October 1878. Once again, a large party of friends and supporters were present for the occasion:

"It was an exceptionally fine day in a week in which there was more gloom than sunshine, and many felt winter had set in before autumn had fairly gone. The new home could not be seen from the railway station – but actually it was not five minutes walk from it. The flys and carriages in attendance were not really needed.

When one thought of the dingy old Refuge and then glanced at the new Home the contrast was so great that it needed the presence of the Secretary on the lawn to smile a cordial welcome and to give to all friends a hearty shake of the hand to enable them to feel that they were really visiting the institution with which they had been familiar for years and were now only seeing an old friend with a new face.

The sense of strangeness vanished, however, the moment you entered the house, for notwithstanding the fine entrance hall, handsome staircase, and fine suite of rooms, here and there you saw the pictures which used to hang in the London refuge, and by and by you heard the murmur of voices which told you the boys were not far off, and were already finding themselves quite at home amid their new surroundings."

The schoolroom and the dining hall were hung with garlands of flowers and leaves, decorations and mottoes, just as on great occasions in the past. One improvement on the old Refuge was the large open-air playground, with a shelter for the boys to use in wet weather.

"There is also an excellent lavatory and bath, on the value of which to such an establishment there is no need to dilate.

Glancing from the dining hall, one obtained a tempting view of one of those good old English gardens, beautiful in its irregularity, and well stocked with fruit trees.

As one rambled through the house, the strains of music seemed to follow us into every room, for the well-known brass band of the refuge was in great force today, and every tune meant gladness and triumph.

We have still the tailors' shop. Lord Shaftesbury's portrait, as of old, will look down upon the little workers. We have also the shoemakers' shop, and rooms in which the other industries of the Refuge can be carried forward.

The opening day was a happy one from first to last. A large tent had been erected in the garden where a good tea was provided, not only for the boys of the new home but for their young companions in the other homes who had been invited to share in the joy of this festive occasion."

Lord Shaftesbury was there of course. He joined with the children in hymn singing:

"A children's temple here we build,
And dedicate it, Lord, to thee"

When he spoke to the adults present, he returned to his theme:

"I speak with all respect of the School Board for London. I am sure they are doing all they can within their limits, but they are so restricted as to be unable to do what is done here. We treat a child here parentally. We train him with due regard both to his temporal and eternal interest. We do not put a child into a kind of grinding machine, and turn away until we at last turn him out. And let a word be said to those who are talking of the overpopulated condition of the country. England may be overpopulated if it is to be the place of security for thieves and vagabonds, but England has not half the population she wants for her true influence and honour."

25 Great Queen Street, where children were received for admission

Lord Shaftesbury had mentioned worries about the increasing population. This was also a concern to the Committee of the Society and the teachers as it was growing ever more difficult to find suitable jobs for their pupils. The best hope for many of the children, they still believed, lay in emigration. The money needed for this, to provide outfits and passage for the boys and girls ready to go, was not always available and frequently the children's families were unwilling for them to embark on the adventure.

The Committee was always anxious about the welfare of those they sent abroad. Within its limited

Boys from the Society's refuges and the Farm School at Bisley bound for Canada, where the Society's Agent placed them with respectable farmers. Many eventually became 'homesteaders'.

means the Society tried to ensure good placements for all the children and to keep in touch with their progress. In April 1883, subscribers were informed that 'we have been urged to purchase a farm in Canada and to place some boys thereon, with a view of giving the lads a good insight into Canadian farming before placing them out in situations.' Funds were not available to buy a suitable property but instead a house in Hamilton, Ontario was leased so that the boys arriving from England would not 'be turned adrift in a strange land' but would have a secure home until they found a job. Old boys already in Ontario would be able to use the house as a temporary home if they were out of work or ill.

Mr. and Mrs. Ward, the Superintendent and Matron of the London Boys' Refuge, travelled to Canada to take charge of the new house. They soon had it in full working order. It had 18 rooms, outhouses and a few acres of land. Mr. Ward kept a paternal eye on the boys in the Home and those working nearby. He reported regularly to the Committee in London and arranged reunions for the boys at which they could meet their old friends:

"In early November last" wrote Mr. Ward to the Committee "I was able to assist about 100 lads from various parts to spend the day with Mrs. Ward and me in Hamilton. In the evening there was a public meeting in the town with the Mayor. About 30 silver medals were presented to those who had remained in their situations with good characters for 12 months."

The House had been taken for three years on an experimental basis. The usual shortage of funds forced the Committee to be cautious:

"When this period expires it may be necessary owing to the expenses to make other arrangements for the reception of the lads, placing them out in situations and keeping the oversight of them. The Committee expect still to have the services of Mr. and Mrs. Ward in this matter."

The 1870 Education Act, which had been responsible for so much change in the Society's work during the period described in this chapter, was reinforced in 1876 by a further Act by which a legal obligation was placed on parents to ensure that their children received at least an elementary education. It was the government measure in 1891, making elementary education at all the Board Schools completely free, that finally brought about the closure of the Society's last remaining Ragged School in Little Coram Street.

Chapter 11
DEATH OF THE EARL OF SHAFTESBURY

'If my life should be prolonged for another year' said Lord Shaftesbury in 1880 'and if, during that year, the ragged school system were to fall, I should not die in the course of nature, I should die of a broken heart'.[35]

The National Refuges, born in 1843, was at the time of Lord Shaftesbury's statement a vigorous and flourishing organization. The men and women who had steered it through crises and upheavals in earlier years were by now themselves elderly. The Society's schools and refuges, which in infancy had been somewhat precarious and vulnerable, had now become sturdy and strong though not without many an alarm and misadventure. The children the Society had cared for in their turn came to show concern for their teachers and supporters.

The Earl of Shaftesbury in his 81st year

The Earl of Shaftesbury towards the end of his life explained how much he owed to the children from the various ragged schools and refuges which he had made his own, including the National Refuges:

"I believe I have been pretty well clothed by day and night by them. I have had all sorts of things made and given to me. I have had slippers and stockings; I have had shoes and waistcoats, and bed linen too; coverlets, counterpanes – well, everything but a coat; I have had desks, I have had arm-chairs, and they gave me such a quantity of writing paper, all well stamped, that I assure you it was enough for all my own correspondence for six months. I love it, however, because it has been all called forth from their dear little hearts, and I prize it all far more than the noblest present that could be given me."[36]

Everyone connected with the National Refuges knew how much he loved the children. One of the Society's supporters wrote:

"Who will ever forget one little feature in our Annual Meetings: As our noble President came on the platform amid the thunders of applause which greeted him from the large audience, he had a special way of thanking the children who were cheering him. He would turn round to them, give them a smile, and a cordial wave of the hand to show that he had heard their cheer above all the rest, and that he thanked them for it."

He had described the ragged schools as a 'dying patient' but they proved tougher than he had imagined. He himself fitted the description better. Anxiety about the fate of deprived and homeless children cost Lord Shaftesbury many sleepless nights. His own health had never been strong; by 1884 he was an old man of 83 and it was clear to all his friends that he had

(35) Hodder, Vol. 3, p.480.
(36) Hodder, Vol. 3, pp.479-480.

only a little time to live. Despite personal worries, disappointments and family anxieties he was determined to use all his remaining strength to further those causes to which he had devoted his life. The children of the National Refuges were never far from his thoughts.

He came to the farewell tea for the boys emigrating to Canada in 1884. He was a little late arriving as he had been at another meeting earlier in the afternoon. He arrived just as the boys, their teachers, friends and supporters were singing a hymn during the service led by Canon Nisbet, one of the Society's Vice-Presidents. The prayers were for the boys' safety on their voyage and success in their new life.

After the service Lord Shaftesbury and the boys listened as Canon Nisbet, who had travelled to Canada two or three years previously, entertained them with stories of whales and icebergs and the awesome weather they might encounter when crossing the Atlantic. He explained to the boys they would find: " ..big rivers, bigger than any you have here, and you will have much colder winters, and much warmer summers, and numbers of other things of which you may have only heard or read."

The boys were excited, eager and apprehensive in equal parts.

Another friend at the party, Professor Tanner, had been to Canada the previous year. 'Imagine a country as large as Europe' he said, trying to give them some idea how vast the country was 'with a population smaller than London's'. Although there was little decent work to be had in the towns of England at the present, he told them, there was plenty available in Canada.

"You may look forward to the time when you will be the occupiers of land. I have known young men go upon land which they have had just enough money to secure but by industry and energy they cultivated it and became prosperous farmers. It is a great thing to look forward to becoming owners of land."

Lord Shaftesbury sat in a chair and chatted to each of the boys in turn; some of them he had known by name for a long time. Over the years he had helped many boys to emigrate to the colonies and many had written to him about their adventures. He spoke to the boys about a letter he had received from a young farmer in Australia who had just bought two rams. He had named one Ashley in honour of Lord Shaftesbury and the other Payne after Judge Payne, one of Lord Shaftesbury's oldest allies in the fight to improve the lives of poor children. 'Now if you get a couple of rams' he told the children 'you should name one after Mr. Williams and the other after Mr. Nisbet – and if you have a third you may name it after me'.

Sid Edwards, one of the emigrants. From simple beginnings many boys prospered in the Colonies.

He raised his voice above their laughter and, turning to the adults, he went on 'it is my belief that you will find finer fellows out on the streets of London than in any other part of the world. The entire history of the National Refuges proves this'. When the party came to an end, he shook each boy's hand, gave him a Bible and wished him well.

In May 1884 at the Annual Public Meeting, Lord Shaftesbury was far from well; it was obvious to everyone how weak he was. He had to be helped to the platform.

At the start of the meeting the children sang the songs they had been rehearsing during the afternoon. Some items were solemn, some were sad but two or three were so funny and the children so amusing that, at times, the audience was convulsed with laughter 'Man the Lifeboat' was sung with such verve and style that they had to give an encore. Lord Shaftesbury loved music and singing. He listened closely, smiling all the time and applauded with great enthusiasm. Everyone in the room clapped and cheered for several minutes when he stood up to speak to them. He reminded the audience of the Society's need for their continuing support. He pointed out the children from each of the schools and said how well and happy they looked. Investing in the children, he said, was investing in the future of the country as well as helping the children themselves.

"Look on my left hand, and see there the lads of the *Chichester* and *Arethusa*. Our mercantile marine, our Royal marine, and those who know the value of good sailors for the protection of our coasts and the extension of our commerce and trade will also thank you from the bottom of their hearts that you have taken such lads off the streets and made them sailors, to carry with them the honour of the English name wherever they go, and to be a credit to all of you."

Memories of his childhood, with loveless parents but a caring, concerned and devoted nurse, Maria Millis, were clearly in his mind as he continued:

"When you see all these little girls fitted for domestic life, fitted to be a comfort to the house to which they go, by the discharge of their duties, you will be able to appreciate their value. They care for your children, set them a good example, and stand in the place very often of a mother to them."

He spoke of his sadness because hundreds of children begging for admission had to be turned away:

".. simply because the public that owes us so much will pay us so little in return. If you look at what these children were, at what they are, and what they will become if you continue your care, does not the question suggest itself – What will become of them if you withdraw your care?"

To finish his address, he spoke of the children's singing:

"While they were singing that thrilling little song 'Man the Lifeboat!' I could almost fancy that they were singing about themselves, and rejoicing in their safety and happiness. You heard them shout 'They're in the boat, They're all afloat! Hurrah! they have gained the shore!' And so they have. They have triumphed gloriously."

Two months later Lord Shaftesbury was well enough to travel by rail with a party of friends and family to Greenhithe to act as Chairman at Prize Day for the boys from the training ships. Many past pupils were present to receive rewards for good behaviour and progress in their subsequent careers. As one young man came forward for his prize Lord Shaftesbury greeted him as an old friend. He pointed him out to the audience and remarked:

"He was one of the earliest trained onboard the *Chichester* and was among those who came to the memorable supper in Great Queen Street. I am happy to tell you that he is now discharging the duty of a detective officer in one of the great Docks. I am truly thankful for his good conduct, and I pray that God will bless him to the last days of his life."

He was so weak in June 1885 that, rather than miss the occasion, he came to the Society's Annual Meeting in an 'invalid carriage'. The hall was packed and the audience was delighted to see among the platform party the well known figure of their President. They had been afraid his poor health would prevent his attending. Nevertheless, he was determined to speak and in a frail voice he told them of a surprise visit he had recently received:

"What do you think happened to me the other day?" he said "I had a deputation of ragged school children to see me, and eight or ten of them came into my room. One of them produced what I could see was a heavy packet. 'What is that?' I asked 'It is money my Lord' was the answer. And true enough it was, for it was nine shillings all in pence, and the gift as it turned out of 147 children."

In his diary that night he briefly noted "took chair in Exeter Hall of Williams' Refuge, quite safe and happy." (37)

His next appointment for the Society was to attend Prize Day onboard the Arethusa on 15th July. When the day arrived the boys lined up in their ranks craning their necks for a first glimpse of their visitors but, as the platform party took their seats, the chair reserved for Lord Shaftesbury stood empty. William Williams opened the ceremony by reading out a letter:

"My dear Williams – I can hardly express to you the deep regret I feel that I must decline to go on my annual visit to the *Chichester* and *Arethusa*. I really have been so ill for the last two days and nights that I am certain I should not have strength to bear only a small portion of the fatigue and suffering that it would impose upon me. Yours truly, Shaftesbury"

John Fordham, the Society's Treasurer, took his place. It was a happy day shadowed with sadness. Before the summer was over Lord Shaftesbury had left London never to return. In the changeable weather of the early autumn he caught a chill which later turned to pneumonia. On 1st October 1885 he died.

The Committee met four days later in response to the news. William Williams wrote on their behalf to Lord Shaftesbury's family that:

"The Committee desire to record their sense of the great loss they and the subscribers have sustained by the death of the Rt Hon the Earl of Shaftesbury KG who has been President of the Institution for so many years and took such constant and active personal interest in the welfare and advancement of the children, who in their turn regarded His Lordship with much honour and affection.

Thousands of respectable and industrious citizens at home and in our colonies owe their successful start in life to the fostering care of this institution which in turn owes much of its successful development to Lord Shaftesbury's unceasing and earnest advocacy, and where his kindly presence was ever looked upon as one of the greatest pleasures alike by inmates, officers and Committee.

The Committee while mourning their great loss, hope to honour His Lordship's memory by carrying on in his own spirit of Christian love and faith the great work in which they have so long had the benefit of his counsel, experience, and above all of his unrivalled example."

The Memorial Service on 8th October at Westminster Abbey was a national affair. William Williams was one of the pall-bearers; children from all the homes and ships attended the service. The next day Lord Shaftesbury was buried after a service for his family and close friends in the village church of his family home at Wimborne St. Giles in Dorset.

Chapter 12

THE BEST MEMORIAL

Lord Shaftesbury's death was a bitter blow to all concerned with the National Refuges - the Committee, its supporters, officers and children alike. At the meeting on 2nd November, members of the Committee were shocked to learn of another death. John Fordham, who had worked for the National Refuges for 33 years and had been its Treasurer since 1872, was taken ill and died suddenly on 12th October 1885, only a few days after his friend and colleague, Lord Shaftesbury. To all appearances Mr. Fordham was in excellent health when he distributed the prizes in place of Lord Shaftesbury on board the *Arethusa* in July. It was little thought that his appearance at that meeting would be the last time he would take a public part in the affairs of the Society.

The question of Lord Shaftesbury's successor as President was quickly resolved. The Committee unanimously decided to ask one of its Vice-Presidents, the Earl of Jersey, an eminent diplomat, banker and landowner, to accept the position. He agreed and the supporters were informed that 'the Earl of Jersey who for so many years has taken a warm interest in the Society has kindly accepted the Presidency of the Institution and for this the Committee are most grateful.'

The 7th Earl of Jersey PC GCB GCMG who succeeded Lord Shaftesbury as the Society's President in 1885

Stepping into another's shoes can never be easy and Lord Jersey was painfully aware of the delicate nature of the task he had undertaken. He had yet to make his mark on the Society, whereas Lord Shaftesbury had been deeply concerned with every aspect of its work from the beginning and was a close friend to many of the staff and children. At his first Annual Meeting as President, in June 1886, he acknowledged the difficulties and he spoke of his feelings of inadequacy. It was hard, he said, to chair such meetings after:

".. our dear and noble friend who for so many years occupied that chair on annual occasions like the present, and who listened with such interest year after year to annual reports describing the growth of an institution which he had watched with feelings of the liveliest interest from its earliest years. We miss him, and shall miss him to the end."

Without Lord Shaftesbury's guiding presence Lord Jersey knew it would be all too easy for the Society to lose its way. He begged his listeners for their forbearance and indicated a path for the Society to tread which would reinforce past achievements and bring further success in the future. Thus, he gave all present a fresh sense of purpose:

"There must be on the minds of every one of us the shadow of the great loss which this Institution – and not only this alone but many other institutions throughout the land – have sustained during last year. And standing here, as I do in the place which the Earl of Shaftesbury occupied for so many years with such regularity, and with such profound sympathy with the great object you have at heart, my difficulty is very great indeed.

I am quite aware that it is impossible (and you can hardly expect it) that his mantle should fall on the shoulders of anyone worthy to follow him; but he has himself set us an example of what a great man can do, and I hope it will stimulate humble individuals like myself to try and do their best."

He urged his audience to continue their support and commitment to the work of the National Refuges. 'You erect to him the best memorial' he told them 'when you insist that this and similar institutions shall be sustained, shall go on and flourish.'

He did not attempt to take Lord Shaftesbury's place but quickly imposed his own imprint on the Society. The hint he gave at the Annual Meeting about honouring Lord Shaftesbury's memory bore first fruit in November 1886 when former residents of the Society's boys' homes were invited to a party at the Great Queen Street premises. More than 100 were present:

"They were supplied with a good meat tea after which a meeting was held with a view to forming a Club for their benefit. The Treasurer, Mr. Hubbard and William Williams with some members of the Committee and the superintendents of the homes were present to meet the party, and a most enjoyable evening was spent. The appearance of the lads and young men was most gratifying."

The purpose of the 'Ashley Club' as it was called was to offer a welcoming place for young men working in London who had been educated at the Society's schools and refuges. The club was open every evening. There was a room set aside for entertainment and relaxation with newspapers, light refreshments and board games available such as draughts, chess and dominoes. During the dark months of winter attendance was good and the young men appeared to appreciate the efforts made on their behalf. It seemed, however, that the freedom to find their own entertainment in London was more attractive. As the summer advanced and 'the long evenings came, the attendance became less.' The Ashley Club survived only a short time. After 1888 it was heard of no more.

Over the years, the schools and refuges had operated from many different buildings in London and there had been frequent moves, additions and changes. In the first few months after Lord Shaftesbury's death, in order to achieve greater efficiency and as a way of saving costs, the Committee sought a building large enough to accommodate all their London operations – the Society Offices, the Home for Working Boys, the Boys' Refuge and the Ashley Club. The one exception was the Ragged School in Little Coram Street for which there was still a local need.

No suitable property could be found so in 1886 the Committee bought a site on the newly constructed Shaftesbury Avenue and commissioned an architect to design a suitable building. The new Shaftesbury House occupied a most appropriate site. The address commemorated the late President and, being in the parish of St. Giles, it was close to the Rookery where William Williams had begun his work. Progress was slower than the Committee wished:

"It was even hoped by those who are not intimately acquainted with the ways of builders that, ere the year closed, the new London Home would have been opened and have been ready for the reception of the lads. Unfortunately, however, the hopes of the Committee in this respect were not fulfilled."

In 1887 Queen Victoria celebrated the Golden Jubilee of her accession to the throne; in honour of her 50 years as Queen, the new building was named 'The Jubilee Memorial Home'. The premises in Shaftesbury Avenue provided a suitable setting for what Lord Jersey had earlier described as the 'best memorial' the Society could offer to its late President, that is, the continuation of care and concern for homeless children.

Through the influence of Lord Jersey, the Prince of Wales had become interested in the project and agreed to lay the foundation stone of the new building on Friday 17th June 1887. On a beautiful, sunny day, 400 children from the

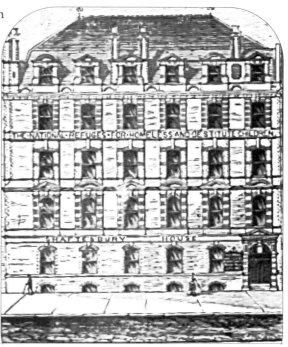

Shaftesbury House, Shaftesbury Avenue, London, opened on 17th June 1887, as a new home for 100 destitute boys and main offices of the Society

Society's homes came to the ceremony which was held in a large marquee decorated with garlands of flowers and banners proclaiming the names of the Society's establishments. The seats were raised so that everyone could see the dais which was covered in crimson cloth bearing the royal coat of arms.

Many visitors arrived early, including Lady Jersey and her two daughters. The boys' band from one of the homes entertained the party with a selection of tunes as everyone waited for the formal proceedings to begin. At one o'clock, a guard of honour of 100 of the Bloomsbury Rifles presented arms and Lord Jersey led in the Prince and Princess of Wales with two of their children, Princess Maud and Princess

No. 77

ADMIT

Mr Williams

TO THE CEREMONY OF LAYING THE FOUNDATION STONE
OF THE
Jubilee Memorial Home for Destitute Boys,
IN SHAFTESBURY AVENUE, ST. GILES'S,
(The New Road from Piccadilly Circus to New Oxford Street,)
BY
HIS ROYAL HIGHNESS THE PRINCE OF WALES,
(Accompanied it is expected by H.R.H. THE PRINCESS,)
ON
Friday Afternoon, 17th June, 1887, at One o'clock precisely.

WM. WILLIAMS, *Secretary*,
25, Great Queen Street, Holborn.
Visitors will oblige by being in their Seats by 12.30.

Mrs William William's invitation to the laying of the Foundation Stone of Shaftesbury House

Victoria. Lord Jersey's daughter presented a bouquet of flowers to the Princess of Wales and girls from the Society's homes presented flowers to other lady visitors.

One of the Society's vice-presidents, the Bishop of Rochester, conducted a short service. The children sang a hymn: "These walls we to Thine honour raise,

Lord may they echo with Thy praise;

Do Thou, descending, fill the place

With choicest tokens of Thy grace."

When the service was over, Lord Jersey told the story of the Society and explained its aims. Turning to the Prince of Wales at the end of his speech, he said:

"The Committee desire to join with the nation at large in devout thanksgiving to Almighty God for the long, prosperous, and happy reign of Her Majesty, the 50th year of which is hailed not only by a united and loving people at home, but also by Her Majesty's subjects in every part of her vast dominions."

Contemporary drawings of the interior of the new Shaftesbury House

In his reply, the Prince of Wales wished the Society well for the future. He spoke of the late Earl of Shaftesbury and all he had done for the poor and for the boys and girls of the National Refuges in particular, saying that the new home would be a great memorial to him and all he stood for. At the end of his speech he unveiled the foundation stone inscribed 'this stone was laid by HRH Albert Edward Prince of Wales KG 17th June 1887'. The children gave three cheers. Then, after the presentation of a silver trowel, they sang 'God Bless the Prince of Wales' and a verse of the National Anthem. The Bishop of Rochester gave the blessing and Lord Jersey invited the visitors to contribute to the furtherance of the Society's work and, as an incentive to generous giving, he announced that the Prince of Wales had donated the sum of £50. The proceedings closed with a grand celebration lunch with a final toast, proposed by Lord Jersey, of 'Prosperity to the Building'.

That day marked the beginning of

a new era for the Society. The hard work and frequent disappointments of earlier years had been rewarded with success and recognition. The Earl of Shaftesbury's ideals infused the National Refuges' workers with zeal for their task. His successor, the Earl of Jersey, led the Society forward to take a more prominent part in national life.

For William Williams, who had been the late Lord Shaftesbury's closest friend on the Committee, the Jubilee Memorial Home represented the culmination of his life's work. Lord Jersey relied heavily on him during his early months as President. 'I must not say what Lord Shaftesbury said of him to me the first time I had the pleasure of attending an Annual Meeting. It might make him wince a little.' Lord Jersey told the Society's supporters on one occasion. Nevertheless, he went on:

"I may go so far as to say that his Lordship told me that Mr. Williams was the most remarkable man he had ever met with for throwing his whole soul and spirit into the work, and that he was in reality the mainspring of the Institution."

Lord Jersey devoutly hoped that 'the mainspring will continue to work in the future as well as in the past'.

Until then, William Williams had been as active and busy as ever but during the winter of 1889/90, his health deteriorated. He was now over 70 and the effort to continue as before was too much for him.

William Williams
c. 1890

When the spring came, he hoped he would feel better with his zest for work restored. It was a shock to the Committee but hardly a surprise when, at the meeting on 31st March 1890, he said he felt the time had come for him to retire.

The Committee urged him to take a long holiday to recover his strength and to rest with his family. This he was unwilling to do as there were many urgent matters he had started and wanted to finish. He proposed 31st December 1890 as a suitable time for him to go. This would give the Committee ample time to appoint his successor.

All counter-suggestions, protests and arguments did not persuade him to change his mind. The post when advertised attracted 185 applications. Nearly half were rejected immediately as not being at all eligible. From the remaining candidates, after some preliminary interviews, three were chosen for a final selection interview.

Mr. H Bristow Wallen was the successful candidate. For the previous ten years he had been Secretary of the Home for Working Boys and his application was backed with excellent recommendations from those who had supervised his work.

Mr. Wallen's first day of duty was fixed for 10th November 1890, allowing time for him to work alongside William Williams and learn as much as possible from him. He formally took up his new duties on 1st January 1891.

On that same date Henry Copeland, who had been William Williams' assistant, was promoted to 'Deputation Secretary' and put in charge of fund raising and publicity, under Mr. Bristow Wallen's direction.

William Williams' letter formally resigning his post is dated 1st October 1890:

"After more than 45 years' connection with the ragged schools and refuges I feel the time has arrived that I should relinquish the actual duties of the secretaryship of your Society. I therefore beg to tender my resignation of the duties which I have had the privilege of discharging for so many years.

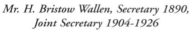

Mr. H. Bristow Wallen, Secretary 1890,
Joint Secretary 1904-1926

As we are now so near the close of the year, which period is a most important one for the finances of the Society, I think it will be beneficial for the Society that I should retain my office until the close of the present year.

In my declining years I still hope to be of some service to the good cause which has so long laid close to my heart. I have to thank you for all the sympathy, help and counsel you have given me in carrying on this important work."

He was awarded a retirement allowance of £250 a year and the Committee, which was most anxious to retain his services in some capacity, immediately nominated him as Vice-Chairman of the General Committee and as a member of the Ships' Committee.

Henry G. Copeland, Assistant Secretary 1889
Finance and Deputation Secretary 1890
Joint Secretary 1904-1928

Chapter 13

WILLIAM WILLIAMS' LAST FEW MONTHS

In his letter of resignation William Williams had written that he wished to continue his involvement with the Society's work. To those who knew him, it was unthinkable that he should want anything else. He regularly attended meetings of the Ships' Committee and the General Committee and at a specially convened meeting in July 1891 he was asked to undertake certain important responsibilities:

"The Committee – considering the deep interest taken by the Founder and late Secretary, for the past 46 years in the spiritual welfare of the children in the National Refuges – believe that it would be of great advantage to the Institution if Mr. Williams would kindly consent to continue the supervision and direction of that most important part of their work."

More specifically, they asked him to be responsible for:
– Organizing religious services at Bisley for children and staff.
– Organizing the monthly meetings for staff from all the homes.
– Arranging regular religious services for children in the other homes.
– The general oversight of the religious education and spiritual development of all the Society's children.

He was also asked to arrange the relatives' and friends' visiting days at the refuges. He willingly accepted all these duties; to his mind what he was doing was the most important part of the work and he revelled in it.

The next year was one of the happiest in his life:

"I have to be thankful" he once said "that God has blest me with a quiet mind, so that if the work before me was one needing to be done I have had no more concern about it than I have at reaching the end of a pre-arranged journey."

His new duties occupied him considerably. There was rarely a function of the Society in which he did not participate.

The monthly staff meetings had been initiated by William Williams himself several years previously. Members of staff from the homes and offices who could take time off from their duties would meet for a short service with prayers, readings from the Bible and hymns. At the tea which followed the staff was encouraged to mention any particular worries or concerns. One who regularly attended these meetings explained 'the gatherings were primarily devotional ones and their main purpose was for asking God's help'. The teachers and other members of staff truly appreciated the time away from their stressful jobs to meet their colleagues and friends and share their problems. William Williams' spirit infused the atmosphere, calming turmoil and soothing troubles away:

"What happy meetings they were" wrote one of the staff "he was not the secretary, more the spiritual leader and guide. His face beamed with delight and he had a wonderful habit of throwing off the cares and worries of his position, engendered doubtless by his strong faith in God."

He led the singing and prayers; he chose the Bible readings (often from the Epistles) and led the discussions which followed:

"He could make us feel not salaried officials but friends and fellow workers for God and the boys and girls. The gatherings will ever be green spots in the memory of the past, for they were veritable oases in the wearying desert of work, incessant labour and anxiety, seasons of refreshments, rests in the shade, enabling us to tread the way of the morrow with a lighter heart."

During the Christmas season of 1891 William Williams visited all the homes in turn as he had always done in the past. Regular features of the celebrations were the parties for past and present pupils. One girl who had gone into service clearly remembered that Christmas. She had been given a day's holiday to spend at her old home. Everyone shared the fun round the Christmas tree. There were oranges and nuts and other treats for the children given by subscribers and well-wishers. The girls, their teachers and friends, all had presents.

William Williams was there, cheerful, white haired and tiny with his clear eyes sparkling. He sat surrounded by the girls. Towards the end of the evening he spoke to them all. He told the old girls at the party to stand up as he wanted all the present girls to see what a fine example they were. He told them they should be proud of their Home and proud of those who had returned for the happy occasion.

When the clapping stopped he turned to the past pupils, 'You are the jewels in the crown of this Home – very precious jewels' he said, 'make sure by your lives that the jewels stay bright and shining as a sparkling example and encouragement to your families and friends'.

At the beginning of the new year, as a result of the Government making elementary education free in all Board Schools, Little Coram Street School had to close. It was the last remaining ragged school run by the National Refuges. The Committee made arrangements with the London School Board for the children who went to Little Coram Street to be admitted to public elementary schools forthwith.

All the children on the school roll were invited with their parents to a special meeting on New Year's Day 1892. Mr. Ware, the oldest member of the Committee, acted as Chairman and welcomed them all. Tea and cakes were available as some slight consolation for the sad news that was to follow.

William Williams explained to the parents what had happened. He reminded them about the history of their School, how a London City Missionary had founded it and how it had grown and prospered under the direction of a man who previously had earned his living as a chimney sweep. Later it had become part of what was now the National Refuges. Although the number of children at the School had lately become quite small, many more had attended in its heyday. Now the time had come for it to close. He announced that:

"The passing of the Free Education Act now opens to all the advantage of the Board Schools free of charge. That being so the Committee have come to the conclusion that it would be the right course to get each child into the nearest Board School. From tonight, therefore, you will understand that your children cannot come again here for instruction unless the School Board Authorities take over the premises. As soon, therefore, as the holidays are over we urge you to take your children for admission, and in the meantime we shall make them acquainted with the names of each of your boys and girls. But now, dear friends, is it not a ground for congratulation that while this door will be closed there is another one open?"

He ended on an optimistic note but it was a truly sorrowful occasion for them all. 'It was painful to witness the parting of the teachers and the children' wrote one of the Committee members who attended the meeting. It was painful too for the mothers and fathers who were saying goodbye to the teachers, their tried and trusted friends.

On 13th January 1892, William Williams attended the visiting day at the Shaftesbury School at Bisley. He was very cheerful and in apparent good health. Five days later he went to the Farm School for another visiting day and again seemed in the best of health and spirits. That occasion was to be the last duty he undertook for the Society. On the following day he was taken ill and he died on Thursday 21st January 1892.

Two memorial services were held for him. The first, on the Sunday immediately following his death, was at the Bloomsbury Chapel in that part of London where so much of the Society's work had been carried out and where William Williams had been a frequent worshipper.

As the Rev. James Baillie pointed out, this Chapel had long been associated with the National Refuges through two other former members of the congregation – Sir Morton Peto, who had served on the Society's General Committee some years previously and also through the Rev. W. Brock, one of the Chapel's former pastors who had been a Vice-President of the Society for many years.

William Williams was buried at Abney Park Cemetery in Stoke Newington, Hackney, on 27th January 1892. The arrangements were kept as simple as possible, as he had always hated ostentation and unnecessary ceremony. Contingents of children from all the Society's homes and the two ships met at the premises in Shaftesbury Avenue, from where they were taken to the cemetery in 'hired omnibuses with seating inside'. The girls were in black and the boys wore black arm bands.

It was a bleak, damp and chilly day. As he would have wished 'every care was taken of the children and the risk of exposure reduced to a minimum'. Members of all the Committees of the Society, the office staff, the superintendents and matrons of the homes, the Captain-Superintendent of the ships and other ship staff travelled together in eight carriages.

"At the gates of the cemetery the body was met by a numerous gathering of friends, subscribers, old boys and girls. The cemetery chapel was only just large enough to admit of the immediate followers, or doubtless many more would have found their way into the building. At the grave-side the service was very brief, to prevent needless exposure of the many friends and children who were present. So anxious were the relatives in deference to the known wishes of the deceased to take care of the children that all singing was dispensed with, and the boys were ordered to remain covered, raising their caps only at the end of the prayers. As the committal sentences were uttered, the dust was sprinkled on the polished casket in the open grave by the hand of the oldest superintendent, Mr. Stallworthy, then followed a prayer and the Benediction."

The second memorial service was held on the following Sunday, in the School Chapel at Bisley. The preacher, who had known William Williams for many years, chose as the text for his sermon a passage from Ecclesiastes (ix.10) 'Whatsoever thy hand findeth to do, do it with thy might. .'.

He spoke of William Williams' gift for friendship for people in all walks of life and all classes of society. He reminded the boys how he had hated 'all kinds of claptrap, sensational advertisements and questionable ways of raising money for work which he was assured was God's'.

The question of how suitably to honour his memory was raised at the next General Committee meeting but no one felt able to make any immediate decision. Instead the members concentrated on making suitable arrangements for the widowed Mrs. Williams. The Committee granted her £50 towards immediate expenses and agreed to pay her the full quarterly allowance which her late husband would have received until April. From that date she would receive from them an annual allowance of £125. A Memorial Fund was started soon afterwards and sufficient money was received by 1893 for the Committee to arrange for the building of four staff cottages at Bisley in honour of the late Secretary.

The Williams' Memorial Cottages at Bisley

When Lord Jersey had spoken for the first time as President, at the Annual Meeting, he had said that the best memorial for a life devoted to helping children was to ensure that the work continued and developed just so long as there were poor children needing help. The memorial that William Williams would have wanted was the further development and success of what he used to refer to as the 'refuge tree'. He first spoke of the Society's work in this way as early as 1874 and from time to time in later years as its work was extended, he returned to the same theme.

Some of the young orphans to whom William Williams and the Earl of Shaftesbury devoted their lives

"It sometimes happens" he said "that when an heir to an estate is born, the father and mother will plant a tree in commemoration of the event. And, as the heir to that estate progresses in years and stature, his eyes will often be fixed on the tree planted on that occasion.

We have come to cast another loving glance at that noble tree which we sometimes call the 'refuge tree'. Our tree was planted sometime out of season, so far as the ordinary time of year for planting is concerned, for it was in July 1852. When the tree was planted we had but five girls and four boys under our care. But the tree grew. It grew rapidly and vigorously."

The growth of the refuge tree, as everyone connected with the National Refuges knew, had

An Arethusa Boy (above) as he appeared when he applied to join the ship and (below) after admission. under Commander G.O. Moore RN.

been made possible through the combined inspiration, work and vision of two men, the Earl of Shaftesbury and William Williams, men very different in background and upbringing but sharing a strong belief and commitment. Each gave much to the National Refuges and each had a high regard for the other. Towards the end of his life Lord Shaftesbury spoke at one of the Society's Annual Meetings of his feelings for his old friend:

"It is not your grand people who make speeches in the House of Commons or House of Lords, who are of best service to their country. They may make a great show, but without such men as my dear friend, Mr. Williams, what would all their speeches do? I hold my friend Williams to be equal to a dozen Secretaries of State, and equal to two Commissioners of police."

Lord Shaftesbury lived in the limelight for most of his life; his work, his philosophy and his ideals are well known. William Williams, in contrast, came from obscure origins. He was unknown in his lifetime, beyond the circle of those connected with his work, and in death he returned to obscurity. His memorial is the Society's continuing service to young people in need of care and support.

The years until William Williams' death had seen success and disappointment, joy and sadness in full measure. Conditions were changing and old friends had died, yet in this period were laid the foundations for the Society to expand and develop its work into the twentieth century. With the death of William Williams and the Earl of Shaftesbury, many of the links with earlier years were severed; different people would now bring fresh energy and new ideas to help the National Refuges care for its children.

The chapters in Part II have covered changes within the Society following the Education Reform Act of 1870. The next section of this book gives more detail of daily life at individual homes and the care of children living in them.

Chapter 14
AN OVERVIEW – THE 1870S, 1880S AND 1890S

We now follow the fortunes of the children in the Society's care during the period which started with education reform in 1870 and continued until around the time of William Williams' death in 1892. This part of the book begins with a survey of the Society's work and then turns to the individual homes for more detailed information.

In 1870 the Annual Report reviewed the numerical and financial growth of the previous ten years:

Year	Annual Income			Av. N° in Refuges	Av. N° Placed Out
	£s.	s.	d.		
1861	5,519	12	1	172	113
1862	4,277	7	9	164	106
1863	4,405	18	1	154	199
1864	5,669	13	11	180	124
1865	5,766	13	7	177	142
1866	10,679	4	11	248	185
1867	15,866	3	2	371	142
1868	19,364	16	7	498	279
1869	20,071	3	5	563	269
1870	20,552	2	10	568	421

In 1871, 667 children were taken into the refuges, but the number which the Society could place out satisfactorily in jobs when they were old enough was only 407. Fund raising was as difficult as ever since the general public tended to misunderstand the philosophy and actions of the National Refuges. Many were unwilling to contribute to what they saw as an organisation giving assistance to criminals. This was not at all a true reflection of the Society's purpose which was and always had been the prevention of crime rather than any punishment or cure. Year after year, the Annual Reports reiterated the same point. As the Superintendent of the London Boys' Refuge wrote:

"Magistrates, themselves, are the first to confess that their hands are tied in the case of young criminals who are brought before them, and they sometimes have to do violence to their best feelings and judgment in committing them to reformatories. Excellent as these institutions are, there is no doubt that the taint of a prison clings to them.

Now, there is nothing of this in our Institution. It is no disgrace to a boy to have belonged to it – it is to his credit rather than otherwise, that from being a poor lad in rags and tatters, with no other facility for getting a livelihood than begging and stealing, he has so profited by the education he has received, as to be able to look the world fearlessly in the face, and to make his way."

The Boys' Refuge in London dealt with all types. In 1871, 577 boys were given shelter there 'whose chief and only letter of recommendation was their destitution'. It was a demanding job to help and train them to develop their full potential:

"We have the sullen and obstinate, who to a great extent have been rendered so by long hard usage, and who have been far more accustomed to a cruel blow than to a kind word. We have the cunning, whose wits have been unnaturally sharpened by a street life, and to whom anything like law or order is at first most irksome. We have the very dull, who seem never to have found out the use of their hands. We have boys of a gentle disposition. We have boys with hardy well-knit young frames, who seem to have a sea-faring life in their very faces."

The Annual Report for 1871 commented on the jobs for which the boys were trained and stressed the importance of establishing worthwhile ambition and good habits:

"The boy who can make his own boots, mend his own clothes, and work at a carpenter's bench, need never become either a beggar or a thief. But it is the constant aim of the Committee and of the industrial staff of teachers co-operating with them that the inmates of the Refuge should be something far better than clever youngsters able to achieve an independence. It is their aim to give them something better than the secular education they receive, good and sound though that may be. They desire to see them entering upon life's journey with the fear of God reigning in their hearts."

In 1871, 445 boys were admitted to the Refuge in London. The table below shows from where they originated:

From various casual wards and other night shelters	63
On the application of parties interested in their welfare	95
On their own application	98
Sent in from the streets by the Secretary and subscribers	76
Brought by the Boys' Beadle	17
Sent by magistrates and policemen as being utterly destitute	17
Sent by London City Missionaries, ragged school teachers and others	44
Re-admitted from the ship	6
Sent from the Newsboys' Home	29
TOTAL	445

The known destinations of the 132 boys in the Refuge on 31st December 1870 together with the 445 admitted in 1871 were:

To the *Chichester* Training Ship	288
To the Country Home and Farm School	36
To various situations	23
Emigrated to Canada and South America	14
Sent to sea	4
Restored to friends to get employment for them	46

Left not liking restraint	12
Sent to an infirmary, incurable	4
Sent to other institutions	2
Dismissed	2
Entered the army as a band boy	1
Total of leavers	432
Living in the Refuge on 31 December 1871	145
TOTAL	577

During 1871, eighty girls were admitted and of those placed out:

> 39 were sent into service
> 8 were restored to friends
> 1 died
> 1 transferred to another home

By the end of 1871 a total of 3,982 children had been admitted to the refuges – 2,972 boys and 1,010 girls. The vast majority came from London and other parts of England but there were also children from Ireland, Wales, Scotland, Italy, France, East and West Indies, Belgium, the United States, Canada and Ceylon. Of those who left the Refuges to go into employment or training:

BOYS

399	Emigrated to New Zealand, Canada, United States, Queensland, Nova Scotia, South Africa etc.
49	Joined the Navy
8	Joined the Army
88	Entered the Merchant Service
381	Found civilian jobs
33	Transferred to other institutions
294	Restored to parents or friends to find them jobs
6	Found apprenticeships
24	Died
1	To college
1,031	Sent to the *Chichester*
268	Sent to Bisley
2,582	**TOTAL**

GIRLS

445	Sent into service
255	Restored to parents or friends to find them jobs
16	Transferred to other institutions
5	Emigrated to Australia
27	Emigrated to Canada
20	Emigrated to New Zealand
2	Emigrated to Tasmania
1	Emigrated to Natal
1	Married
27	Died

799 TOTAL

These statistics do not include children who attended the day schools the Society ran in London where many different activities were available:

At 8 Great Queen Street:
– a Night School for girls on four evenings a week – three for religious and secular instruction and one night for needlework (40 names on the book)
– a Sunday Night School (average attendance 150)
– a religious service for the parents of the ragged school children and other poor people of the neighbourhood, held in one of the rooms of the house (average attendance 40)
– another service on Wednesday evenings (average attendance 20)

At 19 Broad Street:
– a Girls' Day School
– an Infant Day School
– a Sunday School for boys
– a Working Men's Benefit Club
– a Provident Fund for children

At Little Denmark Street:
– a Boys' Day School
– a Boys' Night School
– a Sunday School for boys, girls and infants
– a Band of Hope
– a sewing class for girls attending the Sunday School
– a Provident Fund

At Little Coram Street:
– a Day School for boys and girls
– a Day School for infants
– a Night School for boys
– a Night School for girls

– a Sunday School for boys, girls and infants
– religious services on Sunday and Wednesday evenings

On every Friday during the winter months a good dinner was provided for children from the Society's ragged schools. Pupils had to attend the schools regularly in order to qualify for this meal. A visitor at one of these occasions described the event:

"I noticed that a good many of the children kept some of their dinner over to bring home, and although this is against the rules, the authorities are secretly rather glad to see the smuggling carried on for such a praiseworthy purpose. The dinner consists of hot roast meat, potatoes, and a piece of bread and has been given every winter for six years past. The diners are 300 boys and girls from the Ragged Schools and 150 inmates of the refuge, besides which 200 infants too small to walk to the Refuge, are supplied with soup and bread once a week at their respective schools." [38]

According to this account, the average amount of food consumed on these occasions was 5 sacks of potatoes, 260 lbs of meat and $2\frac{1}{2}$ cwts of bread. Every other week the meat was sent from the Farm school at Bisley.

Every August the ragged school children had their summer treat. This was always paid for from the proceeds of special appeals or donations by individuals such as Mr. J. Duke Hill of Burnt Mill in Essex. In 1892 he provided for nearly 900 children to be taken 'in vans' to Petersham Park, Richmond, where they enjoyed a good dinner and tea.

The teachers enjoyed the occasion because they had 'a better opportunity of mixing with the children and joining in the games in the fields.' The day was a very happy one. Mr. and Mrs. Duke Hill and their household did 'everything in their power to make the day one of real enjoyment'.

A regular Friday Supper was a great encouragement to attendance

(**38**) *The Graphic*, 21 Dec. 1872

The Committee's plan to buy a house in Canada, mentioned in Chapter 10, could not proceed as funds were not available. Mr. Ward wrote from Hamilton, Ontario, to William Williams in February 1886 regretting the decision 'principally for the boys' sake'. He suggested as a compromise that he and his wife should continue their work in rented accommodation and he would try and find a job 'in which I shall have time and liberty to look after the boys'. I will send you a monthly report as usual. We have thought we could carry on the Home upon the above principles for £100 per year'.

The Committee agreed with his proposals and reported to their subscribers:

"Although emigration has frequently proved to multitudes but the fleeing from the ills they had to find others that they knew not of, the Committee have reason to be thankful for the manner in which the lads whom they have sent out have found their footing."

Mr. and Mrs. Ward helped the boys to find jobs, visited them on their employers' premises and discussed their progress. They tried to keep in touch with as many boys as possible, so as 'to speak an encouraging word to them which may help them to persevere in bearing hardness as good young soldiers'. Mr. Ward's monthly reports reassured the Committee that the best possible was being done for the boys they had sent out. 'A feeling of good fellowship is kept up among the boys themselves which, in a strange country to all of them, is of no slight service'.

Expense subsequently forced the Wards to move from Hamilton to cheaper premises in Wingham nearby but in 1888 Mr. Ward reluctantly gave up his attempts to keep the Home going. He could barely manage on the money allocated to him by the Society and his wife was not well. The subscribers were informed that:

"After 5 years' stay in Canada Mr. and Mrs. Ward were, with much regret, obliged to give up the charge of the home, owing principally to the severity of the winters and excessive heat of the summers, which became too trying for Mrs. Ward's health. On their return to England they met the Committee and gave a most cheering and interesting account of the work among the boys."

That same year Lord Jersey came to say goodbye to the boys emigrating to Canada and arranged with his bank that a sovereign for each boy should be remitted to a bank in Canada. The money would be made available to the boys once they had started with their new employers. The following year 24 boys were sent out:

".. under the care of Mr. Pady, an experienced gentleman well known to the secretary. He accompanied the boys to Hamilton and saw them all comfortably placed in good situations and then returned to London. Many of the lads have since written in high terms of the new country and expressing pleasure at the prospects now before them."

In 1892 the Home for Working Boys in Shaftesbury Avenue was renamed 'Fordham House' in memory of the late Treasurer who had frequently made large donations to the funds. The boys could now 'point to their home with pleasure, rather than with fear of stigma'. Mrs. Fordham and her sons kept up their connection with the National Refuges and took a particular interest in Fordham House. Soon after the change of name took place 'Mrs. Fordham paid a visit to the Home, bringing with her about 30 handsomely framed pictures and texts, which have done much to beautify the Home'.

The Carpenters' Shop at Fordham House

On another occasion, the proceeds of a sale of work which Mrs. Fordham arranged provided a piano for the boys which 'has proved most useful in giving the lads some musical evenings during the winter months'. Other evening entertainments were 'harmless games such as bagatelle, chess, draughts, etc., a small library and a generous supply of the daily and weekly papers'.

The Annual Report for 1892 gave more information about the boys for whom Fordham House was intended:

"Many young lads of from 13 to 17 years of age are every year thrown on their own resources and left to make their own way in the world. All these lads for the most part succeed in obtaining employment for the demand for boy labour is large and apparently increasing."

Although there now seemed no difficulty in finding jobs, wages were very low and the boys could not find decent lodgings and become independent unless their rent was subsidised as it was at Fordham House.

In 1893 Frederick Bland had been a resident at Fordham House for three years. He had:

".. kept the same situation, not having lost a single day's pay and earning from 20/- to 24/- per week, left at his own wish to go into private lodgings and as he possessed such an excellent character both in the Home and at his situation it was felt that he ought not to be allowed to leave the home without some slight reward, as an encouragement to him and an incentive to the others to go and do likewise. Accordingly Mr. Wallen and

Hobbies Shop at Fordham House

Mr. Copeland met the whole of the boys and presented Bland in the name of the Committee with two planes which would be useful to him in his business."

The routine of lessons and industrial training at the refuges was relieved by various annual events which were eagerly looked forward to by all the children. The Annual Meeting of the Society was held at Exeter Hall in London and attended by the Committee, supporters and interested members of the public. When the business of the meeting was finished the children invariably provided an entertainment. The singing at the meeting in the year in which William Williams retired was greeted with acclaim:

"A very important and entertaining feature in the evening's proceedings was the singing by the children of a good selection of temperance melodies and other pieces under the direction of Mr. Proudman.

It would be hard to find a more highly trained choir of sweet children's voices than these 700 orphans and their efforts were received with greatest favour by the audience. Such pieces as 'Stanley's Return' meeting with a particularly hearty reception. The success of the evening however, vocally, was a song with a sneezing refrain, which was rendered in such a manner as to fairly convulse with merriment both the occupants of the platform, and the body of the hall.

Another diverting performance by the children, was the skilful manipulation of their coloured song-books, producing as seen by the audience a Kaleidoscopic effect, which certainly bore tribute to the careful and painstaking drilling the performers had received."

This type of entertainment had been one of Lord Shaftesbury's particular delights. Through his insistence it was early established as a feature of any grand occasion for the Society. At the opening of Fortescue House he had spoken vehemently against the opinion that working class children should not be taught to sing as they would never be able to do so without offending the ears of their listeners. 'To say that you must not teach children music because they will never be able to sing Italian melodies' he maintained was a great mistake, 'in all our schools the pretty dears are taught to sing and they do sing, and their hearts come out in their singing'.

Prize-giving was another annual red letter day. Each refuge had its own prize giving day and, once a year, there was a Grand Prize Day for the whole Society when children and teachers from the ships and the homes came together to celebrate. A special dinner with plenty of roast beef and plum pudding for everyone preceded the grand assembly of children, their teachers and invited guests.

The ceremony took a long time as there were many prizes to be given to current residents, as well as old boys and girls who had done well after leaving. Every child had a chance of gaining at least one prize. There were book prizes for needlework, housework, lessons, general improvement and tidiness; money prizes; prizes for boys who had learnt to swim or had improved in swimming since joining the ships; prizes for diligence, Bible knowledge, seamanship and general smartness; prizes for telegraphy and prizes for the most popular boy or girl in each home chosen by secret ballot among the children. Many benefactors and supporters donated money for annual prizes - among them was John MacGregor whose 'Rob Roy' prize, for the best all-round achiever in the *Chichester* and the *Arethusa*, ensured keen competition.

John MacGregor was a barrister who, as a young man in the tradition of Rob Roy, had enjoyed dangerous exploits and adventures. He possessed many skills and influenced all who came into contact with him. He believed in 'enduring hardness' and despised all short cuts to knowledge. He actively sought to promote the teaching of swimming and was a brave, honest and gifted man. He supported the Society for many years and in establishing his Prize Fund demonstrated his concern to bring out the best in young people through physical and mental effort.

Of all the annual events, however, the one that gave most pleasure must surely have been Lord and Lady Jersey's summer treat held in the ground of their home at Osterley Park. The children from all the refuges and the ships came together for a day given up entirely to games, treats and entertainment. The bands played; there were competitions between the various homes, and between classes in each home. Lord and Lady Jersey and their family made certain everyone had a good time and one of Lord Jersey's particular pleasures was in personally serving the cake at tea time. A typical year was 1890, when all the boys and girls and their teachers enjoyed:

" ..an abundance of ginger beer, lemonade, and tea. The swings, Punch and Judy show and cricket were also enjoyed. Lady Jersey had a large store of useful presents for those who were strong enough to run in the races. The unsuccessful competitors and all the smaller children came in for some present, so that no boy or girl left without some token to keep in remembrance of the happy day."

EARL OF JERSEY'S "HAPPIEST DAY."

Contemporary Newspaper cuttings from the Shaftesbury Homes & Arethusa Scrapbook with The Earl and Countess entertaining the boys and girls to a memorable day at their home

At Bisley, after the foundation of the new Shaftesbury School in 1873, there followed a period of consolidation. The number of boys soon exceeded that which could be accommodated at the tiny local Church and in 1874 the Society built its own Chapel, large enough to take the boys from both schools and their teachers. Attached to the Chapel a room was provided for the villagers where they could buy a cup of tea cheaply and meet friends.

The Superintendent, James Wood, who had moved to Bisley when the Farm School was first opened, died in 1876 after a long and painful illness, having worked for the National Refuges for 21 years. He was the man who had struggled to maintain order and discipline, together with Mrs. Edmond, amidst the disturbances at the London Refuges in 1859, mentioned earlier. His death was felt deeply by the boys and the staff at Bisley.

The Bisley School Chapel

In his place Mr. Angus McKay was appointed as the Superintendent of the Farm School. He and his counterpart at the Shaftesbury School were closely involved in a plan to build three cottages which together would be used as a Hospital for the Society's boys at Bisley when they needed more nursing care than could be adequately given by a busy School Matron. The Hospital opened in 1883. The Committee was pleased to announce in the Report for that year that 'although a nurse has been on the premises ready for any emergency, up to the present time her services have not been required. The health of the children has been good all the year round'.

In 1896 the Hospital was altered to serve as staff accommodation after a new, larger and more convenient 'bungalow infirmary' was built so as 'to isolate contagious cases. All the rooms are on the ground floor and accommodation will be for six beds with a day room for small ailments and convalescents, a doctor's room, medical stores and bedroom and kitchen for the nurse-matron'.

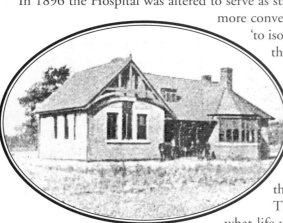

The contract price was £787, plus furniture and other essentials, bringing the total cost to about £887. A few years later the number of beds was increased to twelve.

These few facts give little information about what life was like for the masters and boys at Bisley during this period but the Society's 'Log Book' is

The Bungalow Hospital, Bisley School

more informative. This monthly magazine for subscribers was edited by Henry Copeland, the Deputation Secretary, and it regularly contained news from all the homes and ships. One article described the first few days of a new recruit at one of the Bisley schools. After all the new boys had assembled at the offices in Shaftesbury Avenue, they said goodbye to relatives and friends then walked to Waterloo Station, leaving behind an 'unmistakable aroma from stale clothes.' Their train was met at Brookwood Station:

".. by a smart boy in uniform with three gold stripes on his arm, a school sergeant who had been sent to escort them to Bisley two and a half miles away. Just before Bisley Green they pass the pretty Bungalow Hospital for the sick boys of the two schools, then past the farm bailiff's cottage into and through the playground and then to the Superintendent's door..".

After tea, time in the playground and a bath, the boys were sent off to bed. The next morning, when breakfast was finished, they were kitted out in a completely new set of clothes. The shoemaker master measured them for boots; they were given a haircut and then put on the scales. Three months later they were all weighed again; if their weight had not increased, the school doctor was informed. There were daily inspections 'to see if they are clean and tidy, clothes properly brushed, and boots nicely polished'.

Most boys put on weight after a few weeks and their health improved thanks to regular meals and a plain wholesome diet. Outdoor exercise, cricket, football, other games and 'marching drill' paid dividends. Much time was spent playing in the fresh air and helping on the farm. One of the boys' favourite places was the dairy:

".. where the milk from the cows is distributed to the 300 boys in the two schools. The boys like the dairy, because the eggs from the farm fowls are housed

Helping on the Farm at Bisley

here, and when they get a penny or two from friends they like to regale themselves with a new laid egg."

One of the editions of the Log Book contained an account of the school work and job training:

"All boys up to and including Standard IV are compelled to attend school, after that they become half-timers, attending school either in the morning or afternoon, and for the other half of the day learning some trade. Tailoring, shoemaking, carpentry, gardening, farming, are some of the industries in which the boys take part."

Apart from this routine there were regular treats and events in their school year such as Harvest Home, Guy Fawkes celebrations on the village green and outings at Christmas paid for by local well-wishers and friends. In the summer there were day trips to the coast. In 1889 they went to Bournemouth:

"Early on Friday the strains of military music enlivened the residents on the way leading from the East Station to the Pier and furnished a spectacle rarely, if ever, seen in the neighbourhood, that of a military procession, consisting of well-dressed and well-behaved boys representing the coming Army and Navy of England. There was quite the martial air and spirits, even to the wearing of the caps, and but for the smallness of stature we could not have believed but that a regiment of regular troops were passing our sanctum.

The miniature bandsmen, too, would carry the palm against many a grown up military band. Whether we admired the big drum, the little drum, or the, to us, man-size wind instruments, with our admiration there was no small amount of astonishment at the physique and lung power necessary to produce the results which were exhibited.

Crowds followed the miniature regiment and numbers stood spell-bound to listen to the band on the Pier, and literally to stare at the powers shown by those of the boys who seemed to handle instruments which would soon 'blow' a man. All the public saw must have been convincing proof of the sound health and condition of the boys, and spoke volumes of the care, training and food provided at the schools."

The boys' concert on the Pier was followed by a collection for the Society's funds. The boys then had the remainder of the day to themselves. From the proceeds of the bands' performances in 1892 the schools could afford five new instruments costing over £30 as well as twelve new uniforms for the performers.

The annual treat at Osterley Park was a regular highlight of the summer holidays. In 1892, unlike the sunny occasion described in Chapter 12:

"..we shall never forget our journey home. It was a difficult and dangerous battle with the elements, a three mile forced march with the wind in our teeth, accompanied by drenching rain, vivid and almost continuous flashes of lightning and heavy peals of thunder.

The lightning showed us the way; and though drenched to the skin we all reached home safe and sound. Clothing was quickly changed, prayers said and 'nature's soft nurse' soon visited us. Not one single mishap occurred, nor was anybody the worse next day."

For many years the whole School with several masters and often accompanied by Head Office staff spent a fortnight in the military 'redoubt' at Eastbourne. The Log Book gave a detailed description of one such holiday:

"The redoubt is like a huge well, the rooms being at the bottom round the sides. After tea came the process of allotting the rooms to the boys and officers. Mr. H. Bristow Wallen who was in charge took the guard-room for office and bedroom, another was dubbed the officers' mess-room, a smaller one did duty for store-room, and the rest for the boys' sleeping places."

The Redoubt at Eastbourne

Morning Prayer

The boys came by train. At the station they formed up into line:

".. each boy shouldered his own canvas haversack, the heavy articles having been sent on by van. The bands got into position. The big drum thumped out and then to the step of a swinging pace, the boys marched to the circular redoubt, the bands playing in turn."

The buglers sounded the reveille at 5.45 each morning. Those whose duty it was to prepare the breakfast went to the kitchen:

".. and the rest marched off for the morning dip. Undoubtedly the pleasure most enjoyed by the boys was the bathing, and in consequence of the weather continuing so fine and warm, the boys had a dip twice a day.

It was no slight task to supervise the bathing of 300 boys but, to ensure safety, the Corporation boat was always in the water and the boys were not allowed to stay in the water after the whistle had been blown by one of the officers.

Only one mishap of any kind took place: one of the Shaftesbury boys once got beyond his depth and might have come to an untimely end had it not been for the vigilant eye of the boatman who dived from his boat and rescued the little fellow amidst the cheers of his comrades. The boys at once made a collection among themselves, some giving a half-penny, others a penny, and presented the Corporation boatman with a sovereign."

During their time at Eastbourne the boys were taken on several trips and outings. Sometimes they went to the Circus; one year they visited Pevensey Castle 'conveyed to and fro in a couple of char-a-bancs, each drawn by four horses'.

The band masters asked permission from the Corporation for the boys to play in the bandstands on the Parade:

"Each evening the band played in the parade bandstands to large and appreciative audiences. The visitors were simply astonished that such little fellows could produce such a volume of sound, and all were loud in their praises of the excellent tuition given by the band masters, Messrs. C. Payne and J. Machell. It was undoubtedly due to the bands in the first instance that our boys were brought into such prominence, and also opportunity was afforded for distributing our leaflets and cards, giving particulars of the work accomplished by the National Refuges.

Each Sunday evening one of the bands assisted at the open air meeting in connection with Christ Church attracting a vast audience of those who do not usually attend a place of worship, but who remained to listen to the earnest words of a few selected speakers."

The boys behaved very well for the entire fortnight and received:

"...golden opinions from the visitors, members of the Corporation, clergy, police, etc, and this is the more commendable when it is understood that the boys were allowed to go where they liked all over the parade and town. No punishments of any kind had to be inflicted."

As the party was getting ready to return to Bisley, a local resident handed a letter to Mr. Bristow Wallen:

"Southville,
Royal Parade,
Eastbourne,
Dear Sir,

Permit me to congratulate you and all the officers on the conduct of the lads under your charge, during the time you have been staying at the redoubt, and sincerely hope we may have the pleasure another year of seeing you here again, and that your stay may be longer with us.

I may mention I am part owner of two small boats which lay close to the redoubt, and not once have I had reason to complain of any of your lads damaging them. There have been two Lads' Brigades here before yours, and the conduct and language have been most objectionable, whilst yours have been most commendable.

Yours truly, Mark Hookham."

The golden opinions of the residents of Eastbourne did not always echo the views of the boys' teachers, of course. The Sub-Committee which ran the Bisley schools met once every two weeks and it is from the record of their meetings that we glimpse a different perspective on life at the two schools.

At the Farm school in September 1891:

".. discipline was very lax. The order at meal times and especially in the dormitories was far from what it should be. Several keys and three or four dozen pieces of candle and boxes of matches were found in the boys' lockers. The following punishments had been inflicted during the month: Moore and Thompson swearing, each 4 strokes, Thompson 2nd offence."

To make certain the boys did not get up to any more tricks at night, Thomas Sweetman, a local man aged 28, was appointed as night watchman for both schools. He was paid £1 per week and given a meal each day. Four months after he started work he asked about his summer holiday allocation. The Superintendent of Shaftesbury School referred the matter to the Committee. During the ensuing discussion it came to light that Mr. Sweetman took an evening off duty once a fortnight which the Superintendent thought had been agreed when he was appointed. But the terms of his engagement distinctly stated 'no holidays allowed'; his regular day off was cancelled forthwith and all talk of a summer holiday came to an end. Thomas Sweetman obviously felt hard done by because in June he resigned. Either the boys' discipline had improved or a night watchman had proved to be more trouble than he was worth for the Committee decided not to fill the vacancy.

Another problem that the Committee tackled in 1891 was the case of a boy, Percy Consdale, who complained that he was not getting enough to eat and said that he had been treated too harshly. His medical records revealed no cause for concern. The punishment record book showed he had been caned on one occasion for leaving the premises without permission. He was summoned to one of the committee meetings and questioned about his complaints. Far from being malnourished and cowed, he 'appeared in excellent health'.

The Committee was concerned not only with discipline but with all aspects of life at the Bisley schools. The minutes record staff complaints about the damp in their cottages, the state of the drains and the damage which all their hard work did to their health, information on good and bad harvests, profits from the boys' industrial workshops and all matters affecting the running of the establishment.

The Superintendents and Schools' Doctor reported regularly. Generally all was well, apart from minor ailments, but on 8th May 1891 the Committee minutes carry a record of the Doctor's complaint that:

"Lockyer's eyes were in a very bad condition having been irritated by some application used by the bandmaster. He was strongly of opinion that an unskilled man should not be allowed to tamper with such a delicate and important organ as the eye. The doctor also suggested that no boy should be admitted into the school without being examined by a medical man before or immediately after admission."

Consumption, diphtheria and other diseases took their toll. In June 1892:

"Arthur Passfield died from consumption in Cleveland Street Infirmary, London. A. Ginn and W. Izzart had been sent to the isolation hospital at Chertsey, suffering from diphtheritic sore throats: the cases were slight and they have both returned. Thomas Dunlop was discharged from Guildford hospital with his leg in a splint, but with synoritis setting in the left ankle, he was returned to the hospital. Thomas Macrow suffering from phlebitis had been sent as an in-patient to the Guildford Hospital. Fuller was still under the doctor for enlarged glands of the neck, to be sent to Bartholomew's Hospital."

That same month a recent new boy at the Shaftesbury School was seen by the Doctor who treated him for 'summer diarrhoea and sickness'. The Doctor, seeing him subsequently, noted he was 'nearly well'. Mr. Hopkins, a member of the Society's General Committee as well as being on the Bisley Committee, visited the School the same day. He disagreed with the Doctor's opinion and spoke to the Matron about how very ill the boy appeared. The Matron was unimpressed and hinted that the boy was shamming. Five days later the Doctor visited the School again. He told the Committee later:

"I saw this boy at 4 p.m. on June 13th. I found on examining his chest, signs of pulmonary tuberculosis. He appeared to me to be ill, but I saw no reason to anticipate any immediate danger. I was sent for again at 8.30 p.m. On reaching the school at 10 o'clock, I was informed that the boy had died suddenly at 8.45. It is my opinion that the cause of death was tubercular meningitis, and that, in addition to this, the boy had general tuberculosis. In this particular case, the signs of meningitis were particularly obscure."

This was bad enough. To compound its distress, when the Committee made further enquiries into the boy's death, it learnt that the Superintendent had been absent from the School at the time, accompanying the School Band on a series of engagements. He was severely censured for committing 'a serious error of judgement in absenting himself from the home, when one of his boys had died so suddenly'.

However, adverse criticism was most unusual. The Society's Committee rarely had reason to complain about the management or teaching in the homes. Government inspectors who visited annually to check the curriculum and standards gave good, sometimes glowing reports, with only occasional suggestions for improvements. For instance, in 1890 at Shaftesbury School:

"Out of 109 scholars presented for examination, 96 passed in Reading; 98 in Dictation and Composition and 99 in Arithmetic. The boys were also examined in Grammar and Recitation, Geography (including map drawing from memory), and in Singing from notes."

At the Farm School 98% of the boys passed fully in all subjects:

"The work, the discipline, and the tone are eminently satisfactory, and I have pleasure in recommending the highest merit grant. Music by note, good. English, good. Military drill, very good."

Visitors, whether they were officials, or subscribers to the National Refuges were always welcome. The Rev. G R Merrick, from the Reformatory and Refuge Union, who called unexpectedly that year, wrote to the General Committee:

"I have much pleasure in testifying to the very satisfactory character of everything that I have seen in the School. The moral tone pervading the institution, the perfect yet unforced discipline, industry, happy appearance and application of the boys to their work, reflect much credit upon the management."

Chapter 16

MISS CHIPCHASE AND MISS FROST

By 1872, as mentioned in Chapter 10, all the girls in the Society's care, apart from those going to the ragged schools, were living either at Sudbury Hall, near Harrow, under the care of Miss Chipchase or at Ealing with Miss Frost. These two women supervised the staff and domestic arrangements in the girls' homes, subject to the overall control of a sub-Committee consisting of eminent local supporters and some members of the Society's General Committee.

Emma Chipchase came originally from Tyneside. She was appointed assistant to the Matron of the old Girls' Refuge at Broad Street in 1866, the year a serious cholera epidemic broke out in London. It was so bad that the medical authorities proposed taking over the Broad Street premises for use as a fever hospital. The Committee was unwilling to allow this because the Society had no other suitable

Sudbury Hall Girls' Home

home for girls in London; it offered instead the Little Denmark Street premises. Miss Chipchase's £30 salary was hard earned that year as she struggled with all the extra difficulties and stress of the epidemic.

The following year Miss Dickson, who had taken the place of Mrs. Edmond as the Matron at Broad Street, resigned as 'she had received an urgent invitation to return to her former missionary work in Jerusalem which she was resolved to accept'. The Committee was sorry to lose her because she was a well-qualified and efficient worker. Miss Chipchase applied to take her place and was appointed at a salary of £36 per annum. She then worked for the Society as Matron at Broad Street, and subsequently of Sudbury Hall, until 1911.

The members of the Society's Committee had a high regard for her; all the girls in her care respected her and many of them grew to love her. They knew that after they left the Home they could rely on her support and friendship whenever it was needed. One of the pupils at Sudbury Hall was Selina Amner. She did well at school and won prizes for her work and behaviour. When the time came for her to find a job, rather than leave the place where she had been happy and secure, she stayed as a personal companion and assistant to Miss Chipchase.

A Sudbury Girl

Miss Chipchase established a routine at Sudbury Hall

which remained hardly changed until the early years of the twentieth century when the Home was sold. The girls did all the domestic work, with suitable supervision, each according to her ability:

"Everything that can be, is done within the Home. The washing bill would form a considerably expensive item if the work were done by outsiders, but the necessity for this is removed because the girls do it themselves. Coppers, wash-tubs, wringers, manglers and the like are here in due proportion so that the work may be got

The Kitchen at Sudbury Hall

through without undue labour. Following washing day comes the ironing, and if the visitor happens to be present when the work is in full swing, he or she will feel like being in a Turkish bath. It is a necessary experience for the girls, for we strive to make them proficient for all household work. The large range, spacious ovens and the quantity of crockery fill the newcomers with amazement. Just off the kitchen is the scullery, with two huge coppers belching forth steam like a locomotive.."

The household duties and the system whereby senior pupils helped to supervise the younger ones taught the girls to be responsible. It was not difficult to find jobs for trustworthy well trained girls of good character. Domestic service gave them a home and protection and, in time, they could progress to positions of greater responsibility. The Committee pointed out that:

"A large number find employment in domestic service, and we are constantly telling them that it is undoubtedly the best thing they can do. Some are now comfortably married, and have homes of their own. There are others in Canada, and in all parts of England, that claim Sudbury Hall as their home, and the superintendent as their mother."

New girls, coming from families unable to cope with poverty and misfortune, must have found the life at Sudbury Hall very strange in many ways; security, order, and regularity were key elements in the training in which everyone had her allotted tasks. Miss Chipchase started the system by which an older girl was assigned as a special friend and helper to a newcomer. The older girl's task was to steer her charge through the first few days when she might feel lonely or homesick.

Working in the Scullery at Sudbury Hall

To many of these new arrivals having a single bed to themselves was a luxury never before experienced. On the bed of each

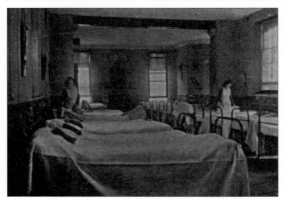

A Dormitory at Sudbury Hall

new girl a doll was waiting to welcome her. It was hers to keep, provided she behaved herself.

Sudbury Hall and Ealing House provided elementary education, like all the Society's homes and this rarely gave rise to any unfavourable comment from inspectors or visitors. An inspection report for Sudbury Hall in 1892 noted that:

"Order and tone are very good and the general efficiency is creditable. The School is improving in all ways and the instruction is becoming more practical. Handwriting and spelling generally and the arithmetic of the first and sixth standards are very good. The arithmetic of the second and fifth standards needs increased attention as regards accuracy, neatness of arrangement and figures, and the mental arithmetic in every class should be a preparation for that of the next class. Greater sweetness and expression would improve the singing. A good beginning has been made in domestic economy. Needlework is good and musical drill good. I hope next year to find a cookery class. A map of the world is needed."

The suggestion about cookery lessons was heeded and for many years subsequently The Honourable Company of Cooks of the City of London paid for an instructor to give fortnightly lessons to about twenty senior girls chosen for their ability and motivation.

Miss Chipchase and her staff went to great lengths to make Christmas and other holidays happy for the girls. They needed some respite from the household chores and without the Society's support many of them would have received no presents or treats at all. The Christmas period of 1897 was a typical one at Sudbury Hall. Supporters from many parts of the country as well as local friends supplied gifts ranging from 'a small knitted coverlet from the Hon. Edith Foljambe' to much larger presents from individuals and companies. Everything was stored away to be handed out on Christmas Day:

"From Major Mackenzie - 100 new sixpences
from Mrs. Robinson - a packet of sweets for each girl and 2 fitted work baskets
from Mr. Collis - 1 case of oranges
from Mr. T. J. Hamp - 3 bushels of Blenheim apples and a case of oranges
from Mr. J. Leete - 14 lbs of sweets
from Mrs. Comber - muscatels and oranges
from Miss Carver - a Christmas letter to each girl
from Miss Sevick - a parcel of useful garments
from Mrs. Crouch - knitted wraps
from Mr. Armytage - 100 Christmas cards
from Mr. Braddick - 100 Christmas cards
from Messrs. G. T. Cox and Sons - oranges."

On 29th December, Sudbury Hall celebrated Old Girls' Day. On this occasion, 80 old girls came for a grand party at their old Home. For many of them this was the one day in the year when they could see Miss Chipchase and their old friends. There were many local people present as well as Committee members with their families.

In the afternoon old girls, present girls and visitors assembled in the schoolroom for the presentation of prizes by Miss Annie Carver, a valued and loyal friend of the Home.

Girls who had kept their jobs for one year and been commended by their employers received ten shillings. A silver brooch was awarded for those still in their jobs after two years; after three years the award was an umbrella. Five years' service was rewarded with an umbrella and a travelling bag.

Annie Carver told the girls:

"I heard someone say that they had too much Christmas dinner and it had made them uncomfortable and miserable. I feel something like that just now, unhappy, because I have been asked to make a speech. I have never done such a thing before, and I think it is too late to begin now.

It was with great pleasure I received Miss Chipchase's invitation to be present here this afternoon. I always like to come and see her and the girls in this home. There is a brightness about the place which does me good. You may have noticed that when a dog settles down for a nap he always curls himself up in a patch of sunshine, and when I pay a visit to Miss Chipchase I always feel I am getting into a patch of sunshine .."

She told the girls to carry that sunshine with them wherever they lived and worked, as it could brighten even the most desolate places.

After tea the girls entertained their visitors in traditional fashion with songs, drill and recitations which they had been rehearsing for weeks:

> "God Save The Queen
> Song: Three Little Heads in a Row
> Recitation: Fancy Fair Bazaar
> Recitation: Girls that are Wanted
> Doll Drill
> Song: So Shy
> Recitation: The House that Jack Built
> Song: Pinafore
> Flag Drill
> Song: Quakeresses
> Recitation: Boys that would not be sad
> Recitation: Half-hour at Willesden Junction
> Statues
> Auld Lang Syne"

Miss Chipchase read out messages and good wishes from many parts of the world. The girls were particularly pleased to receive one which came from a friend living in Africa on the Niger Coast. On Vice-Consulate note-paper headed with two crossed Union Jacks, the

The Dining Hall at Ealing House

message read 'Wishing a Merry Christmas and a Happy New Year to all friends at the Sudbury Home'. The fun, games and dancing continued well into the evening.

At the Ealing home the celebrations were on a similar scale. On Christmas Day:

"The dining hall and school room presented a very festive appearance, being decked with holly, evergreens and flags. Early on Christmas Day the girls sang carols. At breakfast each girl received many cards and a Christmas letter. For dinner they had roast pork, fed at our Farm School, with seasoning, apple sauce and vegetables, fruit and bon-bons and plenty of Christmas pudding. After dinner, the girls' parcels and letters which had been accumulating for more than a week, were given out amidst the greatest glee.

In the evening, the dining hall was given up to amusements and games. Through the generosity of many kind friends each girl received a suitable present from a large bran-pie. Jane Green, the favourite girl in the home chosen strictly by the girls themselves, received a sweet little gun-metal watch given by a kind friend.

During the evening the girls were regaled with cake, fruit and sweets; the festivities on Christmas and Boxing day were kept up until a late hour."

On Boxing day some of the girls performed a cantata 'Jack Frost'. They repeated the performance a few days later when many old girls and friends came to spend the day.

At Ealing, as well as Sudbury, the girls certainly had a good time at Christmas with festivities lasting into the New Year.

Ealing was a well run efficient Home, thanks to the careful management of Miss Frost, but she was held in awe, rather than affection. At times it seemed almost as if the Committee as well as the girls was frightened of her. On one occasion a vacancy had arisen for a Head Teacher at Ealing and two candidates were short-listed for interview. The Committee preferred Miss Sibley, a young, energetic Headmistress of the Girls' School connected with the Wesleyan Chapel in Great Queen Street. Miss Frost, on the other hand, felt 'strongly drawn' to the second candidate, Miss Groom, who was the Headmistress of a School at Sydenham.

A long discussion followed. The outcome was that William Williams agreed to visit Miss Groom's school to watch her

Household Work at Ealing

take a class. If he was satisfied with her teaching and discipline and, if her references were good, then they would appoint her, since Miss Frost was 'so determined to have her'. Some members of the Committee felt that she might be 'a little too old for the job'. William Williams' visit to the School at Sydenham convinced him that Miss Groom was a competent teacher. Her references were in order and fear of Miss Frost's disapproval persuaded the Committee to appoint Miss Groom.

The Laundry at Ealing House

Under Miss Frost's guidance, the girls' education and domestic training at Ealing continued with excellent reports from inspectors, Committee members and the employers to whom the leavers went. The premises were enlarged and improved to make room for more pupils and to ensure they received a sound basic education and first class training as domestic servants. In 1877 the Committee reported:

"Those for whom we obtained situations as domestic servants, will, we trust, do credit to the careful training they received under their good friend Miss Frost. Although very young to enter service, and going of course to their 'first place', it is something to be able to say that they are not sent out as mere novices, and altogether unaccustomed to the work they will have to do. Years ago, as many can remember, the engaging of a new maid was always somewhat an anxious business to the mistress of a household. All can recall perhaps something of the turmoil in the kitchen, to say nothing of the temper in the parlour which generally accompanied the arrival of a new hand. A very wide margin indeed had to be allowed for 'mistakes' and 'accidents', which were of such frequent occurrence because inexperience was so closely yoked either with carelessness or more frequently still with sheer ignorance and timidity. We are glad to say that this trouble, if not altogether got rid of, has to a large extent been diminished by good training, so far as servants from our Institution are concerned. We have progressed with the times, and have endeavoured to meet its new demands in the direction of domestic servants by a wise course of training."

The Committee was taken completely by surprise when in October 1884 Miss Frost wrote a letter resigning her position as Matron at Ealing House. She intended, she said, to start up her own Refuge and a School for small girls. William Williams immediately replied on behalf of the Committee expressing deep regret at her decision seeing that she had been Matron at Ealing with such success for around 18 years.

At the time of her resignation she had not finally chosen where her Refuge would be but she dropped a hint that she intended to stay in the Ealing neighbourhood. It then came to light that she already owned four properties in the area. It appeared a distinct possibility that her proposed establishment would soon be operating as a rival to the National Refuges' Home at Ealing. What happened in the next few weeks is not clear but, on 3rd November, she wrote to the Committee again asking to withdraw her resignation. This was agreed and to everyone's great relief her plans for independence were mentioned no more.

One of the young teachers on the staff at Ealing at about this time was Miss Tufrey. She was unqualified when appointed but Miss Frost was satisfied with her work and encouraged her to take the necessary examination so that she could qualify for promotion. She worked hard and was confident of passing. In January 1885 the Head Teacher at Ealing resigned and Miss Frost suggested to the Committee that the post be left open till March when Miss Tufrey's results were due. If she passed the examination, then she could be appointed as the Head Teacher. No-one at Ealing or on the General Committee objected to this as Miss Tufrey's teaching was perfectly satisfactory. Everything went according to plan. Miss Tufrey was promoted early in the summer and she arranged to take her annual leave with her mother in Bognor at the end of July. On the morning she left, one of the other teachers noticed some money was missing from her room. She reported this to Miss Frost and, although the Home was searched from top to bottom, the money was not found. Miss Frost was none too pleased to learn from her investigations that the likely culprit was Miss Tufrey. Far from going to Bognor with her mother it transpired that Miss Tufrey had gone there with her sweetheart, Mr. Rutt, whom she had been meeting secretly at night during the previous term.

She was not there to defend herself but when she came back from her holiday looking plump and well, she vehemently denied having anything to do with the missing money. Miss Frost questioned her closely but could find out nothing about the theft; it was, however, clear to her that the girl was pregnant. Immediately she wrote to William Williams in alarm about what had happened and on the following day she took Miss Tufrey back home to her mother. She told Mrs. Tufrey nothing about her daughter's pregnancy only that she had been accused of stealing some money from another teacher and therefore her employment at Ealing House had been terminated.

Mrs. Tufrey was deeply upset about this and more so when she learnt from her daughter about her relationship with Mr. Rutt, the unchaperoned holiday and the forthcoming baby. She wrote to the Committee complaining that Miss Frost had not taken proper care of her daughter's welfare.

The Committee wanted to investigate in detail and William Williams wrote to Miss Tufrey asking her to come to the next meeting to give her side of the story. She refused to attend. Miss Frost also refused to talk to the Committee about what had happened and she further complicated matters by writing to Mrs. Tufrey withdrawing the accusation about the stolen money. She steadfastly refused to tell anyone on what grounds she had first accused Miss Tufrey of theft and then had changed her mind. Possibly she and Miss Tufrey (who by the autumn had become Mrs. Rutt), agreed between them that the best course was to maintain silence and hope the matters would blow over quickly.

The members of the Committee were left with little they could do apart from detailing the incidents in the minute book and expressing their extreme displeasure at how Miss Frost had handled the whole affair. Arrangements were made for a special 'Ladies' Visiting Committee' to call at Ealing House as soon as possible to check Miss Frost's management of the Home. This Committee agreed, for the time being at least, that Miss Frost should run the Home under its close supervision. In response, Miss Frost undertook to do 'whatever the Committee want for the welfare of the Home under my care'. But docility and unquestioning submission to authority, even of the Society's Committee, were not in her nature. She resigned four months later.

In spite of all that had occurred the Committee felt satisfied in the main with her work. No fault had been found with her running of the home prior to the time of Miss Tufrey's misdemeanours. Miss Frost departed in June 1886, leaving the Home in excellent order.

Chapter 17

The Ships in their Heyday

In 1874, the year in which the National Refuges acquired a second training ship, a visitor to the *Chichester* described life onboard. He was shown round by Captain Thurburn who explained, in answer to a query about the boys' education before they joined the Ship, that some of them had previously worked in printing offices and received a tolerable or good education. Others could read only with difficulty; some did not know one letter from another and had never learnt a prayer or been in a place of worship. The Captain was impressed by the quick intelligence of his charges and said that it was impossible, in his opinion, to find a more intelligent child in the world than the average London street boy. Finding jobs for them at sea was no problem; it was easy to find good ships 'for double the number we have, either in the Navy or Merchant Service. They have their choice, and the majority choose the mercantile marine'.

Out of the last 267 boys who had left the ship, only 40 chose the Royal Navy. Captain Thurburn explained that, in the mercantile marine, they saw a great deal more of the world and had more opportunity to change ships if they wanted to. When they quit the sea there were many well paid jobs open to them. On a first voyage boys could earn about 15 shillings per month and £1 per month for a second voyage. Their wages would increase to £3 a month when the boys were thoroughly experienced. Captain Thurburn continued:

"This hardly applies to many of the Australian voyages. Our boys have a certain reputation for smartness, and when they arrive in many of the Australian ports, they are frequently

The Training Ship Arethusa, *formerly* HMS Arethusa, *the last British warship to go into battle under sail, moored at Greenhithe, on the River Thames, between 1874 and 1933*

tempted away by country and coasting ships, with offers of £4 and £5 a month."

The visitor, knowing the kind of background from which the boys came, was quite unprepared for their healthy appearance and was surprised to learn that, out of the last 1356 boys who had joined the Ship, only 4 had died of disease. Captain Thurburn was proud of his happy ship and cheerfulness and good humour were everywhere apparent. Just before he left, the visitor joined in with the boys singing a series of sea-songs, accompanied on the harmonium by one of their masters.

Captain Walter, who was appointed to replace Captain Thurburn when he was promoted to Captain-Superintendent in 1874, was 'agreeably surprised at the general behaviour of the boys onboard'. In fact their good behaviour impressed many people who expected otherwise. The Annual Report for 1875 quoted from Lord Shaftesbury's speech in the House of Lords in which he mentioned the 'thousands of boys found to be running about our streets with no means of improvement'. Lord Shaftesbury criticised mistaken prejudice against destitute street boys and:

".. the disgust which has been felt at the thought of inflicting upon the Navy boys of unsatisfactory moral and physical character. If these lads are not at present as physically and morally competent as could be wished they are perfectly capable of being made so."

He quoted statistics about the boys who had been trained onboard the *Chichester* since its inauguration:

"In 9 years there had been sent to sea 1524 drawn from the poorest classes; 1336 to the Merchant Marine and 158 to the Royal Navy of whom the accounts were very good. I sincerely hope, my Lords, that we shall hear no more of employing none but respectable lads of good birth and all that sort of thing."

He told the Lords about the recent visit by a ship's Captain to the National Refuges' Shipping Agent, Mr. Scouler. The Captain had been anxious to tell about the time he had been in charge of a vessel caught off the Cape in a terrible gale. The crew were at their wits' end and thoroughly demoralized. The Captain was afraid to leave the helm but it was vital that he did so; his men were utterly helpless. He called a 16 year old crew member and gave him the rudder. The boy had trained onboard the *Chichester* and 'By God's blessing' said the Captain 'that boy brought us through'. 'What more' Lord Shaftesbury continued 'can be wanted? Respectable parentage indeed! That lad was brought up in the gutter. What more could he have done had he been born in the Mansion House?'

The Committee tried, with Mr. Scouler's help, to

Mr Joseph Scouler, who succeeded his father as the Society's London Shipping Agent in 1880 and was responsible for placing hundreds of Arethusa boys in seagoing billets in Merchant Ships. He retired in 1906 and, until his death in 1914, acted as steward at the Society's annual festivals at the Queen's Hall, London.

Sailmaking Instruction onboard the Arethusa *Training Ship*

keep accurate records of the boys' first and subsequent sailings on Merchant and Royal Navy ships and of their returns. To encourage the boys to stick to their jobs, the Society promised to pay two shillings and sixpence to each boy reporting back to the Society after a voyage. Boys who reshipped after first or subsequent voyages which lasted for a year or more were given 'some useful present of clothing, say of the value of five shillings'. Each boy 'who had borne a good character for 18 months after leaving the ship' received a silver watch.

In April 1875 many old boys returned from voyages and visited the training ships. Among them were some 'who had been to Australia and returned in their ships without deserting although the rest of the crews were tempted away by the higher wages offered at Melbourne'.

In October Captain Thurburn resigned on health grounds. Captain Walter transferred from the *Chichester* to become Captain Superintendent onboard the *Arethusa*. Captain Boxer RN was appointed to take his place in the *Chichester*.

On 22nd December 1875 the London School Board Training Ship *Goliath*, under the command of Captain Bouchier, was destroyed by fire as a result of a paraffin lamp being upset. There were 480 boys onboard at the time with training officers and teachers. All their lifeboats were out of action because of a violent storm the previous evening. Captain Walter, with officers and boys from the *Arethusa* and the *Chichester* helped in the rescue operations by which large numbers were saved. During a presentation ceremony at the Mansion House a few weeks later the Lord Mayor of London publicly acknowledged their bravery. Captain Walter received a silver medal and a framed testimonial inscribed:

"CAPTAIN FREDERICK WALTER, R.N.

of the Training Ship *Arethusa*,

under whose gallant command three boats from the *Arethusa* and two from the *Chichester*, proceeded a distance of three miles, and saved during the fierceness of the fire, no less than 30 lads. Captain Bouchier attributes his own safety entirely to Captain Walter's efforts which were most heroic."

The nautical Examiners' report for 1876 was as usual highly satisfactory:

"In the rule of the road and seamanship, we gave them a severe examination and it is certainly very praiseworthy in both the trainers and the lads for the quick answers given, many of the questions put would have puzzled many an older head than theirs."

The Examiners wrote that they 'would be pleased to see such valuable institutions better supported'. The Committee of the National Refuges endorsed this view. They still received not a penny from the Government which, instead, gave funds to the reformatory ships for convict boys.

At the Annual Meeting in 1876 one of the *Arethusa* boys received a prize for outstanding bravery. Lord Shaftesbury read out the letter from Captain Walter which described what had happened:

"A little boy, about 9 years of age, fell from the Ballast Wharf, astern of the *Arethusa* (about 100 yards) into the water. Our dinghy was under the stern painting. Those in the boat, seeing the child fall, shoved off, and pulled for the shore. On arriving, the child was under water,

A class under instruction in the Chichester *Training Ship*

and the boy, James Henry Drew, jumped out of the dinghy into the stream, and saved the child. I believe it was a very close thing, and the boy Drew deserved commendation. By the Register, I see he has neither father nor mother."

The boy was called to the platform, and presented with a Bible inscribed 'To James Henry Drew, of the Training Ship *Arethusa*, for jumping into the river Thames, and saving the life of a little boy who had fallen into the river'.

'I have great satisfaction in saying' Lord Shaftesbury told the audience 'that if he goes on in the way in which he has begun he will be an honour to his country'.

1876 was a successful year for the training ships; more boys were sent to sea than in any year since 1866.

The Committee felt greatly encouraged as the Annual Report noted:

"Perhaps no other calling would better suit those overgrown, over-aged and neglected lads for many of whom it would be no easy task to find good situations on shore. Life on shipboard has supplied the discipline, the habits of restraint and obedience without which they could have made no headway in the world.

Working in the Bo'sun's party onboard the Arethusa

The difference between poor ragged Tom as with downcast look he stood in the Secretary's office asking for admission, and Tom of the *Arethusa* as he is seen a few months afterwards rollicking up the rigging to 'man yards' is almost inconceivable.

The lad has awakened to a purpose in life at last and feels that there is something worth striving after."

The Society received many grateful letters from old boys saying how useful their training had been. 'Sir' wrote one in 1876 'I am pleased to say what I learned onboard the *Chichester* has come in very handy indeed to me and it has saved me from a good many whacks, I can assure you'.

By 1878, the outlook for employment in ships was not so hopeful as in previous years. The Annual Report noted the trend by which:

"Year after year steamers are more and more superseding sailing vessels, the size of steamers is being constantly increased while their crews are being rather reduced than otherwise, all of which facts tend to diminish the demand for our boys."

In addition to the change from sail to

steam, other factors made it hard to place the boys when their training was finished. The *Chichester* and *Arethusa* had been followed by a number of publicly funded training ships. *Warspite* had increased its complement of boys by 100; the *Exmouth* 'supported by the rates of Poor Law Unions' had nearly 600 boys; the reformatory ship *Cornwall* trained 240 boys every year for sea. It was even more frustrating for the Committee that:

"A new ship has been placed on the river which is moored in the proximity of our ships, which has been named The *Shaftesbury* after our noble President. On The *Shaftesbury* which is designed to accommodate 500 boys there has been expended by the School Board of London, exclusive of its original cost, in fitting up and rigging a sum of over £35,000. The cost of fitting up our two ships the *Chichester* and *Arethusa* which would together accommodate the same number came to under £14,000."

Besides the new and unwelcome competition thus provided for the Society's shipping agent in placing boys in ships after their training, there was confusion in the public mind between the Society's two training ships supported wholly by voluntary donations and the new *Shaftesbury* funded by the London School Board. Requests for donations were frequently met with a blank refusal because 'you are the people that have spent all that money and saddled us with a heavy rate'.

In comparison with these problems, it was a small matter that, onboard the *Exmouth*, *Shaftesbury, Cornwall* and *Warspite,* the boys had white bread and a certain quantity of biscuit per day rather than the brown bread then provided in the Society's ships. The boys complained and Captain Walter arranged with the Ships' Committee for a change to white bread. This livened up what must have been a rather tedious diet, as can be seen from the daily dietary scale which, for many years, remained as:

soft bread	1lb
biscuit	8 oz
fresh meat	7 oz
potatoes	8 oz
cocoa	3/4 oz
tea	1/8 oz
sugar	2/3 oz

and sometimes green vegetables. On Sundays a special treat of 4 oz flour and 2 oz treacle was allowed for pudding and twice a week another 4 oz flour was allocated for 'sea pies'.

The depression in trade and hence in shipping continued in 1879 but, as the Annual Report stated:

".. this has not in the slightest degree interfered with the work done in our training ships. Nevertheless the fact cannot be denied that in consequence of the continued decrease of sailing vessels the difficulty is increased of shipping as many lads as formerly."

There was, however, no difficulty in finding employment on shore for those boys who could not find ship berths so the Committee began to consider whether one ship might not be more practical than two. Training would then be offered only to those boys who had a reasonable chance of a berth after qualifying. The money spent on a second vessel could thus be put to

The Arethusa *Training Ship at Greenhithe*

better purpose in training more boys for shore jobs.

In June 1879 it was decided, therefore, to reduce the complement of boys in training from 400 to 300: all to be berthed in the *Arethusa*. From then on the *Chichester*, after the rigging was altered to make it easier to handle, was used as a drill and exercise ship for all the boys to give them better and more thorough training than was possible when the two vessels were being worked independently. Captain Walter believed that the change would be an improvement, because:

"Although the shipping may not improve sufficiently for us to send as many boys to sea as in past years, those we do send will be decidedly better qualified."

The decision was implemented on 18th November 1880. Captain Boxer left to take up the post of Harbour Master at Folkestone. The saving achieved by this reorganisation was estimated at £2,000 per annum. All the boys who had served more than two years in the training ships were found employment on shore. Frustration at spending longer in the training ships than expected probably explains the most serious disorder recorded in the Ships' Committee book. This occurred in June 1879 when a few of the older boys tried to set fire to the ship. On Captain Walter's advice the Committee decided that the ring-leaders should be handed over to the police as an example to the other boys.

By 1881 there was a revival in shipping. The Committee was heartened to note that:

"The Captains and owners of our large steam fleets are beginning to see that the lads trained on our ships are capable of doing the work which it was supposed could only be done by those who had a different if not a special training for it."

Consequently boys were kept onboard for 13 to 14 months only instead of the previous 20 to 24 months. More boys could thus be trained for a smaller outlay than previously. For the first time, Captain Walter was able to report 48 more boys placed in steamers than in sailing ships.

The Nautical Examiners' report for this year commented that:

"The discipline apparently observed onboard is perfectly quiet but firm and the result is a smart and willing obedience and general cheerfulness, regularity and good order very difficult to obtain and most satisfactory to all concerned whenever successfully accomplished, as it is at present onboard your ships *Chichester* and *Arethusa*."

The improved state of the shipping trade prompted the Society to consider increasing once again the number of boys onboard the *Arethusa* to 300 or more, and even to have 50 boys permanently back onboard the *Chichester*.

Captain Walter advised against this, however, unless more staff were available:

"It is more especially during the spare time and recreation hours that supervision is necessary. My object is to prevent the possibility of boys getting into mischief and doing wrong, by having instructors on duty in all parts of the Ship to which the boys have access."

The number of boys shipped decreased again in 1883. One of the reasons, as the Committee acknowledged in the Annual Report, was that bigger steamers were regularly being used, and these needed:

".. only able and experienced crews. The

The Depot at East India Dock Road

lads who are taken onboard such ships come of respectable parentage or have wealthy friends who are able and willing to pay a fair sum by way of premium."

The work of the Shipping Agent, Mr. Scouler, was invaluable in placing the boys and helping them on their return from sea. The *Arethusa* 'Depot for Trained Sailor Lads' at East India Dock Road in East London could accommodate 12 boys who were on the spot when Mr. Scouler spoke to Captains of merchant vessels on their behalf. The boys were equipped for their first voyage with:

2 serge shirts	1 set of tins, needles, thread, etc
2 singlets	4 lbs soap
2 striped cotton shirts	1 bag
2 duck jumpers	2 cloth caps
3 duck trousers	1 pair drawers
1 pilot jacket	1 belt
2 pairs half hose	2 combs
1 pair blankets	1 comforter
1 rug	1 towel
1 bed	1 pair boots
1 oiled suit and wester	

The Annual Report for 1890 gave more details about the changes in the shipping trade and the Royal Navy's work:

"The whole course of maritime business has undergone a most remarkable change, and especially during the last 10 or 15 years. Large ocean steamers have taken the place of the small sailing ships which used to trade from port to port, and sometimes all round the world. Onboard these ships, which are now almost becoming extinct, there were fine opportunities for boys to learn all the duties of a sailor's life, and eventually of becoming well fitted for doing their part in carrying on the commercial trade of the country, or for its defence by entering the Royal Navy.

Everything nowadays must be done in the shortest possible time, and the old vessels which for so many years held their own on the ocean have gone the way of the old stage-coaches, and large mercantile steamers easily obtain and quickly carry the manufactures of the country, as well as the passengers going out to foreign ports. These monster ships supply very few openings for the employment of our sailor lads."

The Chichester *Sailing Brig, purchased in 1889 for £500 by the National Refuges for Homeless and Destitute Children. The* Chichester *was originally a two-masted schooner named* Ballerina *of Cowes, length 83ft, beam 19ft, and was converted into a brigantine with squaresails at the forward mast. She was used to provide sail training for the boys of the Training Ship* Arethusa *which lay on the River Thames at Greenhithe between 1874 and 1934. In 1917 she was sold to Messrs Richard and William Massey of County Wexford for 500 guineas.*

The Committee consequently decided to sell the *Chichester* (which had been on loan from the Admiralty until 1889 when it had agreed to give her to the Society) and the Society received £12,500 from Messrs. Castle & Sons for her disposal. With a small part of the proceeds, it was decided to acquire:

"..a smaller and more modern craft, so that during the year the boys can be taken out for a cruise, thus familiarizing them with duties of which the best drill and exercise of sails on board a stationary ship must leave them in ignorance."

After a good deal of searching and deliberation, the Committee purchased the *Ballerina* from a Mr. George Marvin of West Cowes for £500. She was renamed *Chichester* and altered:

".. from a fore-and-aft schooner to a brigantine in the early spring. 15 cruises of a few days at a time with about 28 boys, to Harwich, Brightlingsea and other places were managed before the middle of October when the prevalence of fogs rendered it prudent to discontinue them for the winter."

The Captain Superintendent, who by this time was Captain G.O. Moore, submitted statistics in his report for the year ending 31st December 1890:

Onboard or with Agent at 1st January 1890	171	
Admitted during the year	158	
TOTAL	329	
To:		
Merchant Service	130	
Royal Navy	17	
Army	2	
Friends, etc.	17	
Onboard, and at Agent's at 1st January 1891	167	

The boys who were sent to merchant ships had spent an average of 13 months onboard; their education and training increased their self confidence. Their improved health was measured by the increase in their height and weight during the period. As an example:

	Height	Weight	Chest Girth
On joining	4ft 11ins	91 lbs	28.25"
On leaving	5ft 2ins	108 lbs	30.75"
Increase	3ins	17 lbs	2.5"

The years from the early 1870s, when the National Refuges established its second Training Ship, until the late 1890s were characterised for the Committee by concerns arising out of the change from sail to steam and the fluctuations in trade which, in turn, led to a varying demand for trained boys. Nevertheless, during these years, young men who had been in the *Chichester* and the *Arethusa* proved the value of the training they had received. By the time the nineteenth century drew to a close the Society's national standing and reputation for seamanship training were unsurpassed.

Commander G.O. Moore RN, Captain
Superintendent of the Arethusa *Training*
Ship from 1888 until 1905

Chapter 18
The Turn of the Century

Previous chapters have related the story of the training ships and the homes at Bisley, Twickenham, Ealing and Sudbury in the 1870s, 1880s and 1890s. It is now time to examine how the Society as a whole changed and developed at the end of the nineteenth century and in the early 1900s.

In 1896 the London Boys' Refuge at 164 Shaftesbury Avenue was converted into a Technical School for older boys from the Society's other homes. The Log Book for May 1896 explained that:

"Boys will be brought from our country homes when they reach the age of 14 – not before – and will then be given 18 months or two years' thorough and practical training in tailoring or shoemaking, under efficient trade instructors.

There is no doubt that their transformation from schoolboys into young tradesmen, the greater liberty which will be granted to them, and the contact they will necessarily have with business men, will considerably tone their rawness, and will put the boys, when their training is finished, in a much better position to earn their own living."

Mr. E.W. Dixon, the tailor master at Fortescue House, became the Superintendent. He had joined the Society almost by chance more than 20 years previously as a result of a visit to London from his home in Easton, Northamptonshire. He had heard much about the work of the National Refuges and called in at Great Queen Street to see for himself the kind of work that was done:

"Upon being shown the tailoring department" he wrote later, "I was surprised to see it without a trace of skilled labour and in quite a neglected state. Mr. Williams informed me he required a tailor master very badly, and asked me if I would be kind enough to try and find him someone whom he could rely upon."

Try as he might, he could not find anybody suitable who was willing to apply for the job. William Williams wrote shortly afterwards asking him to come to London and fit the boys with the new suits they needed for the Annual Meeting. Mr. Dixon left Easton at once:

"My heart told me that this labour was my mission. I decided to throw my lot in with the Institution, and in May 1871 I found a buyer for the tailor's business I had at Easton at a fair price, which unfortunately for me was never paid."

Mr. Dixon put the Society's tailoring on a professional footing. With the boys in their tailoring workshops he made, at various times, all the clothes needed for the ship boys, outfits for the boys who were about to emigrate and all the uniforms for Shaftesbury School.

When the General Committee was considering setting up the Technical School he gave his support to the scheme, because:

"I thought the idea a grand one. Previously

Mr Dixon's Tailoring Department at Fortescue House

few boys continued the trade, of which they had acquired a slight knowledge; consequently more unskilled labour was put upon the market, instead of skilled, and the work of teaching was completely thrown away."

The Technical School was soon well known for the high standard of its training and professionalism. In 1898 the boys in the shoemaking department 'had the honour of making a pair of boots for royalty .. an order

The Shoemaking Shop at the Technical School, Fordham House

(through Mr. F. H. Clayton, a member of our General Committee) for a pair of boots for King Kamswaga of Koki'. A photograph in the Log Book of the finished boots placed on end with the soles upwards next to a pair of 'large sized ladies' boots' against a brick wall showed the king's boots as approximately twice the size of the other pair and extending upwards to a height of five bricks. The Technical School was well established by 1899 and the Society's Committee could look with pride at its achievements as well as the success of the ships, the homes at Bisley, Sudbury, Ealing and Twickenham and Fordham House, the London Boys' Hostel.

King Kamswaga of Koki's boots. Mr F.H. Clayton had been asked by the Rev. Clayton, MA, a CMS Missionary in Uganda, to provide a suitable pair of boots

Christmas in 1899 and the New Year of 1900 were celebrated by the children and their teachers in a traditional way with carols, church services, music, visits and treats. The girls at Ealing performed a cantata 'Lazyland' for their visitors. At Sudbury Hall, everyone enjoyed a visitor's lecture on kindness to animals 'with dissolving views'. Miss Chipchase was delighted to see many old girls and was surprised and gratified to receive an 'Oxford reading stand and revolving bookcase' as a gift from some of her former pupils who could not attend. Selina Amner, her companion and helper, had arranged the collection and old girls from many parts of England and one from Canada had contributed. The boys at Twickenham enjoyed a slide presentation about Nansen's attempt to reach the North Pole and a friend paid for them to go out for a celebration tea with bread and butter, jam and cake.

The boys in the Technical School and Fordham House, being older, mostly spent the Christmas period with friends or relatives, but at the schools at Bisley Christmas Day started with morning service at 10.30; lunch was at 12.30 with roast beef followed by plum pudding 'with oranges and romps in the evening to the accompaniment of the band'. There were two performances of the cantata *Robinson Crusoe* 'to which Mr. Mollett devoted so much time and labour in bringing the boys to a successful rendering'.

In its Annual Report for the year 1900 the Committee defended its policy of placing their children in separate homes rather than in one large, central institution, although this would have been cheaper.

"Anything like the barrack system is wholly unknown in our work, each branch of the Society being really a home, and every child personally known to the Superintendent and Matron. The children are rescued from unhealthy dwellings, frequently from demoralising neighbourhoods, and are received into well-lighted, properly ventilated homes situated in the country and suburbs."

The Report highlighted the Society's concern and care for children but value for money was always a high priority to the members of the public who supported charities. In the previous year, for instance, the Society received a cheque from a Miss Boord, with the promise of more money in future, provided the children were not accustomed to 'more comforts than were necessary for health and life, or luxuries out of keeping with working homes in the lowest ranks of society'. Consequently, the Annual Report highlighted the children's diet which was nourishing, wholesome and economical. It was a rule of the Society that Superintendents and Matrons should be present at the children's dinner time to see that the food had been properly prepared and cooked and was well served. The custom at Bisley, in the early years,

The Dining Hall, Bisley School, c. 1922

of selling produce from the farm to raise revenue for the Society was modified at the beginning of the twentieth century so that:

"All the fruit and vegetables consumed by the children are furnished from the gardens of the homes and the sale of any surplus is prohibited so that the children know that the whole of the produce is for their entire use and benefit. Each child is weighed on admission, and again three months after, and the additional weight gained is simply astonishing. The children are warmly clad; first rate quality cloth is supplied at advantageous prices through the kindness of some wholesale firms."

The Committee members felt great satisfaction in the first few weeks of 1900 that thanks to careful management the finances of the National Refuges were in good shape to face the new century. Particular thanks were given to Henry Copeland, the Deputation Secretary, for his imaginative approach to raising funds. One of his schemes, to increase awareness of the needs of poor children and encourage generous giving, was to target young people from comfortable homes by forming the 'Victoria League' for girls and the 'Arethusa League' for boys:

"Mr Copeland has made a vigorous onslaught on the Sunday Schools of our land, and has secured many openings in drawing rooms, but perhaps the most important part of his labours has been his entrance into many of our Public and Prep schools for boys. His addresses, illustrated as they are by lantern views, must eventually be the means of raising up for our Society an influential body of helpers and subscribers.

The Deputation Secretary will attend any meetings which can be held during afternoons or evenings, in drawing rooms, lecture halls or elsewhere. The apparatus has been now so perfected, that this can be done in the ordinary afternoon meetings, without any disturbance of furniture, disarrangement of walls, or darkening of the room. The lectures are illustrated by a powerful oxyhydrogen light and specially prepared views, and are given without charge, the Society relying for aid upon the offerings of the audiences.

To any one who is preparing a lecture series for the winter, think of this possibility. Very suitable for Sunday schools, Temperance Societies, Bands of Hope, Young People's Guilds and other societies. Where it is not cost effective to send a speaker, the slides are sent out free of charge, the only condition being that the hirer pays postage both ways and holds a collection."

A printed lecture was sent with each of the three sets of slides. The first set gave an overall view of the Society's work in London and the country; the second set showed the life of boys who had emigrated to Canada, and the third set covered training for a life at sea.

The Committee was delighted, in November 1900, to note that the lantern slide lectures had made a clear profit of almost £300 during the nine months to 30 September.

Another way of raising funds for the Society was a system of local agents. The Committee constantly appealed for interested people to act as agents, whose task was to receive donations, disseminate information and encourage initiatives which would benefit the Society. Local agents made a valuable contribution to the funds, though there were occasional difficulties. Bogus collectors from time to time tricked the public into parting with money which made it more difficult for genuine agents to operate. The Society's advertising consequently stressed that no door to door collections were carried out on its behalf.

Much support for the National Refuges was achieved by a policy of encouraging visitors to see for themselves the regime in the homes:

"The Committee desire it to be distinctly understood that all the homes and training ships are open for inspection throughout the week (except Sundays) at any time of the day. Ladies and gentlemen desiring to pay a visit are cordially invited to do so on presentation of their card, any weekday or evening."

The total destitution of the Rookery dwellers which had moved William Williams in 1843 to found the National Refuges and the appalling social conditions against which Lord Shaftesbury had campaigned had by now been largely overcome. Many social ills however, such as poverty, disease, cruelty to children and the break up of families were still commonplace. Every application for admission to the homes was considered on its merits; no child was turned away if an emergency had arisen. All that was needed was a letter of recommendation from a clergyman or other person of standing who could testify to the applicant's genuine need.

On 7th January 1900 a great benefactor of the Society, Alfred Fennings, died at the age of 84. He had made his first contribution to the Society's funds in 1870 and until his death had given some £86,377-10s-0d, from the proceeds of his business which manufactured and sold popular medicines. At his request, he was known to the Committee as 'Alf' and all his donations had been acknowledged in the regular list of supporters and benefactors as 'Anonymous'. His contributions were made on the strict understanding that the money was to support destitute boys of London and that none of it should be used to train a boy for a life at sea; nor, indeed, were any boys who had been assisted by his contributions to be urged or helped to go to sea. On the Wednesday before his death he sent a cheque for £1,375 to support an additional 24 boys. Mr. Bristow Wallen attended his funeral on behalf of the Society, with a wreath:

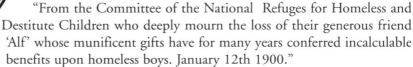

Alfred Fennings known as 'Alf'

"From the Committee of the National Refuges for Homeless and Destitute Children who deeply mourn the loss of their generous friend 'Alf' whose munificent gifts have for many years conferred incalculable benefits upon homeless boys. January 12th 1900."

In his will he provided for named relatives and family until their deaths following which all profits of the Company were placed in trust for the benefit of the National Refuges with the proviso he had made earlier, to support 'vagrant street boys of London or elsewhere, and it is my desire that none of the said children who shall be so boarded clothed and educated shall be trained for or induced to adopt a seafaring life'.

Alfred Fennings had established a very successful business selling medicines for the treatment of a wide variety of conditions. Fennings' Cooling Powders, Childrens' Powders, Fever Curer, Lung Healers and later, Little Healers were some of the products which had made 'Fennings' something of a household name in the early part of the twentieth century. The business generated good profits from sales at home and abroad and, in accordance with the will, the profits were paid to the Society.

These financial contributions, with full tax relief, from the Foundation of Alfred Fennings, were substantial. The money had to be used for the boarding, clothing and education of boys but any surplus could be invested or used to purchase or improve buildings. Since the Foundation was established, well over £2,000,000 has been paid by the Trustees of Alfred Fennings to the Society. The money enabled the Society to continue through difficult times and indeed ensured its survival. Whilst William Williams had, with Lord Shaftesbury, worked tirelessly to establish the great work of the National Refuges, Alfred Fennings had become its greatest financial benefactor.

The story of Fennings is fascinating and could justify a book of its own but the financial commitment to transfer all profit to the

Society led to problems. The products sold well in the period up to the outbreak of the Second World War but, since the Society was entitled to all profits, the business was starved of investment capital. This situation led, inevitably, to decline. In other circumstances, Fennings might have developed to become a leading pharmaceutical company. With insufficient funds to undertake research, its remedies became less effective than modern alternatives and it became difficult to renew product licences. The Fennings' Trust still exists but the right to market Fennings' products has recently passed to another concern. The Society continues to benefit from income generated by the Trust's assets.

June 1902 saw the Coronation of Edward VII. As Prince of Wales he had long taken an interest in the Society and his continued support as a Patron, after he became King, further enhanced its reputation. The General Committee authorized expenditure at the rate of 6d. per head for the children to mark the occasion.

The royal endorsement of the Society's work and the children's regular appearances at national events such as the Lord Mayor's Show, the Earl's Court Exhibition, the annual Church Congress and many other national occasions ensured that public support continued. Many rich and influential patrons and friends, as well as several City Livery Companies, endorsed and contributed to the work in the early years of the twentieth century and the Society was probably the largest of all charities helping orphaned or destitute children and young people.

It was a sign of more modern times when, in July 1902, Henry Copeland made his report to the Committee and submitted proposals for better office accommodation and equipment

The Committee worked hard to raise funds to provide a home for girls such as these

including 'a new typewriting machine and manifolding apparatus'. That same month the Committee further modernised the Head Office by accepting the quotation from the Post Office Telephone Service for 'fixing up the telephone apparatus and maintaining same for £5 a year with the minimum charge of £1-10s-0d per annum or 360 calls at 1d.'

The Diamond Jubilee of the National Refuges was celebrated in 1903 and the Committee planned to mark the occasion by opening a new Home for Girls who needed care but were too young to be sent to Ealing or Sudbury. Although the Society was by now a well known and respected national charity and legacies formed a considerable part of its income, it could not afford to go ahead with the project immediately.

A problem arose when a small legacy from a supporter in Chile could not be claimed, as according to Chilean law of the time, only Incorporated Societies were recognised. The Secretary had to make an arrangement with Dr. Barnardo, whose Society also benefited under the same will, suggesting that he claim the whole legacy and afterwards give the National Refuges its share. Thanks to Dr. Barnardo's help, a way through the legal tangle was found and the Society received its bequest. This was one of the reasons why, in 1904, the Society applied for and gained Incorporated status in accordance with the Companies Act of 1867. The Trustees of the Society were thus relieved of personal financial responsibility and the Society was able to hold its own property.

In 1906 the Society bought a $5^1/_2$ acre site at Royston in Hertfordshire as the new Home for young girls. The property was less than a mile from the station and only ten minutes walk from Royston Heath on 'a fine stretch of elevated common'.

In the meantime, until the Home was ready for occupation and rather than turn away really urgent cases, the Society reluctantly resorted to 'boarding out' very young girls and boys with suitable private families. Great care was taken 'to secure foster parents of irreproachable character and to ensure proper supervision'. The age range of these children was from five to eight. When they were nine years old they were sent to one of the existing homes. This scheme generally worked well and, for most of the children, it provided a safe, secure home. When the Royston home opened boarding out was still used in urgent cases but the

Committee preferred, if possible, to have all children under the full-time care of its own staff.

One of the young boys who was placed in foster care at Tolworth, in the early years of the twentieth century, still remembers the family who looked after him:

"Mr. and Mrs. Searle were like a loving mother and father to me. They treated me as their son, and we were friends for years after I left school. I kept in touch with each of them till they died, and went to their funerals. I owe them more than I can say."

The Little Girls' Home at Royston in Hertfordshire was built by the Society to accommodate some sixty children and opened in 1908. It took five years to raise the £7000 to pay for it.

'Shaftesbury House' at Royston was formally opened in November 1908. Over the years its use varied from admitting young girls or young boys and, in some periods, it became a home for both.

A few weeks after the opening of Royston, Mr. Dixon, the Superintendent of the Technical Home in London retired. He felt justifiably proud of what had been achieved since its inauguration. 300 young men had gained enough skill to go on to earn decent wages or start their own businesses. Together with the residents, he had saved the National Refuges a great deal of money and had made a healthy profit on outside commissions:

"My full trade in the Tailoring Department in 1907 was £1039-1s-3d, against £320-0s-1d in 1897, showing an increase in 10 years of £710-1s-2d. My outside trade for 1907 was £543-5s-0d, against £117-19s-0d in 1897 showing an increase in 10 years of £425-6s-0d."

The School Room at Royston in 1908

Miss Chipchase retired in 1911. Selina Amner, who had worked at Sudbury Hall as her helper, resigned at the same time in order to look after her at her new home in Worthing. The farewell party was a quiet occasion at Miss Chipchase's request. However many Committee members with their wives and families, old friends and past and present pupils were there to wish her well. She received a cheque which was the result of collections among the many people she had befriended over the years. In the Society's Log Book for 1911 Henry Copeland wrote:

"We know that she has been deeply touched with all that has been said, and all that has been done to make her comfortable in her new home. It will please the Old Girls especially to know that she calls her new abode 'Sudbury'".

This edition of the Log Book gave a record of Miss Chipchase's work for the Society:

"Forty-five years of faithful and efficient service is a record of which anyone may be justly proud. The National Refuges have had the untiring and patient devotion of Miss Chipchase in the care and training of poor girls since 1866, first as the Matron of the Girls' Refuge in Broad Street, Bloomsbury, and subsequently, when the work was transferred to Sudbury. From the commencement Miss Chipchase had the entire confidence of Mr. William Williams, the founder and first Secretary, as well as the Committee. It is not surprising that at her advanced age of 75 she should find her strength inadequate for the work, and desire a time of quietude and rest.

The Committee has made suitable provision for her remaining years and thank God for her long life of usefulness and her consistent Christian character and influence. Nearly 1500 girls have had her kindly care and training, and she will carry into her retirement many happy memories of those to whom she has acted a mother's part."

Mrs. Swaffield, the Head Teacher at Sudbury Hall since 1901 was appointed in her place. She had worked for the National Refuges as a school teacher a few years previously but had left to get married. On the death of her husband she had turned again to teaching to provide for herself and her family. She loved music and often produced cantatas and song recitals with the girls from Sudbury, winning praise for her abilities and dedication.

Henry Copeland, the Deputation Secretary, travelled all over the country year after year to talk about the National Refuges in schools, clubs and at meetings of every kind. By 1914 he admitted to himself and the Committee that he felt mentally stale. He needed a change and persuaded the Committee to grant him £75 for a two month trip to Canada. He planned to visit as many past pupils as possible, to learn about local labour and employment conditions and to promote the National Refuges as far as he could. He left with Mrs. Copeland on 14th April 1914 and an account of his travels was published in the Log Book. One of his first contacts was an old boy from Twickenham living in Montreal. He was in 'an excellent situation and doing very well'. From there he went to Winnipeg where he saw:

"..about a dozen of our old lads who had come into the city from various towns and from homes in the city itself. The agent to whom our lads are sent on first arrival is an excellent man, and with him the boys are in good hands. The Twickenham, the Farm, and the Shaftesbury Schools were all represented by those whom I saw, and to a Twickenham lad belongs the honour of being the first to give me a contribution towards the support of the work. This was followed

Some of the Society's young people on their way to Canada

by several gifts, reaching the sum of five dollars with promises of more later on, so that the 'Old Boys' Dollar Fund' is now established. I am looking forward to seeing other boys on my return to Manitoba, and in Ontario on my way home. In Wetaskiwin I spent a delightful time with one who left the Shaftesbury School thirty years ago, a man of interesting character, full of affection for his Bisley Home."

The first years of the twentieth century saw the Society in good shape as a vigorous, influential and respected national organization. The Committee felt confident about the future.

Chapter 19
The First World War

The beautiful spring of 1914 moved a boy at Fortescue House ('the Poet Laureate of our Twickenham Home'), to express himself in poetry, which was proudly published in the Log Book:

"What means this freshness in the air?
What new wonders to declare?
Light the snowdrops answer sweet
Gently birds the sound repeat -
Spring is here!
Spring! the new birth of the year
Hope reviving season dear
Nature's gifts, so good and rare
Soon will be lavished everywhere -
Spring is here!"

In June Henry Copeland returned from Canada. His trip had been an outstanding success in every way. The fund raising and publicity campaign had produced good results and to his delight he met many old boys and girls who were comfortably settled and happy in their work. One of his letters described an invitation he received to visit an old boy:

The Technical School at Fordham House, 164 Shaftesbury Avenue, prepared boys for a trade which enabled them to find employment and a secure future despite their disadvantaged beginnings.

".. to spend a few days on his farm near Niagara. We were fortunately able to spare a week-end and greatly enjoyed our visit. The welcome which we received from this old boy and his wife and family was hearty in the extreme.

The next farm that we visited and the last before we turned our steps homewards, was owned by another old lad, and is about eight or ten miles from Ingress. Here he was cultivating about 50 acres. He is living in a temporary dwelling, for he is building himself a capital new house a little further away."

Two deaths marred the summer peace and enjoyment. The Rev. Thomas Turner who had been associated with the Society for 36 years, died on 13th June. He had been a good friend to Mr. and Mrs. King who ran Fordham House and was a frequent caller there. In his will he left £800 to be invested for Scripture prizes each year for boys and girls in the various homes. Another good friend died on 25th June 1914, the *Arethusa* boys' Shipping Agent for 26 years, Joseph Ralph Scouler (son of the first Shipping Agent employed by the Committee). Associated with the sea from the age of 15, he had taken over the job of Shipping Agent from his Father when he retired from the post in 1880. When he retired in 1906, Mr. Joseph Scouler kept in touch with many old *Arethusa* boys, and never voluntarily missed a Society function:

"He delighted to render help as a steward at the Society's great festivals at the Queen's Hall, London, and was never happier than when associating once again with those old colleagues who had known and respected him in the years gone by."

Splendid weather enhanced the Society's many grand occasions that summer - the fetes, prize days and reunions. The children enjoyed their sports days, treats and holiday outings.

The announcement of war in August brought the summer holiday mood speedily to an end. The Log Book for September showed the alarm the Committee members felt and their anxiety to do the best for the children under their care. They were equally anxious to support old boys and girls whose lives would be affected by the conflict.

"The declaration of war has plunged the nation into a state of anxiety. The Committee have at once resolved that there is to be no curtailment of admissions, for the children will need our succour and help now, more than is usually the case.

Breadwinners will fall in the conflict, and the Committee desire it to be known that they will be prepared to receive into their Country Homes boys and girls who may have the misfortune to lose their father, and other boys in similar distress to whom the *Arethusa* will afford a welcome home and training.

It is earnestly hoped that a Society like ours, which has sent such a large number of lads into the British Navy and Army, and has so many of them at the present moment throughout our Fleet and the other arm of the Service, may not lack for the necessary means of maintenance.

During the continuance of the war the Committee have decided to give full pay to the families of the staff who have been called out, at any rate until such time as remittances can be received from the husbands, and after that half-pay, as we did in the case of the Boer campaign. Further, to prevent distress and unemployment in trade quarters we are issuing orders for printing and other matters in the usual way.

Let our closing note reiterate the fact that our subscriptions and donations are hard hit by the war, and difficulty in procuring them is enhanced by the appeals for our soldiers and sailors. We are full of hope, however, that the generous public will rally to our aid and see that the work we are doing for 1,200 boys and girls is not allowed to suffer."

At the outbreak of hostilities, as well as the many old Arethusans in the Merchant and Royal Navies, old boys of the Society were serving in 74 Army regiments. The Committee considered how it could best assist the war effort without decreasing care for its resident children and former pupils. Members resolved to admit into the Society's homes any boys or girls whose fathers were killed or disabled in the conflict, as far as numbers would allow. They volunteered the tailors' shops in the boys' schools, to make up shirt material for the troops.

Thirty of the senior boys from Fordham House joined the Army and their places were taken by teenage boys who had fled from Europe as refugees. The Log Book gave some information about a few of the first arrivals:

"One of our two Belgian Boy Scouts was shot in the leg at Liege. Their father is a soldier in the Belgian Army, and their mother has been working in the Belgian Red Cross Service. Three others are from The Malines. Their father who kept a café there died some months ago, and their mother was carrying on the business when the Germans arrived and they had to flee."

The Committee's fears about the Society's finances were soon confirmed. 'The war is hitting our Society very hard' subscribers were informed. 'We began the year with a deficit from 1913 and this year we are face to face with a prospective heavy diminution of subscriptions and donations. The Committee earnestly appeal for additional helpers'.

Strict economy was needed because 'the cost of food and materials has considerably increased, flour alone having gone up 7s. per sack'.

An Old Boy serving as an A.B. in the Royal Navy

By October, the first sad news was reported:

"Among the missing officers of HMS *Pathfinder*, sunk in the North Sea by one of the enemy's submarines, was one of the very old *Arethusa* boys, viz: Gunner H E Morrison. He had retired from the Service, but immediately rejoined when the war broke out. All honour to him and to the other brave men who lost their lives in the same event."

The year finished with an appeal:

"The Committee are full of hope that the Society may not be forgotten during the Christmas season, especially as we are being so hard hit by the war. May we say to every reader, 'Let this be your Society for Christmas, and for aid throughout 1915'. Think of its splendid record and of its work of today.

We want again to bring brightness into our homes at Christmas time, and shall be glad if our readers and friends will think of the 900 boys and 300 girls distributed throughout our branches. Gifts of toys, books, dolls, games, etc., will be most welcome."

Their hopes were not disappointed. In January 1915, the Log Book conveyed the Committee's thanks to all the friends who 'sent such a good supply of dolls and toys and games to brighten the Christmas season in the Society's various branches'.

The National Refuges' pride at this time was naturally in the stories of their former pupils, particularly those in the

Another Old Boy serving in the Royal Horse Artillery

fighting lines. Sapper L. A. Sycamore of the Royal Engineers, who had been at Fortescue House, was recommended for the Distinguished Service Medal, as was Signaller John Walter Johnson for service on 16th December 1914 onboard HMS *Hardy*, off Hartlepool. He was wounded when his ship was chasing German cruisers from the coast. He remained at his post although he had received seven shell wounds.

On 31st May 1915 the Earl of Jersey died at the age of 70. He had been the Society's loyal and hardworking President for 30 years. He was 'a dear and generous friend whom the Society can ill afford to part with'. His funeral was at Middleton Stoney in Oxfordshire on 4th June. A Memorial Service was held in St. George's, Hanover Square, attended by boys and girls from the Society with the Superintendents of their homes and Mr. Bristow Wallen and Mr. Copeland.

The boys and girls missed him. It was his friendly interest in the day to day details of their lives that had marked him out as special. The Farm and Shaftesbury School boys remembered his surprise visit when they had to line up for inspection. 'Take your shoes off, everyone' he told them 'I want to see who's got holes in their socks. None of you boys should ever wear undarned socks'.

When in 1890 he had been appointed Governor of New South Wales, he told the young people emigrating from the National Refuges' homes that if they went to Sydney they were to pay him a visit at his residence, Government House. Several took him up on his offer and were warmly welcomed. His Lordship's regular annual treats at Osterley Park had been unforgettable highlights of summer holidays for many years. Even when he and Lady Jersey were in Australia, arrangements were made for the event to take place as usual. Many boys and girls developed a passion for reading through his encouragement – being himself a great lover of books. Dickens was a particular favourite. He had once nearly choked, so the story goes, laughing over 'Pickwick Papers'.

As the war continued contributions, subscriptions and donations fell. Prices rose. Staff were called up. Every possible economy was made at the Homes and in the running of the Society. Consignments of food received through the London Chamber of Commerce came as gifts from as far away as Australia and New Zealand. The *Arethusa* received:

4 carcases sheep	12 cases syrup
12 bags sugar	8 cases preserved meat
10 cases rabbits	8 cases jam
10 sacks flour	4 cases boiled mutton
6 boxes butter	

A meeting of brother and sister at Osterley Park. The boy is from the Bisley Farm School, the girl from Sudbury Hall

Staff and pupils at the homes managed as best they could. Mr. King from Fordham House was called up, so Mrs. King managed the home without him. When

Mr. Hoskyns, the master in charge of the shoemaking department at the Technical School, was away seriously ill, his senior pupil A. E. Wales took over and ran the Department. Mr. Dodkins, the superintendent of the Home, spoke highly of the boy.

"He has done excellent work during Mr. Hoskyns' illness. In the Cordwainers' Technical College list of the winners of certificates and prizes he was second highest prize winner for the session. He was anxious to join the Army, although he was under age, but we advised him to stop and help Mr. Hoskyns."

In spite of all difficulties work, training and play continued at the homes as normally as possible. One of the boys at Fortescue House during this period still remembers it as one of the happiest times of his life. He is now in his nineties but his childhood is vividly clear in his mind and he loves to talk about his school-days:

"We had all the usual lessons but, above all, they taught us how to behave and how to get on in life. All the masters were very friendly. Just before I left school, the headmaster Mr. Holloway told me 'This is your home and you are always welcome to come back any time. There's no need to knock at the front door. Walk straight in through the side entrance.'"

When he was in the top class at Fortescue House he was chosen by Mr. Holloway to be one of the 'house boys':

"In the week we house boys were at school in the mornings and then in the afternoon we did jobs. Only two or three of us were chosen, and it was a great privilege. We helped in the kitchen, served at table, opened the door to visitors, and ran messages. Mr. Holloway came into the kitchen once when I was helping with the washing up. My hair was all dishevelled and he said 'I chose you because you were always neat and tidy – and now look at you!' At Christmas time I helped the cook make the Christmas puddings. The ingredients were tipped into a great bath, and I rolled up my sleeves and stirred. The mixture came up to my elbows. Of course, there was much less food with the war on but we did not go without. Because of being a house boy I got to know all the Committee when they called. Mr. Clayton used to call often, and we became quite friendly. He was a really lovely gentleman. I met him and his wife several times over the years after I left and he never forgot me, not even many years later when he became Chairman and Treasurer of the Society, and then Sir Francis Clayton.

When we left school we were all given a Bible and a prayer book, and I've kept mine to this day. We had to go to Shaftesbury Avenue to be fitted out with a complete set of clothes and a cap. Three months later we had to go again for another set."

Inexorably, the number of In Memoriam notices in the Log Book grew. It was only to be expected that the strain on the staff would tell. Whether poor Mrs. Swaffield's nerves were affected by anxiety over running Sudbury Hall or by worrying about her son Lt. H. G. Swaffield we do not know, but she was finding it ever more difficult to cope with her job. Junior staff at Sudbury Hall had to cover for her on occasions when she was not fit for work. Eventually matters came to a head and in April 1916 a special Committee Meeting was called because Mrs. Swaffield 'had been seriously ill and her illness had again been caused by intemperance'. Her son asked the Committee to be tolerant and give his mother one more chance but it was a risk they did not feel could be justified. It was unanimously decided that she be asked to resign at once. She left Sudbury Hall within the week. Bearing in mind that she had worked for the Society for 17 years, the Committee awarded her three months salary and £1 per week for three months. Her place was taken in September by Miss Lyle Browne from the staff at Colston Girls' School, Bristol.

In 1916 the Society announced a deficit of over £6,000. The Committee was unanimously against any diminution of the work. The need was too great. It was an inappropriate time to sell any investments or property as the market was so depressed. All that could be done was to work to attract a larger number of subscribers and donors and at the same time exercise all economy.

Accordingly, in the Log Book, emphasis was placed on war news and on the distinguished part played by old boys of the Society. There were photos and letters from those at the Front and news of old boys who had been captured or killed in action.

Over 600 former pupils serving in the Army wrote to their old teachers that year. The Society managed to send 120 parcels to old boys in the forces. Mr. Clayton in particular, personally organized the despatch of 30 Christmas parcels. A Fordham House old boy, A. Birch, received one and wrote: "Many thanks for your kind letter and the parcel which followed. I received the letter when we were up in the line, and the parcel during our few days out. We spent Christmas and New Year in the trenches and had quite a good time. Many thanks for the Log Book. I enjoy reading of the doings of all the old fellows. There will be some tales to tell when this job is finished."

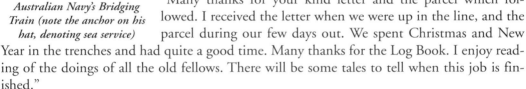

Driver W.H. Field of the Royal Australian Navy's Bridging Train (note the anchor on his hat, denoting sea service)

The Log Book was a life-line to old boys in the fighting forces during the War but by the early months of 1917 it was hard to keep it going:

"In view of the difficulty of obtaining paper and the heavy cost of the same, it is very probable that we shall have to restrict the issues of this magazine. As a beginning, this number will do duty for February and March."

In February the Committee sold the sailing brig *Chichester* for 500 guineas and organized a collection among city firms in the marine, insurance and shipping industries. The result was wonderfully cheering and the deficit was reduced to a mere £1,600.

Since the outbreak of hostilities, 900 old boys had joined up. Of these, 52 had been killed, 14 invalided out of the services, 9 had been captured as prisoners of war (one of whom was exchanged) and

Private George Moles, Highland Light Infantry, buried by a shell and taken prisoner at Loos

many more were missing or wounded. Several had received commissions.

The teachers in the homes made every effort to maintain normality and lessons, vocational training and extracurricular activities continued as normally as possible. When the end of the war came, life had changed for all the Society's children.

They had learnt first aid and air raid drill; they had listened to talks from old boys who had been invalided out of the services and from Commanding Officers on leave and many had learnt the realities of losing a close relative. Many old friends had been killed. Boys from the *Arethusa* entertained wounded soldiers in Ingress Abbey Hospital at Greenhithe with recitations, singing, comedy sketches, a sailor's horn pipe and a mouth organ quartet. An enthusiastic report in the Dartford Express praised the 'real star' quality of their performance. The boys in the band from Shaftesbury School entertained troops in camps in the locality. At Sudbury Hall:

"Mr. Hallam from Harrow spoke to the girls about the war, and Mr. Wiggins, Chairman of the Fire Brigade, Wembley, visited to see what provision was available in case of fire by bombs."

The Medical Officer attached to the Home before the war, Dr. Major Goddard, when home from active service, came to Sudbury Hall and spoke to the girls about his experiences at the Front. He brought photographs and specimens of shells and bullets. The girls tried on some gas masks, life saving waistcoats and collars that he showed them.

C.E. Malden Esq: Chairman 1917–1925. Served for a total of fifty years on the General Committee

On 10th January 1918, the Society's Chairman and Treasurer, William Egerton Hubbard died. He had worked for the Society for 50 years, having joined the Committee in 1868 at the age of 23. Mr. C. E. Malden took over his responsibilities. He too had been a long standing member of the National Refuges, having joined the Committee in 1873. This was the year in which his Father had resigned as Society Treasurer after more than 20 years' service. Francis Clayton was appointed Deputy Chairman. In May 1918 William Williams' widow died, aged 96, in her home in Ilminster, Somerset. She was buried in the same grave as her husband and sister at Abney Park Cemetery.

The Society's new Chairman, Mr Francis H. Clayton

The nightmare days of war ended in November 1918 and at the beginning of December the Committee put on record its thanks to God for seeing the Society safely through the crisis and their pride in all their old boys who served in the forces, those who died and those who had returned home.

"The Committee warmly thank the Staff of their homes and

office for their efficient labours during these four and a half years of warfare. Notwithstanding the depleted staffs, temporary officers, and constant changes, and the recent scourge of influenza, rendering the work difficult and arduous, it has been carried on unimpaired and the care of the children thoroughly maintained.

To mark their grateful appreciation of the excellent services rendered, the Committee resolve to present a small monetary Christmas gift to each member of their staff – i.e. £2 to each married and £1 to each single member, and 6d. to each child under the care of the Society."

The Society's old boys had served their country with bravery and honour during the war years, and the Committee, the staff and the children were justifiably proud of them. The Annual Report for 1918 noted that:

"It will take some time to obtain complete records of the part played by *Arethusa* old boys in the war, but we know that there was scarcely a vessel flying the White Ensign without them. Many have, alas, given their lives and others have endured much suffering. All the world knows of the daring exploit of HMS *Vindictive* at Zeebrugge. There were eight old *Arethusa* lads on board at the time, seven of them were awarded the DSM, and the remaining one, Albert E. McKenzie AB secured the Victoria Cross."

Albert McKenzie had joined the volunteer storming party at Zeebrugge Mole. He advanced down the Mole with his machine gun, under the command of Lieutenant Commander Harrison who, with most of the party, was killed in the early stages of the action under intense enemy fire. McKenzie continued to press home his attack and, though severely wounded, he survived. He was selected by the men of the *Vindictive, Iris II* and *Daffodil* to receive the Victoria Cross. He did not live long to enjoy the peace that came in 1918. He was recovering satisfactorily from his wounds in hospital at Chatham but succumbed to influenza and died in the last few weeks of the war. At his funeral a message of sym-

Able Seaman Albert E. McKenzie, VC

pathy from the King and Queen was read out stating that 'Their Majesties were grieved to hear of his untimely death and to think that he had been spared so short a time to wear the proud decoration which he so nobly won'.

The Committee and the staff looked ahead hopefully to a period of peace and stability in which they could continue their work. They knew that requests for help would increase through the hardship and bereavement many families had suffered.

Chapter 20
CHANGING TIMES

With the return of peace, came many changes. The Education Act of 1918 involved the Society in:

".. a fuller development of physical training on new and more interesting lines, more development of the social and artistic side of the children's school life, as well as mere bookwork."

The Committee was hard pressed to meet the expenses involved. They saved on administration costs by combining the two schools at Bisley into one, with the juniors at what had been the Farm School and the Seniors at the former Shaftesbury School. In 1920 they had to sell investments amounting to £8,500 to meet their liabilities. The extra costs, which included higher staff salaries, led to new arrangements for educating children in the care of the Society. In 1920 subscribers were informed that:

"Negotiations are now proceeding whereby in some cases the schoolrooms of our branches will be taken over by the Authorities and in cases where this is not done the children will be sent out to schools near at hand. In either case the Society will be entirely relieved of having to pay the teachers' stipends and will be free of the expense of school stationery and books and generally of the cost of warming and lighting the schoolrooms."

A government inspector visiting Fortescue House, Twickenham, in 1923 was pleased with what he saw. 'When the inspector has no suggestions to offer it may be taken as high praise' commented Mr. Copeland in the Log Book. The inspector's report was reproduced for the subscribers to see:

"The recent change of status by which this School has become a public elementary school maintained by the Authority has involved no change in staff or organization. The boys enter this School at various ages, at any date, and from very different origins; so that the good level of attainment is most creditable to all concerned. The standard reached in school subjects remains high, and the organization is effective.

In Arithmetic the written work was well set out and extremely accurate; mental arithmetic throughout was equally good. Handwriting and spelling were both good in all classes. Composition in the top class was very accurate and neat, though not many boys tried to produce anything original. Questions in history and geography were answered clearly and carefully; even the boys who have been but one year in the School are able to think out the meaning of each

Masters at Fortescue House: Mr Holloway (Headmaster, seated) and (l. to r.) Mr Howick, Mr Turner and Mr Walker

question, and so all answers are intelligent.

Pencil drawing remains good and now some satisfactory colour work is being done. More than half the boys get practical instruction, either in woodwork, tailoring or shoemaking; many also assist the skilled gardener. The new rooms for art and woodwork are proving a valuable adjunct. The school library is large and well managed; it contains mainly stories and it is possible that the inclusion of some more serious books as well as some of higher literary merit would produce much advantage in broadening the boys' knowledge of what can be found in books.

The discipline is excellent. The boys work hard; they are keen and eager and there is no sign of severity or suppression of natural enthusiasms. Much help is given to the boys over school age. Those capable of intellectual occupations are catered for as carefully as those who enter the industries or trades."

A letter reproduced in the Log Book was further evidence of the benefits of the Fortescue House regime:

"Bonchurch, 27th August 1923

Dear Sir,

I have this morning had the great pleasure of a visit from Basil Martin, a boy who has the good fortune to be in your school at Twickenham. His mother brought him to see me, and I could not believe he was the little untidy, reckless, defiant boy whom I had known nine or ten months ago before he came under the excellent influences prevailing at Twickenham. Instead of the little boy I have described I found a well set up, well spoken boy who looked me straight in the face and was perfectly civil and well mannered, with neither awkwardness or boldness."

Since the death of the Earl of Jersey in 1915 the Society had been without a President. During the war, all the Committee's energies had been devoted to caring for children in the homes, supporting past pupils in the services and helping the nation's war effort. Any decision about Lord Jersey's successor had been postponed until the return of peace. When the news came that the Prince of Wales, who was later to become Edward VIII, had agreed to become the new President, there was great rejoicing. One of the first decisions in which he was involved was to change the Society's name. The National Refuges for Homeless and Destitute Children was a name borne with pride since the early days of its work. The Committee and many of the Society's supporters were now beginning to feel that the old name was out of keeping with the times. It carried no reference to Lord Shaftesbury nor to the training ships and no longer gave a clear picture of the work. Miss Lyle-Browne

The Society's President (1919-1935),
HRH The Prince of Wales

spoke for many members of staff when she complained about the title on the notice-board at the main entrance to Sudbury Hall. She said the stigma of the words 'For Homeless and Destitute Girls' was very upsetting for the children in her care. Most people who knew the Society's work referred to 'Shaftesbury Homes', so the National Refuges became the 'Shaftesbury Homes and Arethusa Training Ship'. The Chairman explained the change in the Annual Record for 1920:

"In our appeals to the colonies, the former name was a serious drawback, and we suppressed it as much as possible, for it gave the impression that we were dealing with degenerates, a type which the dominions will not have. Let it be clearly understood that no change whatever in the character of the work is intended. The same class of children will be helped in the future as in the past – those of the poor who have suffered bereavement or misfortune or are destitute."

The idea that homes were 'institutions' was now unacceptable and great effort went into ensuring, as far as possible, that they were indeed 'homely'. The Matron of Ealing House encouraged more contact with the local community than had occurred previously:

"With a view of humanising the training and of breaking down an institution atmosphere, and for bringing the girls into contact with the outside world, a company of Girl Guides was formed at our Ealing School in May, and its members are entering upon their work with great enthusiasm, and already the results are gratifying. Several won prizes for good essays, and at a rally of neighbouring companies in October our Ealing company secured the third position for efficiency."

At Sudbury Hall Miss Lyle-Browne introduced a prefect system to encourage the girls to help each other and help in the running of the School as she believed that 'all this deepens the sense of responsibility, tends to bring out resourcefulness and tact, and to strengthen the all important notions of honour and straight dealing'.

For boys in the Society's care, there now was a far wider choice of career than in earlier times. Those with academic ability were encouraged to train for teaching or other professions. For those who were willing, emigration was still a possibility. A former pupil from Bisley School, now living in Canada, remembers the events that led to his leaving England. He was at Bisley until November 1923 and was trained in the shoemaking and repairing workshop 'which' he said 'has been handy and useful all my life'. When he was old enough to leave Bisley he found a factory job in London and lived at Fordham House. One evening after he had finished work, the Superintendent asked him if he would like to emigrate to Canada. His job in the factory was boring and badly paid and so he had jumped at the chance. He sailed in March 1926. 'It was the best move I ever made'. His first job had been on a farm, where the lessons learned at Bisley were put to use immediately.

The boys at the Technical School in Shaftesbury Avenue earned a weekly wage, part of which went towards their keep. They were encouraged to save regularly from what was left so that they could buy their own clothes. The standard of the training and workmanship was high and they frequently received prizes and awards which were listed year after year in the Log Book:

"One boy has lately won a scholarship at the Regent Street Polytechnic for tailoring, while gold and silver medals, prizes and certificates have been gained at the Cordwainers' College and the Trades Training School. In the Tailoring Department boys enter for the Exhibition of Apprentices' Work arranged by the Proprietors of the 'Tailor and Cutter'. Last year prizes were gained for each exhibit."

The 50 Fordham House boys received their training through arrangements made for them by the Society with their employers. In 1919 the list of their occupations included engineering, electrical work, metal work, carpentry, woodcarving and office work. By 1924, however, the range of careers had increased. According to the Society's records boys were working or training as:

Clerks and office boys	Engineers
Electrical engineers	Carpenters
Coach painter (motor)	Motor mechanic
Motor trimmer	Cabinet makers
Wood cutter (machinist)	Buhl cabinet work
Film maker	Map maker
Photographic work	Brace maker
Radiator and lamp maker	Dental mechanic
Warehouse work	Store keeper

The choices of career available to the girls were more restricted. Most of the girls still went into domestic service; some of the more able ones trained for teaching; some girls chose nursing. Opportunities were limited and many people still believed that a woman's place was in the home. The matter was of sufficient concern in April 1926 for the Society's Ladies Association (a group of women associated with the Society which campaigned, raised money and supported the work) to arrange a conference on the 'Education and Training of Girls, Their Maintenance and Careers'. The talks and discussions covered work in this country, the Dominions and the Colonies.

Lady Jersey took the Chair and spoke at length regretting that mothers sometimes were over ambitious for their daughters. Although sympathetic to high aspirations she felt that in many cases it could lead to disappointment: "I sometimes wish that those who have the training of girls would point out that they are not only being trained to be servants, but are being educated in the management of a home, to know how to cook and to become wise mothers." Another speaker discussed opportunities for working abroad:

"There are not many vacancies for trained teachers; there are not many vacancies for trained nurses; and the young women on the spot are anxious to take these posts. But there are an enormous number of vacancies for all forms of domestic work. Now of course, I suppose the most important item regarding emigration is the redistribution of population. Here we have two million more women than men and in the Dominions there are two million more men than women .. the great problem for the Empire is the redistribution of population in order that the young men, splendid young men of the Dominions whom we saw when they came over to the war, may find good wives."

In answer to complaints that it was wrong to 'over-educate the working classes' one lady emphatically maintained that this was not so:

"Most of the ills from which we suffer are due to the fact that they are either under educated or wrongly educated for life".

She went on to say that she did not approve of girls taking up lower grade clerical work as this did not equip them for their lives ahead as wives and mothers. The opinions of most speakers at the Conference reinforced the Society's commitment to training girls for domestic service.

Miss Lyle-Browne devised a system of training in Sudbury Hall based on the original scheme by Miss Chipchase whereby all the girls gained experience in every aspect of domestic work and learnt to be responsible and trustworthy at the same time:

"The girls have what is called the 'round', which comprises the Parlour, House, Kitchen, Scullery and Laundry. Two girls have charge of each department, an 'upper' and a 'lower' and they occupy this position for 12 weeks at a time, the 'upper' teaching the 'lower'. At the end of this time they pass one step higher.

The girls are by no means angels, and if, after warning, a girl repeats a serious offence, then her punishment is to lose her 'post' and she has to take a lower one. Occupying a certain position for 12 weeks gives each girl in the Home an insight into every kind of work."

Miss Lyle-Browne's regime was well thought out and her firm discipline ensured its success. Miss Carter, in charge of Ealing House, did not seem to organize her girls quite so well. In 1928 she reported that:

"She had experienced trouble with six of her girls who had refused to carry out their duties and locked themselves in a dormitory. As they refused to behave themselves she had been compelled to ask the Chairman, Mr. Clayton, to come and speak to them."

She was forced to give corporal punishment to two girls, one for 'throwing a knife at Miss Biddle' and another for 'pushing her downstairs'. Miss Biddle was the woman in charge of teaching laundry work. The Sub-Committee which investigated this incident pointed out that, as Miss Biddle was blind, it was not surprising she had difficulty in keeping order and this fact accounted for a great deal of the misbehaviour of the girls. Some girls 'had been at work in the laundry now for from 7 to 10 months'. It was arranged that Miss Carter would look for a new laundry teacher. The washing was reorganized and the girls had instruction there for periods of no longer than a month.

Mr F. Brian Pelly AFC
General Secretary, 1927 – 1953

In November 1926, Mr. Charles Edward Malden, the Chairman and Treasurer, died at the age of 82, after 53 years of service to the Society. He was succeeded by Francis Clayton, the Deputy Chairman. Mr. H. Bristow-Wallen and Mr. Henry Copeland, whose work spanned the years since William Williams' death, both retired within the next eighteen months. The new General Secretary was Mr. Brian Pelly whose previous experience had been in mission work, banking and in the administration of the United Services Fund and its hospital. In April 1928 the Society acquired the Newport Market Army Training School at Darrick Wood, Kent. It had been founded in 1863 in Newport Market, Soho, with William Gladstone, then Chancellor of the Exchequer, as its President. The original aim was to train poor boys with musical ability aged between 9 and 14 who wanted to join army bands; by 1928 1,140 boys from the school had succeeded in doing so and 625 had gone into civilian employment. In 1929 the name of the school was changed to 'The Newport Market Army Bands School' so as to reflect more closely the kind of training offered.

One problem Francis Clayton tackled in his early years as Chairman was to secure a new home for the girls and staff at Sudbury Hall. In February 1928 when a builder was repairing the roof it was found that 'the whole condition of the laundry was in a very unsatisfactory state which necessitated the roof being at once shored up and the wall sup-

Lieutenant Colonel C.H.Jaeger, OBE, Irish Guards, a pupil of the Newport Market Army Band School, who rose to become the Chief Instructor of the Royal Military School of Music, Kneller Hall

ported'. By October it was found that 'numerous small repairs are necessary to ceilings, window frames, fire grates etc.'

Early in 1929, after a period of frosty weather, several pipes burst with consequent damage to ceilings and walls. During the year plaster began to flake off the walls in increasing quantities. The House had been built on clay and the Society's Surveyor reported that its foundations did not go deep enough.

By this time there was a very serious crack in the main central wall of the building which ran almost to the roof. The ceiling in the staff dining room was badly cracked and unsafe. The grate could not be used as the smoke went through to the other side of the wall. There had been movement in the walls, so that various doors and windows would not shut and

Prince Arthur of Connaught inspecting the Guard of Honour from the Newport Market Army Bands School at the Society's Annual General Meeting at Queen's Hall in 1930

others would not open. The roof leaked badly. The rivets holding the tiles were all badly worn and the leaded areas were perforated. There was a serious leak in Miss Lyle-Browne's bedroom and a large crack on the outside front wall. Many of the floors were in a dangerous condition. One of the window bays was so badly cracked that it had to be shored up. It was abundantly clear that Sudbury Hall could not be retained and the Committee began an urgent search for another home.

A former pupil had vivid memories of her time there between 1923 and 1929. She recalls nothing about the cracks, leaks or flaking plaster but will never forget the rigours of the housework, getting up on cold mornings to rake out the cinders of the kitchen stoves, scrubbing the length of the dining room floor and rubbing her clothes clean against the washing board in the laundry. Hard as the routine was, for this girl Sudbury Hall primarily meant dancing, music, singing and poetry brought alive by her teacher Elizabeth Keen, herself a former pupil.

Elizabeth Keen passed on to her pupils a love of music that for some would provide a lifetime of pleasure. Her classes sang every day; their repertoire included songs by Handel, Holst and other great composers. The girls sang on every possible occasion. For the old girls' reunions, a particular favourite was a song for three soloists and chorus – 'Three Little Heads in a Row':

> "Three little heads in a row
> Looked over the garden wall.
> They heard the blackbird whistle low
> And the merry thrustle call.
> 'The spring, my dear,
> The sweet of the year,
> Its beautiful sounds I know.
> We shall have sun
> The whole day long.'
> Said the three little heads in a row."

Three girls were hidden behind a curtain, and as they sang, they popped up one at a time so that only their heads were visible. They sang on joyous occasions and on sad ones. When Princess Marie Louise, one of their supporters, died the girls sang her favourite hymn and the 23rd Psalm.

In 1926 the best dancing team from Sudbury Hall performed a display of 'eurhythmic' dancing for the Annual Meeting at The Queen's Hall, Langham Place, in the presence of the Prince of Wales. Miss Lyle-Browne was convinced of the value of this style of dancing, which she believed gave the girls poise and self confidence. It was a method of teaching the elements of music while providing enjoyable and graceful exercise.

Elizabeth Keen also taught the girls poetry; they had to learn by heart many passages from Shakespeare and other poets. 'I didn't fully understand the poems at first' said a pupil of the time 'but I loved them all the same. I still remember the words and they mean much more to me now. I often recite them to myself'.

Meanwhile, the search for a new home continued. In June 1930 the Committee was able to buy Esher Place, a magnificent country mansion in Surrey with grounds of approximately 10 acres. It was large enough to accommodate the girls of Ealing House and Sudbury Hall together. The cost of adapting Esher Place and the necessary structural alterations and additions was estimated at around £8,000. It was hoped that the cost would be covered by the sale of Sudbury Hall and Ealing House. Miss Carter retired when the move took place and Miss Lyle-Browne became Matron of the new Home.

The Dowager Countess of Jersey attended the last old Girls Reunion Days of both schools and presented prizes. At Sudbury Hall past and present girls sang together for the last time their School Song, ending with the words:

"It's up to me and up to all
  To do our best for Sudbury Hall."

From then on, all the Society's girls would have to do their best for Esher Place.

Princess Marie Louise, accompanied by Mr Francis Clayton, at the Society's General Meeting in 1936

Chapter 21

MEMORIES OF THE 1930s

Esher Place had an interesting history. The original fifteenth century building was a Bishop's palace. Cardinal Wolsey repaired and partly rebuilt it; it was later acquired by Henry VIII. There were many subsequent changes of owner until the Society bought the property in 1930, by which time the old palace, apart from the gate-house, had been long demolished and a beautiful French Chateau style house built on a different site within the grounds.

Esher Place, acquired by the Society in 1930

The new Home was formally opened in November 1930. The girls from Sudbury Hall had previously worn green and those from Ealing House had worn blue. The new uniform for Esher Place was a combination of these two colours. Portraits of the Earl of Shaftesbury and William Williams decorated the walls of the entrance hall as well as pictures from the previous homes.

Francis Clayton, as Chairman, spoke at the opening about the history of Esher Place and his hopes for the girls who would make this their home:

"They often come to us in sadness, poverty or bereavement, but whatever it may be, may they find love and affection, with bright, happy influences here, and go out to do God's work and will in the world."

View of the Dining Hall at Esher Place

Many of the pupils at Esher Place in the 1930s still remember the building with awe and affection:

"The library was a beautiful room, and I was utterly charmed with all the books. There were big bay window seats looking out onto the terrace and a great fireplace. I remember a very old musical box in the room, the kind with long metal rollers covered with spikes, and a cabinet gramophone.

There was a wide marble staircase in the hall. We had to clean the marble and wrought iron banisters and their brass rail. I loved doing that because I used to imagine I was in high society. I often remember the words 'I dreamt I dwelt in marble halls' and think of Esher Place.

Grace before meals at Esher Place

The only time we were allowed to go on that staircase was Christmas Day. The Headmistress used to put a radio on full blast in her sitting room and we all congregated on the stairs with the staff to hear the King's speech.

One of the larger rooms was used as a theatre with a box for the Headmistress and staff. We were allowed to play there on winter evenings. It had a beautiful oak floor and it was one of our jobs to polish this. The older girls used to put the polish on and then tie rags to their feet and slide."

In the grounds were flower beds, shrubs, lawns, statuary and a greatly admired tulip tree which was reputedly 250 years old. There was a large sunken garden, which the

The Society's 30,000th child

girls called the 'Greek theatre'. It had lawns levelled off in tiers and dancing and gymnastic displays took place there.

The next major event in the Society's history was in 1932 when the *Arethusa* after 59 years service, was condemned as unfit for further service. An inspection report a few years earlier had warned that it was approaching the end of its useful life:

The Arethusa *Training Ship at the end of her days at Greenhithe*

"It is noticeable that the decks are leaking in many places and have become so thin that they cannot be caulked. Rot has set in many of the transverse beams and serious looking cracks are appearing in some of them. There is a serious leak by the stern post and the old Ship makes a considerable amount of water. This leak should be stopped as soon as practicable. The time has arrived when it must seriously be considered whether the ship is safe for further service."

The Committee and the Captain Superintendent considered a number of ships on the market, including the *Parma*, before eventually choosing the *Peking*, a four masted steel hulled barque of 3,191 tons built at Hamburg in 1911. At the outbreak of the first world war she had been at Valparaiso and, in the distribution of the spoils of war, she was awarded to Italy who resold her to her original German owners, Ferdinand and Carl Laeisz in 1923. She was one of a once famous fleet of trading vessels (*Parina, Privall, Padua, Parmir, Pluto, Parma* and *Passat* were others) and had previously been employed on the nitrate trade with South America. At first it was thought that the Society's President, the Prince of Wales, would object to the purchase of a German ship but he accepted that, if no suitable British ships were available, then the *Peking* could become the new *Arethusa*. The lease on the berth at Greenhithe was due to expire in March 1934 but already the Port of London Authority had indicated that the Society's Training Ship lay in the way of visiting steamers and should be moved due to the demands of trade at Greenhithe and a proposal by the British Portland Cement Company to build a jetty.

The *Peking* was purchased for £6,250 and converted to a training ship in the Royal Dockyard, Chatham, under the superintendence of Mr. E. W. Roger, and renamed *Arethusa*. When her conversion was complete, at a cost of some £30,000, she moved, in July

The Peking *in full sail*

1933, to a permanent mooring on the River Medway at Lower Upnor, near Rochester.

On board the new *Arethusa* the regime was restructured so as to allow boys with ability to

The new Arethusa *Training Ship on the River Medway at Lower Upnor, near Rochester*

move on, after their initial training in seamanship, to an advanced course for potential officers. It was a custom of the Society to present a watch to those ex-Arethusa boys who obtained their Second Mate's Competency Certificate or their Radio Officer's Certificate, and a pair of binoculars to those who passed the Master Mariner's Certificate. Those who reached commissioned rank in the Royal Navy were presented with a sword.

Boys who trained in the *Arethusa* in the 1930s are unlikely to forget their time onboard. Unforgettable for many was the numbing experience of standing on the ice and frost on the upper deck, in bare feet, during the winter months and then having to run down the main deck ladder afterwards, catching frozen feet on the metal strips put there as protection. If the boys were not quick enough, 'Nippy' Downs the bosun whacked them with the end of a rope. Hammock drill was always a memorable occasion with the instructor 'Granny' Longmore and his cane which he used like a scythe round the boys' legs when they did not get into their hammocks quickly enough.

The tradition of presenting swords to Commissioned Officers in the Royal Navy continues. Pictured above are Sub Lieutenants Renwick and Jacklin with the Society's Chairman, Captain Christopher Knight, in 1977. Colin Renwick subsequently became a member of the Society's Council of Trustees

Members of the Ship's Committee visited regularly and on these occasions there was a slice of cake for tea as a treat. There was also a slice of cake awarded to the members of the cleanest mess each week:

An unforgettable experience for the Arethusa *Boys*

"We were one big happy family united against authority," remembers one of the boys "we seldom won but we had some great times trying to outwit them. They knew all the answers. I can honestly say that I have not regretted serving on board the *Arethusa* – it was one of the highlights of my life and if I could have my time over again I would still go there. We had a pride in being Arethusa boys because we knew we were better than the rest."

After the inauguration of the new *Arethusa,* the work in the various branches of the Society continued and flourished. In 1935 the Society was approached by the 'National Society for the Protection of Young Girls (Princess Louise Home)' with a view to amalgamation of the two organizations. This charity, established in 1835, was in financial difficulty and had been forced to close its Home at Kingston Hill two years previously. The Presidents of

HRH Prince George speaks at the Inauguration of the Arethusa *Training Ship on 25th July 1933*

the two Societies, the Prince of Wales and Princess Louise, Duchess of Argyll, agreed that the proposed merger should go ahead. Henceforth the Girls' Home was called 'Esher Place (Princess Louise Home for Girls)'. The Annual Report informed the subscribers that the Society was:

".. benefiting now from having taken over the Princess Louise Home for Girls by dividends on their investments which form a very useful little endowment towards the cost of our Esher Place Home. We should like it distinctly understood that girls taken into Esher Place are accepted under the same conditions that we have always adopted."

Just as the building made a deep impression on those who lived there, so also the training the girls received and the friendships they formed were rarely forgotten. The regime at Esher Place is still clear in the minds of many past pupils:

"It stood us in good stead, but it was tough. The elder girls helped the new ones to settle in; they could be very loving and caring. Most young ones attached themselves to one or two. I made friends with three sisters. I loved them all. They were so kind to me.

We had slippers and plain black lace-up shoes which were passed on. Anyone who needed a new pair queued up to try some on. If you managed to get some that were brand new - well!! We had to sew our names onto the tongues. Young as we were, we were taught to be independent. I could not get the needle through and I remember pushing it with my teeth. It slipped and stuck in my tongue. I had to pull it out - but I never did that again.

I loved going to church on Sundays. It was part of being normal. We went in a crocodile and had a special part of the church saved for us. The older girls used to make eyes at the choir boys. They used to have secret meetings at night. If they were caught they would be punished for it but, of course, that did not stop them. When we were confirmed, we wore white dresses; the teachers made it special and it was a big occasion at Esher Place.

One Christmas one of the ladies in the parish living not many yards away

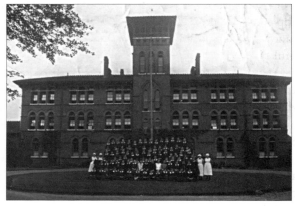

The National Society for the Protection of Young Girls (Princess Louise Home) at Kingston Hill, incorporated with the Shaftesbury Homes and Arethusa in 1935

from the home invited a few of us for tea. We were all scared but excited. It was a wonderful treat going into someone's house. The lady made us really welcome; she poured our tea herself and served us from a silver tea set. She had a maid whose job it was to answer the bell which was fixed under the tea table. One of the girls, being nervous, was fidgeting and her knee kept pressing against the bell by mistake. The maid kept running in and out; we did not know whether to laugh or not."

The Society's Patron, HM King George V, died in January 1936. According to the editor of the Log Book:

"His interest in our Society began as a boy at the age of 10 when, with his brother, he attended our Annual Meeting in 1875. He was present when King Edward VII, then Prince of Wales, laid the foundation stone of our Shaftesbury Avenue Headquarters. In 1899, he opened a new wing of our Fortescue House School, at Twickenham. He has been our Patron for many years, and has shown his interest in many ways in our developments, latterly in the taking over of the Newport Market Army Bands School, provision and equipment of a new *Arethusa,* the 90th Anniversary of our foundation and the amalgamation of the Princess Louise Home for Girls with Esher Place."

The new King, Edward VIII, relinquished his role as the Society's President and became one of its patrons. The events which led to his abdication and the Coronation of his brother, King George VI, cast a shadow over the Society's work. The Committee informed subscribers that:

"No Society has been better served by a Royal President than was the Shaftesbury Homes and Arethusa Training Ship by whom we now know as HRH the Duke of Windsor. During the 16 years prior to his accession to the throne, all matters of importance in the life of our Society were referred to him as President, and more particularly at the time of the giving up of the old *Arethusa.*

He was most insistent that every British source should be explored for the acquisition of a new ship before looking to foreign parts. When the new ship was acquired, with his entire approval, he himself wrote and signed as President, the letter of appeal to the public for funds, and as is well known, the response enabled us to purchase and fit out the present beautiful ship.

We wanted him as Prince, and we wanted him during his short time on the throne. At Christmas time he remembered us, and within a few weeks of his abdication, he sent the *Arethusa* a dinghy as a personal gift. After his visit to the distressed areas in the North, we at once admitted at his suggestion a number of children from those areas into our homes and Ship and have since continued to do so.

To Their Majesties King George and Queen Elizabeth our hearts go out in sympathy, loyalty and affection. We welcome the news that His Majesty King George VI has graciously consented to become Patron of the Society."

In 1937 the Committee sold Fortescue House and bought a more suitable building in Twickenham large enough to accommodate the Newport Market Army Bands School as well as the boys from the old Fortescue House. As a way of cutting costs the move was a great success,

Fortescue House School, Twickenham, formerly a Police Orphanage, purchased by the Committee in 1937

although for a time it was hard for the two schools with their different identities and cultures to merge into one, with the hybrid name of Fortescue House (incorporating the Newport Market Army Bands School). Nevertheless, the boys from both schools created a favourable impression by their achievements and behaviour. The Headmaster encouraged them to take the opportunities offered them and to enjoy life to the full. The annual school productions of The Gondoliers, The Mikado and other Gilbert and Sullivan operas played to packed houses for a week at a time. Specially chosen boys from the school acted as ball-boys at Wimbledon each year and boys from the old Newport Market Army Bands School regularly lined the forecourt at Buckingham Palace for the State Opening of Parliament.

All this, and the fact that their uniform included stiff collars, did not endear them to their peers at Bisley who concealed their jealous feelings by heartily sneering at them whenever an opportunity occurred.

By this time the two schools at Bisley had been reorganized into one with a Senior and a Junior Department under one Headmaster. The boys' academic achievements had merited a change of status to a 'central' school and the Royal Society of Arts examinations were taken at the end of their last year. The boys were put into 'A' classes or 'B' classes depending on their standard at entry. Those in the 'B' groups learnt trades (tailoring, shoemaking and some engineering) whilst the 'A' groups concentrated on working for their leaving examinations.

Billy Jean King meets Denis Payne of Fortescue House School at Wimbledon in 1967

The Senior School had four houses, Cavaliers, Ironsides, Knights and Crusaders with about 50 boys in each. Each house had prefects and the Head Prefect of the house was in sole charge of the boys in the house dormitory until first parade for breakfast.

Every month, all the boys were judged on their scholastic work and behaviour. Everybody was anxious to do well as there were financial rewards for good marks. The system worked smoothly. Because the standard of education at Bisley was good, the boys did not find it difficult to get employment when they left:

"My RSA certificate" writes a pupil who was there in the 1930s "gives passes in Economic Geography, English, History, Science and Shorthand and passes with credit in Arithmetic, Book-keeping, Commerce and Mathematics. The day I left was one of great sadness for me but I got the first job I applied for as a Junior Clerk. The job involved book-keeping, shorthand, typing and acting as relief cashier. I remember I had to suggest a wage, and stated 25 shillings a week.

A proud moment for one of the boys at Bisley School when the Earl of Athlone inspected their Empire Parade in 1936

The interviewer wondered why I had asked for so much."

It was not only by passing examinations that the boys gained a good reputation. Just as in earlier times, music was a very important part of life at Bisley. It was an honour and a great achievement to get into the School Band. The standard was high and there was a waiting list for those who wanted to join. Bisley School Band won high acclaim for its public performances and professionalism:

The Bisley School Band in 1943

"We practised every day - we were that keen. The Headmaster Mr. Read loved music and used to come and listen to rehearsals sometimes; if he heard a wrong note he would stop us.

After morning school we would quickly have lunch and then go to the band room for 20 minutes practice. After tea, same again. On Saturday mornings we had to clean our instruments until they shone to perfection, and then from 11 o'clock onwards we had to practise marches for Sunday Church parade. If our Band Master was not satisfied, we had to stay there until we had got it right, so we learnt pretty quickly. We had to work hard.

Two o'clock on Saturdays was the tuck shop hour, when we could buy sweets. If we hadn't got the playing perfect by then, we didn't go. We were stuck in there practising; there was no messing about. That's why we were champions."

Boys no longer worked in the grounds or on the Farm but undertook cleaning jobs, known as 'domestics', on Saturday mornings. Because it had originally been a 'Farm

Headmaster, Mr B.L. Read, BSc

School', a good deal of fruit and vegetables was still grown :

"There were wonderful orchards. We could eat fruit till it came out of our ears, but of course we still climbed out of the windows at night to go and nick it. If we were caught we got the stick."

The boys were encouraged to garden for themselves:

"There was a large field behind the School and if you were interested you were given a plot to grow what you liked. If you asked, the gardeners would tell you anything you wanted to know. We had our own rubbish disposal dump – no plastic, all organic. When it rotted down, we used to dig into this. It was absolutely alive with worms. We got to know that this was the right thing for our gardens and we got spadefuls of this stuff and used to dig it in. We grew wonderful stuff.

We had weekly inspections by the professional gardeners. One weed lost you one point - they were very strict about it and on sports day there were prizes for the best plot on the day and the best plot on points through the year."

One of the Bisley boys went on to Fordham House after he left the school and recorded his impressions:

"Arriving at Fordham House I was met by Mr. Dodkins ('Dee') a kindly old gentleman with sparse silvery hair on a shiny bald pate upon which was placed a large piece of sticking plaster. He had been attacked by thugs who thought he held money in his office.

He chatted to me, looked me over and said 'Hmm .. I think we will send you to Bennetts' – a prestigious architect of the time with offices in Bloomsbury Square. That must have been the most basic careers assessment ever carried out, but Dee got it right and I was launched on a career of some 50 years as an architect.

Fordham House had its own tailors' and shoemakers' shops both staffed with old boys from Bisley and Twickenham. The standard was exceptionally high and the shoemakers had a large clientele. Each client had a 'last' made to his measurements and this was labelled and filed away for future shoes. I was kitted out with two suits and two pairs of shoes and how proud I was. No Regency Buck strutted along Shaftesbury Avenue as lordly as I did on my first day.

We were well looked after at Fordham House, but discipline was strict. The entrance door was shut at 9.30 sharp and woe betide anyone having to ring the bell after this time. The food was good, well cooked and plentiful. We handed over our wages intact; something was kept back for when we needed new clothes, and we were given our pocket money of 1s-6d per week which was enough for our

HRH The Duke of Kent, KG, inspecting the shoemakers' shop on the occasion of his visit to Fordham House in January 1939

basic needs. I doubt very much that our wages kept us in food, shelter and clothing. We were expected to be well mannered and of good behaviour at all times.

As for entertainment, free seats were to be had at West End cinemas by the simple expedient of chatting up the usherettes. If no luck, then we could always walk to Kings Cross to the local flea pit and get in to a show for 6d. We joined a Boys Club and enjoyed indoor sports. A local café was a good meeting place for us and on many a cold night we spent the evening there chatting to the Proprietor. He was a first generation Italian immigrant who was pure gold to us and we were greatly saddened when he was interned at the outbreak of war.

During the summer and autumn of 1938 it gradually dawned on the British public that Hitler really did mean business. It rapidly became clear to us boys that we would be the ones to do the dirty work. A number of the older boys joined the Territorials and during the long summer evenings it was a common sight to see them parading in their finery. We were all fervently patriotic and genuinely proud of being British and Hitler had better beware. We loathed the Blackshirts and their parading with the Union Flag. They often held court at Seven Dials and we enjoyed barracking at their meetings."

In 1939 the Society said goodbye to Mr. Dodkins and Miss Lyle-Browne who retired after 40 years and 22 years service respectively. During the year 415 children in all were admitted to the homes and Training Ship; 402 boys and girls left, including 129 boys who joined the Royal Navy and 32 who went into the Merchant Service. At the end of the year the Society was caring for a total of 1,200 children.

The Log Book reports on the regular pleasures of the summer. At Bisley, there was the usual Empire Parade on 14th June, with a ceremonial march past and trooping of the colour. At Esher Place, there was the annual Garden Party with a tea and a sale of work arranged by supporters and girls at the Home. The proceeds were in aid of a Fund to send the girls to the seaside for a month during the summer holidays. The Society's greatest triumph of that summer was the occasion when the Bisley School Band broadcast from the BBC Concert Hall on the afternoon of Friday, 30th June.

Those children with parents who could take them went home for their holidays. The remainder went on holiday trips, visits and outings arranged by their schools and funded by supporters. But the holidays came to an end and, in the words of the boy at Fordham House, Hitler really did 'mean business'. At the beginning of September a girl on her way back to Esher Place remembers:

"I was at St. Pancras; my Mother was putting me on the train at the end of the holidays. Every nationality you can think of was at the station that day – Australians with their hats turned up, Scots in their kilts. My Mother stared in amazement, saying 'and they tell us there is not going to be a war? I don't believe it.'"

The next day war was declared.

Chapter 22
The Second World War

The news of the outbreak of war had an immediate effect on the work of the Society as a whole and on life in the homes and Training Ship. The Treasurer told subscribers that:

"The last four months of 1939 proved a very anxious time. Subscriptions in some cases were late in arriving and others were reduced owing to the unexpectedly heavy taxation reverting back to April. Then the heavy expenses connected with air raid shelters and, in some cases, evacuation all tended to produce the deficit shown in the Society's accounts. The cost of food and clothing and indeed, everything, is mounting."

Twelve months later things were no better and in his report he commented:

"It is impossible to keep the various Homes up to standard or even to keep them going at all without the wherewithal to cover the necessary expenditure, now increased owing to rising prices. It certainly is a time of great crisis for the Society and its various homes and the Ship."

As many children as possible were sent back to their parents to make room for children orphaned or homeless as a result of the war. The homes were provided with underground shelters for the children to sleep in. By 1941 the number of children in the Society's care had fallen to 800, whereas in 1939 the number had been 1,200.

The *Arethusa's* mooring on the Medway was in an officially designated evacuation area. Consequently, with the exception of 50 older pupils who were shortly to enter the Royal Navy, the boys were temporarily returned to their homes. The Ship's on-shore swimming bath was converted into a dormitory for 100 boys and covered trenches were built close by in case of raids. In 1940, the Training Ship was taken over by the Admiralty to be used as accommodation for naval ratings. The boys on board at the time were evacuated to the Tides Reach Hotel at Salcombe, South Devon, where they played a full part in local community life, helping with various activities such as the settling of evacuees or fund raising. One of their first tasks was to help build the defence boom across the Harbour. 'We also had a few excitements in the way of bombs and lost a Cutter on the rocks' wrote the Captain Superintendent later in a report for the *Arethusa's* magazine, 'The Fo'c's'le'. At Fordham House Hostel in London, the ceiling of the basement was shored up and a blast wall erected. 42 bunks for the boys were put in an old locker room and sleeping berths for male staff were placed in the adjoining lobby. The women slept in the swimming bath. The

TS Arethusa *at the Tides Reach Hotel, Salcombe, Devon*

Superintendent was called up; his wife, the Matron, like her predecessor during the first World War, ran the Hostel with the help of the tailor and shoemaker instructors and whatever other help she could find.

Both houses at Bisley School were provided with underground shelters; Esher Place already had well built cellars and an additional exit was made leading from them into the garden. At Fortescue House there was a passage slightly below ground level running right through the main block. This was fitted out with bunk beds for the boys; it felt cramped, airless and cold. One boy remembers:

"Bedtime was a particular hardship for me. The boys all slept in close confinement along the low dark passage, and in various rooms off it. All windows were boarded up with stout timbers."

The Society's President, the Duke of Kent, was tragically killed in an air crash in 1941. He had been President of the Society for five years only but, like so many members of the Royal Family, he had been a loyal supporter for many years.

In 1943 the Society celebrated its Centenary. In happier circumstances there would have been grand celebrations in all the homes and the Training Ship, with perhaps a new commemorative building or venture. As it was, the occasion was marked only by a Thanksgiving Service held at St. Martin's-in-the-Fields. The Archbishop of Canterbury addressed a congregation including HRH The Duchess of Kent, one of the Society's new Patrons, children, staff and friends. Shortage of paper forbade all but the briefest reports of the events of the year. The Annual Report and the Log Books gave only outline details of Society finances, appeals for support and a summary of events.

We learn most about the Society and its staff and pupils during the war period from the memories of those who were in the homes at the time. All the schools helped the war effort in various ways. The girls at Esher and the little children at Royston picked herbs and wild plants for food and medicine. At Bisley and Fortescue House the boys' metalwork lessons were used to make small lathe turned parts of various kinds for the Services. One pupil remembers:

"They had to be made to a certain size and we were taught to use a micrometer. I was never any good at using that gadget, so I hope whatever they were we turned out were not of some critical impor-

HRH The Duchess of Kent, one of the Society's Royal Patrons, at the Centenary celebrations in 1943

tance. That worry has nagged me on and off for most of my life."

All the Society's schools used their available land to grow vegetables. The 'Dig For Victory' campaign had an enthusiastic supporter in the Headmaster of Fortescue House, Mr. Leslie Pierce. The end part of the playing field was dug up to grow vegetables and the gardening was done by parties of boys after school, before supper and on Saturday mornings. Mr. Lily the gardener presided over the scheme, supervising the double trenching for potatoes and a

Leslie Pierce, Headmaster of Fortecue House, in battledress, accompanying Colonel P.R.O. Simner CB, DSO, DL at the Cadet Corps Inspection

great pit which was dug to receive the leaves from the many trees on the Estate, to rot down for compost. The gardening boys wore wooden clogs with leather uppers which had been made in the shoemaking work-shop. These clogs were not popular as they were stiff, cold and uncom-fortable. Mr. Pierce's enthusiasm for vegetable gardening produced excel-lent results. In 1943 the school was self-sufficient in vegetables; none of the Society's other homes achieved so much, not even Bisley where, in ear-lier times, so many of the boys had been encouraged to enjoy gardening and farming either for pleasure or as training for future employment. No written records are available to give details of life at Bisley during the war years. Lack of information, however, was not the only effect of the paper shortage. One old boy remembers:

"No toilet paper was ever kept in the toilets, for it disappeared too fast. We therefore had to seek out the 'Quartermaster'. He was always hard to find. When at last you found him and told him what you wanted, he used to pull out a sheaf of the stuff from his pocket, and sup-ply us with precisely three sheets, one at a time. He histrionically licked his forefinger between handing over each sheet, intoning the never to be forgotten phrase 'One up, one down, and a polisher'."

Finding enough clothes for the children proved difficult for the care staff, even though the numbers of children had been drastically reduced. The Log Book reports ended with appeals for unwanted and second-hand clothes:

"The coupon system for a family of 800 has meant a good deal of extra work. The rationing, as well as the cost of clothing, is a problem we have to face. Suitable clothes for boys and girls from five upwards will be welcomed at our Head Office. Not only have we to provide clothing for the children under our care, but outfits for them on leaving."

Another headache for the staff was providing food for the pupils. There was always enough, but only just. Past pupils have vivid recollections of the food – and the lack of it. 'We never went without, but we always seemed to be hungry' a pupil from Esher Place remembers. The girls sang a song:

> "Egg and bacon we don't see
> We get sawdust in our tea.
> That's why we gradually
> Fade, fade away .."

Fortescue House boys made everything go further by converting it into sandwiches between doorstep slices of bread; whatever turned up for a meal was sandwiched if possible. On the rare occasions when a cake arrived, perhaps as a present for one of the boys, it would be eked out in between layers of bread.

One meal vivid in the memory for a Fortescue House pupil was provided by the US army stationed nearby at Bushey Park. For their pudding, the boys were given slices of fresh pineapple. This was a new experience for all of them. It was served on the plates they had used for their first course.

The Americans entertained the girls at Esher Place too and put on a concert for them at Christmas:

"One great fat man had us all doubled up laughing when he sang 'I must have been a beautiful baby, because baby, just look at me now.'"

At Esher Place a local Air Raid Warden came to live in the home. He was a member of the local Amateur Dramatic Society which presented plays at the King George's Hall in the village. He arranged for the girls occasionally to go to performances there. The senior girls, when it was safe, were also allowed to go to early evening performances at the local cinema:

"We carried gas masks wherever we went. When the air raids started we used to go to the cellars to sleep, taking blankets with us. These cellars were very roomy, with white-washed walls and stone floors with strongly buttressed arches. We felt quite safe there although it wasn't very comfortable sleeping on the floor, no matter how many folded blankets we lay on.

One night there was a direct hit. We heard the explosion and felt the impact through the stone floor. Fortunately the damage was mostly confined to the dental room and a store-room near the kitchen. Many windows were broken and it was quite late in the morning before we were allowed to come out of the cellars; we had to stay there while the staff and older girls cleared the rubble and broken glass. When she was helping to reorganise the store-room one girl helped herself to a catering size tin of baked beans with pork and invited a select few of us to share the booty. We ate the beans cold, straight from the tin and they tasted delicious."

Another girl remembers:

"When the war came the sirens used to go nearly every night. The Headmistress blew a whistle and all of us went from the dormitories to the cellar which was whitewashed, clean and safe. One night an incendiary bomb dropped in the grounds. There was a big hole in the lawn and the playroom's glass roof caved in. After that we didn't go to bed in the dormitories but instead went straight to the cellar every night. We changed into our night things and put our coats on for extra warmth as the cellar was so cold. We slept on big bristly doormats, with a pillow and a blanket.

We took turns to sing and tell stories until we fell asleep. My family hadn't got a wireless at home and so I didn't know many songs. You could tell who was better off as they knew lots of songs."

One summer during the war ten of the girls, chosen for their good manners, went to live at Sundridge, Kent, in the home of Lady Plender who was a loyal friend of Esher Place. They slept in the servants' quarters. When they arrived at the house, Lord Plender gave each girl 6d, wealth indeed for some of the party. One of the girls remembers:

"I loved our time in Kent. We used to walk round the lovely gardens with Lady Plender, and she would play with us. Once we played 'I spy' and she said 'Something beginning with O'. We could not work out what it was. The answer was 'orchid' – but none of us had ever heard of them.

She used to have a little service for us on Sunday afternoons, and she would play the piano. We told her we did not know what prayer to say when we bowed our heads, so she taught us one. I say it even now when we bow our heads in Church."

After the bombing at Esher Place the Home was evacuated. The girls went with their teachers to stay at a school in Bradford.

Fortescue House staff and children suffered badly. Mr. Pierce, a military man, was admired and respected by the boys but it must have saddened him to see the sorry state into which his school had fallen. The fun, companionship and respect which masters and boys mutually shared in pre-war years had gone. It was a struggle to keep it open at all. A pupil there has vivid recollections of one particular master:

"Mr. Wheale, Sergeant Major of the Cadet Corps, was a master the boys actually loved. He was a real tartar on the parade ground, every inch a military man, but when doing duty as a housemaster he was possessed of compassion for the boys and would do a kindness here and there if anyone seemed unhappy or had a problem."

Other masters, however, who were too old to be called up, seemed to lack the energy to cope. They struggled to keep discipline:

"They could only assert their wills on us boys by a day to day struggle that involved shoutings and boxings of ears. Many ears got boxed in those days, but little heavy caning was done."

For a time the School Cadet Corps Band kept up its practising and played whenever an opportunity occurred but, as the war progressed, the School routine became more and more disrupted and Band practice became irregular and less frequent. The 1942 Inspection was the last time the Cadet Corps wore its old red coat uniforms. After that they were affiliated to the Home Guard and Territorial Army and put into khaki uniforms. The School still retained something of its earlier military connections:

"We were trained in the throwing of hand-grenades, elements of unarmed combat, how to dismantle and re-assemble a Lewis Gun, and crawling round the school field with out hats on backwards to deceive the enemy; neither live nor blank ammunition was ever used by the boys."

Two flying bombs fell on the School premises in 1944; one landed in a playing field and did little damage beyond destroying the cricket pavilion but the other fell one afternoon as the School weekly bath routine was in progress:

"Suddenly there was an unexpected crash and bang, quickly followed by the noise of tinkling glass .. 'Oh, my flat!' exclaimed the Mistress. She shot off up the little staircase to see what had happened. Meanwhile the masters on duty gathered in the bathroom where the unshuttered windows had blown in on the boys sitting in the baths. Soon a crocodile of naked and bleeding boys proceeded to the hospital building. The Mistress came down the staircase again 'My boys, my poor boys' she said loudly 'My first thoughts were for my poor boys'. Those of us near her when it happened knew otherwise but none of us challenged her over it."

For a short period after that the boys passed the nights in the shelters of a school nearby. Each boy wore his day clothes and took one blanket. They had to attempt sleep either sitting on a wooden bench or lying on the concrete floor. Later they were evacuated, some to South Wales and the rest to Bucklesham, near Ipswich, where they lived in a nissen hut camp with poor facilities and no sanitation except buckets and oil drums:

"We used to drink cocoa with no milk, and we used to eat a lot of corned beef and scrambled egg made with water and dried egg powder. There were compensations, however. We got to eat lovely sweet chestnuts that abounded in the area. We helped a local farmer with potato picking and the local girls came to inspect us all."

Later still, Fortescue House was evacuated to Pontefract in Yorkshire where the Headmaster had to care for nearly 200 boys with only four masters including himself.

When victory came in 1945 the schools and Training Ship returned to their own premises as soon as this could be arranged.   The Society had particular cause for thanksgiving as was noted in the Log Book for Christmas 1945:

"It is with deep gratitude in our hearts that we bring to our readers our first real Peace Log. As we look back over the long weary war years, so full of danger and anxiety, we realise that we have been wonderfully blessed. Of our widely scattered homes only Royston escaped undamaged, but nevertheless, not one child or member of our staff was injured."

The boys from the *Arethusa*, although the first to be evacuated, were the last to return. Most of them had enjoyed their time in Salcombe, Devon. The Log Book noted:

"Staff and boys enjoyed their stay in beautiful Devon, and they will be greatly missed by the inhabitants. One particular friend, Lady Clementine Waring, always readily offered her beautiful grounds for the annual Sports and Prize Giving. On 29th July the *Arethusa* boys attended their last Parade Service at Salcombe Church and, in the following week they proceeded on leave, with happy memories of an interesting time, spent amongst kindly and generous people and yet with an eager anticipation of later joining a real ship whose name they bear. 17 boys went to Bristol in July for their Royal Navy examination, and all passed."

When the *Arethusa* was returned to the Society by the Admiralty in 1945, the staff and boys returning from evacuation were delighted to receive as a gift the radiogram,

Helping with the move from Salcombe

three loudspeakers and wiring installation which had been used on board:

".. as a token of appreciation of the happy times so many Naval ratings have spent in this Ship between the years 1940 and 1945 when chartered as a Naval Accommodation Vessel attached to the RN Barracks, Chatham."

Sadly 80 old boys lost their lives in fighting for their country. Many gained awards for courage and service. The death of the Dowager Countess of Jersey, aged 95, on 22nd May 1945 was a cause of much sadness among the members and staff of the Shaftesbury Homes and Arethusa Training Ship. She had been devoted to the Society's cause from the time when her husband, the 7th Earl, had first taken a part in the work of the National Refuges. Later, her involvement increased when he became President in 1885. After her husband's death in 1915, she had continued to work with and for the Society.

The first aim of all the staff in the homes, Training Ship and offices after the war was to get back to normal as soon as possible. Many children orphaned or traumatised by war need-ed help, as well as those already in the Society's care. The Chairman pointed out that 'Now we are returning to normal and the number of children in our Homes is rapidly increasing, with very many coming from families whose homes have been broken up as a result of the war'.

Raising funds to continue the work was more difficult than ever. Mr. Francis Clayton, the Chairman and Treasurer, noted in his report for 1946 that:

"All our establishments have required renovations after the war years, coupled with improvements and alterations in some cases, and this at a very expensive and difficult time. The cost of maintenance has largely increased and the salaries of staff likewise. Fortunately, during the war years, with reduced numbers and the Admiralty payment for the use of the *Arethusa* we were able to put by and invest a considerable sum in Savings Bonds, some of which are now being realised to meet this heavy capital expenditure."

As the next chapter will show, money worries were not all the Society had to cope with in the years ahead.

Chapter 23

POST-WAR CHANGES

Although Mr. Clayton, members of his Committee and all the staff longed for life to return to what it had been before the war, this could never happen. The world was different; attitudes were changing and the British way of life would never be the same as before. Nevertheless, as far as possible it was business as usual in the homes and Training Ship, at least initially; the forces for social change, however, were strong and the coming years saw the Society struggling to adapt, reorganize and above all find a new role into which its energies could be channelled successfully.

One of the first signs of change was in the summer of 1946. Those children whose parents could afford to send the fare went home for the holidays whilst others spent time with temporary 'aunts and uncles'. This, in contrast to previous practice, was in response both to the publication of the Curtis Report (set up to enquire into the conditions in Children's Homes) and to a general and growing belief that children needed, as far as possible, to experience life as part of a secure and loving family. For some of them this was their first taste of family life.

After the war, as part of the move towards the Welfare State, the Government began to develop a coherent policy for dealing with social problems in an effort to create a fairer, better and more just society. Previously charitable and voluntary organisations had been largely responsible for the care of deprived and neglected children. Now legislation introducing the National Health Service, National Insurance and Family Allowances was set to alter policy towards large homes for deprived children and the views of the public who gave to charity.

The Education Act of 1944 which ensured free primary and secondary schooling for all, made it necessary for Bisley and Twickenham to be reorganized as secondary schools. The Committee was anxious to be allowed to retain the primary departments at these homes, for experience had taught them that children, deprived of a normal home life, benefited from a continuous education with as little change as possible. In case permission was not granted, they started to look for a property to use as a separate primary boarding school for boys who would eventually be transferred to Bisley or Twickenham.

While changes were planned for the education and care of the younger boys, there was a change too in arrangements for the older ones at Fordham House which:

".. has vacated its old premises at 164 Shaftesbury Avenue and moved to a much more spacious property in Hampstead. The Technical School, which trained boys as shoemakers and tailors, has had to be disbanded, but all the lads have found work in the neighbourhood through the good offices of the local Labour Exchange, the tailors and shoemakers continuing in their trades. The great move took place in November, but the staff and boys worked very hard and soon had the new Fordham House looking like home again."

In 1947 subscriptions and donations were less than in previous years. Nationalisation of major companies was reducing investment income and money was not as freely available to many people as in the past. Some supporters felt that, with the advent of the Welfare State, the role of the voluntary societies would become redundant.

Difficulties over accommodation and facilities at the boys' homes were still unresolved; the Committee remained firmly in favour of continuous education at one school:

"Our children so often come to us from broken and unhappy homes that we deprecate transfer to another school at 11 years of age. We prefer moving them up from the primary to the secondary department at the same school. Boarding schools for children admitted from all over the country should, we consider, receive separate treatment from day schools in this respect."

Whatever the outcome of the discussions was to be, Mr. Clayton was under no illusions as to the consequences:

"Whatever is decided upon, it will (when building on a large scale is once again permissible) entail heavy expenditure in remodelling and providing additional buildings under the new Act."

The Committee decided, as a cost-cutting measure, to sell the freehold interest in the Society's Head Office in Shaftesbury Avenue. The offices on the ground floor were vacated and a smaller suite of rooms rented on the first floor. The new owners of the building quickly started an extensive programme of alteration and improvement so that, for the next twelve months, the Society's office staff:

".. had to contend with engineers, electricians, builders and decorators. However, by the end of the year the central heating plant was in working order and the shaft for the installation of the lift was completed, so that life could go on more normally."

By the 1948 Children Act all homeless and unprotected children became the responsibility of the State, through local councils who henceforth had charge of any children in their district who, for whatever reason, were in need of care. This Act also established regulations for the running of homes by charitable and voluntary organizations concerned with child care. Initially, more children than ever before were taken into care and, for a time, the large

An Esher Place girl receiving her prize
from HRH Princess Elizabeth in 1948

boarding schools such as Esher Place, Fortescue House, and Bisley flourished. One old boy remembers Fortescue House in the immediate post-war years with affection. 'The good days I call them. I was very proud of myself and the School. To me they were happy days. Fortescue House was the only home I knew; it was a fine place'. Many of the Society's subscribers and friends, however, were confused as to how much support the State provided. Mr. Clayton informed them that:

"The 'Children's Charter', as

it has been called, does not affect the work of voluntary homes and the Shaftesbury Homes and Arethusa Training Ship is carrying on precisely as it has done hitherto. Several of our subscribers have written to enquire whether, because of this Bill, we are now nationalised or whether we receive any financial help. Under the Children Act the larger Societies (of which we are one) are not receiving any financial assistance; indeed the reverse is the position, as it seems that we shall be involved in heavier expenditure to comply with the regulations of the Act."

Costs and expenses continued to rise in 1950. During an Easter Sunday Broadcast Appeal the Secretary, Brian Pelly, pointed out that the cost of running the Society was 90% higher than it had been before the second world war. It soon became evident

HRH The Duchess of Kent receiving a bouquet on the occasion of her visit to Fortescue House School in 1948

that part of the work would have to be curtailed so as to maintain the overall standard. Reluctantly the Committee decided to close Fordham House in Hampstead:

"In recent years the need for the Hostel has not been so acute as lads can earn much bigger wages and a parent or guardian who in pre-war days wished a boy to go on to Fordham House for training in tailoring or shoe-making now wants the boy to live at home. For the past year the Hostel has not been full and it was therefore arranged to transfer the boys to other hostels in London towards the end of the year. The Society however still keeps in touch with these lads through its Welfare Officer who visits them regularly."

The outcome of the discussions with the Ministry of Education about the Society's boys' schools was a deep disappointment:

"To comply with the act Bisley Boys School has to be a secondary school for boys of 11 and over and Fortescue House a primary school for boys from 7 to 11. The financial position makes it necessary for the Society to further curtail its work and discussions with the Home Office have taken place with a view to further re-organization which will mean a reduction in the number of children in the Society's care."

All the boys of primary school age in the Society's care were henceforth educated at Fortescue House and transferred at the age of 11 to the reorganized 'Bisley School, incorporating the Newport Market Army Bands School'.

The Headmaster of Bisley, who implemented the changes there, was Mr. T. T. Barnes. He took up his appointment in 1948, coming to the School with excellent qualifications and teaching experience in both state and public schools. Under his leadership the School became

Mr T.T. Barnes, Headmaster of Bisley School from 1948 until its closure in 1959

a shining example of what could be achieved when enthusiasm and hard work are linked with a determination never to accept second best. At the first Speech Day after he took up his post, he spoke about the warm welcome he had received from boys and staff alike. He thanked the hard-working staff and the prefects, saying that the boys had been magnificent in their kindness to him and his wife during their first term. 'I could not wish for a better lot of boys' he said. He set about reorganizing the time-table to meet new requirements and to give the school a real secondary curriculum incorporating the best contemporary educational ideas. At the end of his second year in office, he could report that all the boys who had entered for the RN and RAF Artificer examinations had passed and for the first time in the School's history some boys had sat for the School Certificate.

Changes introduced by Mr. Barnes affected every aspect of school life. Art, music and drama became more important than previously, with the establishment of a Drama Society and a full School Orchestra and various ensembles. One of their productions was 'Let's Make An Opera' by Benjamin Britten. The composer himself came to watch one of the rehearsals and to offer advice; he sent a good-luck telegram on the first night. The success of this venture encouraged Brian Schlotel, one of the masters at the School, to write an opera 'To Freedom' for the boys which was subsequently performed successfully. The School magazine was published regularly again after a long absence and the school competed with other schools at athletics, games and sports. All the boys took part in extracurricular activities and the senior boys walked at least five miles each day in the course of their normal school life.

General Certificate of Education results were good and in 1953 two Bisley boys took and passed Advanced Level subjects. Mr. Barnes hoped that this would encourage more boys to stay on and do the same.

While the School at Bisley was going from strength to strength, the 1950s was a time of crisis for the Society as a whole. The editorial in the Report for 1950 was pessimistic:

"1950 will go down in the annals of the Society as, perhaps, the most momentous through which it has yet passed. Many of our friends can no longer

A group of the Society's officials, Mr Barnes standing on the right and Mr Thorp, Assistant Secretary, on the left

help us to the same extent as formerly, and at the same time, in spite of every economy, the cost of maintaining the children and the homes and Ship has risen steeply. These two factors meant that income no longer covered expenditure and the Society has been obliged to dip deeply into its reserves."

Mr. Clayton, the Chairman and Treasurer for 25 years, retired in 1952 after nearly 60 years of service to the Society. The following year, to the delight of all his friends and colleagues, he was knighted in recognition of a lifetime's service to children.

Esher House, 48 Palace Road, East Molesey

The year 1952 was momentous in the Society's history for other, sadder reasons. It was one hundred years almost to the day since the opening of the Society's first refuge that Esher Place and Shaftesbury House at Royston were closed and sold to meet some, though not all, of the deficit which had accumulated. The Committee bought a much smaller house in East Molesey which they named 'Esher House' and which could accommodate 20 girls. This was reserved for those the Committee judged to be most in need of support and those who had won scholarships to grammar schools and needed to stay with the Society to finish their schooling.

In 1953 the Treasurer was pessimistic about the future developments of the Society's work:

"The drain on our reserves has not yet been halted, and I estimate that in 1953 it will again be necessary to make further inroads into our reserves, which have already been adversely affected by the present monetary trend."

In 1954 the homes and *Arethusa* were full to capacity with 750 children; finance was a continuing anxiety. The Annual Reports echoed the Committee's concerns:

"Our programme of essential building renovation is not yet complete and cost almost £10,000 in 1954, but both Bisley and Fortescue House Schools and the Girls' Home at East Molesey are nearing the standard of maintenance and modernisation necessary to provide bright and convenient surroundings for the boys and girls in them. Within the next two years it will be necessary for the *Arethusa* to be dry-docked, the moorings renewed and the pier between Ship and shore rebuilt – all at a cost of approximately £5,000."

Mrs E.M.M. Cubbin and Mr R.A. Colby Cubbin

However, it was cheering that in 1955 the Society received a bequest of the ocean-going steam yacht '*Glen Strathallan*' under the will of Mrs. Cubbin of Douglas, Isle of Man, for 'use in the training of boys for the sea services'. The yacht was given a permanent berth alongside the *Arethusa*.

After-care had always played an important part in the

The Glen Strathallan *bequeathed to the Society in the will of Mrs E.M.M. Cubbin with the proviso that, when the vessel was no longer of use to the Society, she should be towed out to sea and scuttled. In 1970 Mrs Cubbin's descendants agreed that the unique reciprocating engine should be removed and donated to the Science Museum before the vessel was scuttled*

Society's work and during the 1950s it began to expand. During their last term at school the boys and girls received a visit from the Society's Welfare Officer who:

".. visits the schools and interviews all leavers to discover what kind of work they want to do. He then sets about finding suitable openings for them, or puts them in the way of further training, arranging hostel accommodation for those in need of it. He visits certain of the homes from which children are admitted if there is any doubt as to the suitability of the home for the child to return to for holiday periods. Hardly a day goes by but there is a call at the office from an old boy or girl who wants advice on personal problems or about their particular work."

In 1956 financial worries were mounting. Increasing costs far outweighed the savings from the limited economies which were possible without impairing the standard of care offered. One of the main expenses was for the dry-docking of the *Arethusa* and the *Glen Strathallan*. The following year after much heart-searching the difficult decision was made to close down the School at Bisley and sell the property. In future all the boys not in training onboard the *Arethusa* would be educated at Fortescue House which would be reorganized and expanded into two separate schools, one for juniors and one for seniors on the same site.

Research work carried out in the 1950s resulted in a change in the 1960s from a 'child-centred' approach to one which was more concerned about the child's wider family and community, and to the concept of preventive work with families. Large residential homes lost favour as more emphasis was placed on fostering and smaller family units.

Aerial view of Fortescue House before reorganization

These emerging theories, together with concern about numbers being received into care, were factors leading to the Ingleby Report of 1960 and the 1963 Children and Young Persons Act which followed it. This Act placed the Local Authorities, for the first time, under an obligation to undertake work to prevent the break up of families and to prevent the reception of children into care. Later, the Seebohm Committee led to the 1969 Children and

Young Persons Act and a more unified approach to work with families in need, with Social Services Departments developing family 'casework'. These developments, with all the good contained within them, had initially a devastating effect on the Society's work. More financial uncertainty and further difficulties over increasing costs of the Society's large establishments were a feature of this decade.

In 1966 the Chairman shared the Committee's concerns with the subscribers:

"What of the future? The changing patterns and values of life in the sixties, vastly different as they are from those other sixties of the last centu-

Bedtime stories at Esher House

ry, have not lessened the demands made upon us for help. As always, we admit children primarily upon a basis of need and it is perhaps an anomaly of the Welfare State that the need for our Society is as great as ever. True, the need is of a contemporary character and not simply the uncomplicated 'destitution' of the last century, and we have to move with the times in order to meet it."

Although there was a recognition that a change was necessary, it was by no means clear what the change should be. A possible way forward was suggested when local authorities began to look to the Society for help where children were in need of short-term care. One of the earliest of these cases involved two families of boys and girls between the ages of two and five who became homeless and, after spending two days and nights in the open, were sent to Esher House. They stayed until their parents had been re-housed and the families were then reunited. The girls at Esher House enjoyed having these young children staying with

Chairman of the Esher House Committee, Mrs E. Kennedy, at Hansler Grove with Lt Cdr England, General Secretary and Reginald Marsh, the actor. in the foreground, with Miss Ethel Stokes, Matron and Sir John Child, Chairman, in the rear

them; they helped to bath them and read them stories at bed-time. The staff at Esher House were pleased and the Committee judged the experiment a success.

The economies had to continue. In 1967 the Head Office moved from 164 Shaftesbury Avenue, following the expiry of the lease, to smaller accommodation at 229A Shaftesbury Avenue. Early in 1968 the girls and staff at Esher House in East Molesey moved from the house in Palace Road to a smaller one, close by, in Hansler Grove.

In line with the new mood towards integration with the Community, the Headmaster at Fortescue House reported in 1968 that:

"It is difficult in such a limited space to report the increasing number of activities in which the boys are engaged at Fortescue House and the immediate neighbourhood. Integration has been the keyword since November – integration with local organizations thus enabling the boys to feel that they are members of a much wider community. For example, the Air Training Corps Squadron in Richmond and Twickenham – the Sea Cadet Corps Units of TS *Goodwin*, Richmond and TS *Saumarez*, Twickenham – TS *Steadfast*, Kingston - St. Mary's Church Choir –

Arethusa *spirit to the end*

St. Johns Ambulance Cadet Unit, Twickenham Theatre Workshop. Voluntary work has also been undertaken daily through the Council of Social Service at the West Middlesex Hospital."

By the beginning of the 1970s fewer boys were interested in training for a life at sea than formerly and, as far as it was possible to judge, this was unlikely to change in the future. Consequently, after much discussion it was decided to alter the aim of education on board the *Arethusa*. The accent henceforth would be on academic achievement and the chance of going on to further or higher education; the lesson curriculum would be combined with adventure activities and confidence and character building exercises.

Mr Henry de B. Staveley-Hill, Chairman, 1971–1973, responsible for the reforms to meet modern day requirements

Although much hard work, enthusiasm and good will had gone into all their projects since the war, it was obvious that a new initiative was needed if the Society was in the future to play a useful and relevant part in helping children and young people in need. Clearly the time for large residential homes had passed but the way ahead was uncertain. It was therefore decided to engage a firm of consultants, Peter F. Hunt & Associates, with special knowledge of child care and education to make recommendations for future development in the light of the Children and Young Persons Act of 1969.

As a result of this Review and the detailed Hunt Report which followed, three major changes took place. First, the Committee decided to continue to run the *Arethusa* not as a Training Ship but as a secondary boarding school afloat, offering not only a secondary education of a high standard but also a unique type of adventure and character training. Secondly, the

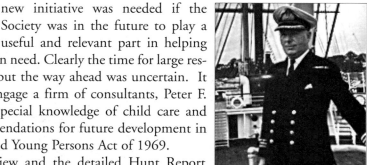

Commander M.H. Le Mare, RN, the last Naval Captain of the Arethusa *Training Ship, retired after 20 years' service in 1969, when the ship became a 'boarding school afloat'*

Pictures of the Society's first hostel for young people in Dealtry Road, Putney

work of the Society would be expanded by opening a hostel or hostels for homeless school leavers, to be run as closely as possible to a family unit. Thirdly, a 'Social Service Secretary' with suitable experience and qualifications would be appointed to co-ordinate all caring aspects of the Society's work with professional expertise.

By carrying out these recommendations, it was hoped that the reverses of the last few years would be halted and the Society would once again be able to play a major part in helping young people in need. The experience of the post-war period had shown that 'paradoxically, the Welfare State produces more problems than it solves. One day, perhaps, the State will be able to take over the work of voluntary societies, but not for a very long time yet'.

This rather pessimistic view is not borne out by the story of the Society's development after the implementation of the recommendations in the Hunt Report. On the contrary, Local Authorities and the voluntary societies began to redefine their aims, methods and areas of concern, resulting in collaboration rather than conflict. The children and young people in the Society's care have benefited greatly from these changes. After more than thirty confusing years the Society emerged from the turbulence with renewed vigour, a new image and a clear vision of the way ahead.

Major Piers de Bernière-Smart (r) the Society's General Secretary, who had the unenviable task of supervising the closing of the large schools and the Training Ship and reshaping the Society to meet the needs of the future, shown here with HRH Princess Margaret

Chapter 24
A New Direction

After years of serious financial concern, the Hunt Report had pointed a path by which the Society could continue to take a positive and active role in the support of young people. The Council (as the Committee was now called) accepted the recommendations and adapted to new methods, new style projects and a new outlook with the intention of introducing modern professionalism with enough flexibility to cope with changes in the years to come.

In 1973, the Council acquired a building in Putney to be converted into the Society's first hostel with a small residential staff for ten boys in their late teens. The house next door was bought soon afterwards to be run as a 'progress hostel':

"The idea is that, whereas the first hostel will provide close care and supervision for those in need of it while finding their feet in the adult world, the second will consist of self-contained flatlets for those who have reached a state of stable independence which renders close supervision unnecessary."

Shortly after this, the Society branched out into a new area of work. Esher House changed from being run as a children's home to become a supported hostel for vulnerable young single mothers with their babies.

A further development in 1976 was to give practical and financial support to the Centrepoint Night Shelter in Soho, which provided temporary accommodation for homeless young people in London. The crypt of St. Anne's Church was used for emergency accommodation for up to about 30 young people a night. It was open 365 nights a year from 8 pm to 8 am and was run by a team of five full-time workers, assisted by about 50 regular volunteers. Some of the young people who used the shelter were subsequently offered accommodation for up to six months at Centrepoint House in Hammersmith. The background of those selected varied:

".. it may be someone who has just left home, young and not experienced in living on their own; or it could be someone who has experienced a recent crisis, such as a bereavement or rape, and who is unable to cope on their own at that time; it may be someone who has been on their own for a while, lonely and unable to make relationships."

These new projects were funded by the sale of the grounds of Fortescue House for residential housing and the House itself to the London Borough of Richmond in 1974. The Society bought The Old Rectory at Hanworth, Middlesex and transferred the remaining residents of Fortescue House, now no longer a School but a Childrens' Home, to the new property. That same year was the last for the *Arethusa* as a boarding school afloat. It was expensive to maintain and recently had, for some years, been under-used. Repairs estimated at around £100,000 were urgently

The Old Rectory at Hanworth, Middlesex

needed. The vessel was sold to the South Street Seaport Museum of New York where she was restored to her 1911 built condition and reverted to her original name, the *Peking*.

It was unthinkable, however, that the Society's link with the sea should be completely severed. Lord Shaftesbury's dream whereby sea training coupled with a boy's sense of adventure would together develop his potential and instil self confidence was equally valid in modern times. The Council planned to make use of the *Arethusa*'s shore buildings for the benefit of many inner-city children and to launch a new sail training project: "We plan a new and excit-

The Peking *in the South Street Seaport Museum in New York*

ing venture which, if we can achieve it, will benefit a greater number of children and young people in a way particularly suited to the sociological needs of the present time. We want to adapt the shore buildings to provide an Environmental Study Centre for schoolchildren who would not otherwise have a chance to explore the natural mysteries of land and water, and to revel in the discovery of these things.

We have started to look for a small sea-going schooner which, under the command of a qualified master and mate, could take young people to sea for several days at a time."

The Venture Centre at Upnor in Kent was successfully developed and attracted the support of the Inner London Education Authority which made extensive use of the facilities for the benefit of large numbers of children from the

Activities at the Arethusa Venture Centre

densely populated areas of the City. It gave then and continues to give, an opportunity to hundreds of children, from towns and cities, to spend a week or so learning much, in new and exciting surroundings, whilst enjoying fresh air, exercise and adventure, away from the restrictions of town life. Living, working and playing together, they are introduced to new challenges and encouraged to look to the future with determination and greater enthusiasm.

In 1975 the Society bought a 'superb new 71 foot ketch' to be its third *Arethusa*. This was able to take groups of young people on sea voyages to the Continent. Many of the young crews had never been to sea before and gained tremendously

An introduction to Sailing

The first offshore ketch Arethusa *built to the order of The Shaftesbury Homes and Arethusa by the Ocean Youth Club, Falmouth Yard, to a design by Robert Clark. In service with the Society 1975-1982 as an offshore training ketch for young people*

from the experience of life on board. This first ketch was replaced in July 1982 by a purpose built vessel, also named *Arethusa*, capable of increased performance and versatility. Today, the *Arethusa* continues to provide exciting opportunities for many young people who would not otherwise have an opportunity to benefit from the exhilaration of life at sea and experience a sense of achievement from the challenge of working and living together in a sometimes hostile environment.

The environment was indeed hostile to one 14 year old who described a personal battle against the elements fought and won while on an adventure expedition at the Centre:

"The fog silently, smoothly dropped like a blanket engulfing everything. I could not see more than two feet in front of me .. The fog was like a prison, with no end; you could plough on through it and never come to a halt.

My friend was quite used to these conditions and I had faith in him, but every now and then I had a mad idea of never returning to civilisation. The fog made everything seem sinister and forbidding. It had the power to change a nice sunny dry day into a cold, damp, murky, sweaty gloom.

Suddenly, as quick as it had come, the fog started to go. Visibility grew stronger and stronger. My friend pointed to the jetty which was rapidly grower clearer as we drew close ... My encounter with the sea had made me realise in full how lonely you can be even with company."

Two other projects maintained the Society's link with the sea. The first, the *John Collett* Barge, was a floating School for children in the London Borough of Southwark who had difficulty in coping with mainstream

The new purpose-built sail training ketch designed by David Cannell, being built at Fox's yard, Ipswich. She was launched by The Countess Mountbatten of Burma on 6th July, 1982

education. These children received individual help and support onboard the Barge and were encouraged to return to their schools when their difficulties had been overcome. The Head Teacher, speaking at the Annual General Meeting in 1982 described two of his pupils:

The John Collett *barge at her permanent moorings on the River Thames*

"Ruth had threatened one teacher and attacked another. The way she could string words together was totally unbelievable. Basically she needed to know how far to go, how to gather self-discipline, how to adapt to a different way of behaviour, how to communicate with her peers and with adults. Her basic skills were limited."

Her time on board was a life-line. When she left the *John Collett*, she got a job with a book-binding firm. She held the job, negotiated herself a pay rise and

View from the Arethusa Venture Centre at Lower Upnor, near Rochester, with the Arethusa *ketch at her moorings*

as evidence of her success rang up her old Headmaster who was thrilled when she 'asked me out for a pint!'. Chris was another child at the school who could not be easily forgotten. He had 'eighth of an inch hair, braces, tattoos, rolled up jeans'. He spent his days roaming the streets, but after he had spent some months in the *John Collett* his teacher commented:

"Still the same clothes, but how he's changed! He's gentle, kind, humorous. He's intelligent and considerate. So many qualities emerged. There's still a long way to go but the Barge may well be the only kind of situation for him. Why? Because it's small; it's homely, and we have time to treat each child as an individual."

Shy, frightened children came to the *John Collett* as well as aggressive ones. 'I came to school on the Barge because I had problems at home' wrote one in an essay 'I didn't have any school uniform and people used to say things that I didn't like so I didn't bother going to school.'

Yet another link with maritime tradition was the *Sir Alan Herbert*, a Thames barge, in operation from 1980 to 1985. She was a sailing barge, chartered from the East Coast Sail Trust, equipped with canoes and camping gear. She operated, most successfully, from her base at Brightlingsea in Essex and was used by inner-city children and young people from schools, clubs and homes and those on court orders. The Captain felt encouraged that 'almost without exception, the youngsters who visit the Barge would like to return', bearing in mind that 'we have no television or radio on board, all the cooking and cleaning is done by the youngsters and all sail handling and anchor work is manual'.

Another new venture in the 1980s was the MacAndrew House Family Centre in Clapham. This provided for parents who had difficulty in coping with their children. At the Centre, the Society's social work staff

The Sir Alan Herbert, *the Society's mobile sailing/adventure centre, based at Brightlingsea, on the Essex coast*

Katie Boyle visits staff and families at the MacAndrew House Family Centre in Clapham. The funding of this project was made possible by the legacy of Mr Vernon W. MacAndrew

helped the mothers and fathers to gain confidence and acquire skills to become good parents. In the majority of cases, those who attended had very low self-esteem and needed help from staff to 'develop themselves as people in their own right. We provide play for both the children and the parents, many of whom have never had the opportunity to play when they were children themselves'.

The activities at MacAndrew House were perhaps reminiscent of the classes in ragged school days when the teachers organized lessons for mothers and fathers as well as children of all ages:

"The most popular activity has proved to be cooking. After hearing from most of the parents that they 'couldn't boil an egg' they have in fact produced some delicious meals. The mothers plan a week's menu for the Centre, consisting of cheap, well-balanced meals and work out a shopping list from this. We then take the parents shopping to the most local and cheapest shops."

The parents decided what craft activities they wanted and helped each other. Some learnt knitting and dressmaking. One of the fathers offered to teach woodwork. There were regular swimming sessions at a local Pool and outings to the coast in the summer.

With all the new projects the Society provided after-care and support for the young people involved. The Council was anxious to ensure that 'once young people have become part of our family there should always be a link and a supporting shoulder when they go out into the world'.

Support for children outside the classroom and after they have left school has been a feature of the Society's work from the earliest days when the Ragged School teachers became friends to their pupils and their families. In 1855 Mrs. Edmond, the Matron of the Girls' Refuge, had said that she felt she was in charge of a family rather than a School and went on 'it has been my constant aim to bring about this very desirable feeling'. The two Mr. Scoulers loyally supported old boys from the *Chichester* and *Arethusa* whenever there was need. Mr. and Mrs. Ward in the 1880s had been mother and father to the boys who settled in Canada. Miss Chipchase became the lifelong friend of the women she had cared for as young vulnerable girls.

The Society demonstrated its concern for those leaving care by establishing an After Care Department and appointing a full-time social worker to co-ordinate this vital aspect of its work.

By the 1990s the changes initiated following the Hunt Report had produced good results. The Treasurer optimistically announced that he was:

".. very encouraged by the results for 1991 which show clearly that although more work has been undertaken our financial position has continued to improve significantly. Our day to day operating costs have fallen; the Society is in good heart and in sound financial shape."

The role of the voluntary societies which had previously declined as state intervention grew is now, once again, vital in caring for children in need. With increasing calls on their limited finances, many Local Authorities are seeking ways to economise in the provision of child care services. The Shaftesbury Homes and Arethusa has recognised that, in the modern world, it must be able to compete for this responsibility by providing a high quality service at an economical cost and it is actively seeking opportunities where it can make a contribution towards higher quality standards in all aspects of care and concern for children and young people.

The Society established a Youth Justice Centre in Ipswich, run in conjunction with Suffolk County Council and aimed at diverting young people away from custody and the spiral of detention and a criminal life by offering credible alternatives to the police and the Courts. Experience shows that many young people fall into the way of offending or antisocial behaviour simply because they are bored and have few interests to occupy their free time. Many are easily led astray by their friends and soon find themselves in trouble.

With a great deal of professional counselling and a variety of remedial work, staff at the Centre can usually persuade these young offenders that there are many more productive and rewarding ways of occupying their time.

One very successful method of motivating these youngsters has been through providing opportunities for motorcycle scrambling. Whilst this may be seen to be a reward for bad behaviour, it is quite the reverse. Only those who show a willingness to behave are included in such activities and the responsibilities of the activity are soon brought home to them when they settle down to the more onerous tasks of cleaning and maintaining the machines. This all helps them develop an abiding interest in an absorbing pastime which will keep them away from the long arm of the law.

Another recently established project, also in Ipswich, is the Young Persons Support Team. The Society was successful in obtaining funds, through a Central Government initiative, to develop a service aimed at providing advice and

'Scrambling back to the right track' at the Ipswich Youth Justice Centre

practical support to young people with family and housing problems. The aim was to reduce the number of vulnerable youngsters arriving in London with nowhere to live. Since its inception, it has achieved considerable success and done much to improve prospects and motivation for many young people from the Ipswich area.

Local authorities make strenuous efforts to avoid splitting up families and communities and will, wherever possible, attempt to provide childcare facilities within their own boundaries. In most cases, children in need of care will be placed in foster homes within the Borough so that they can be brought up in a family environment and remain part of the local commu-

The Society's team at Ipswich gives hope and practical support to large numbers of young people who have drifted away from their families

nity in which they have been born or spent their early years. There will always be cases where suitable foster parents are not available, where an existing fostering arrangement breaks down or where the child does not wish to be placed with foster parents. There will also be cases when, for behavioural or psychological reasons, a foster home placement would be totally inappropriate. In instances such as these, residential care in registered children's homes can provide a very positive and sometimes rewarding solution. It is particularly in this field where the Shaftesbury Homes and Arethusa continues to make its mark.

The work carried out today, in the Society's residential homes, is not unlike that of the large schools for boys and girls which have featured so prominently in the Society's past history. Emphasis has always been on the development of children as individuals and their preparation for a worthwhile and happy adulthood. Education and career development continue to be important factors in the upbringing offered today. Many young people coming into care have suffered from all manner of deprivation and often serious abuse. This requires expert and professional counselling. The fundamental aim of today's homes is to prepare the young person to have the confidence and the ability to become a happy, self-sufficient and responsible citizen.

Although young people generally leave care at the age of eighteen and tend to be allocated flats or other accommodation by their Local Authority, the Society is well aware that many of them will have no family or friends to fall back on in times of difficulty. Through its Aftercare Department, the Shaftesbury Homes and Arethusa continues to provide practical and moral support to the members of its 'family' long after they have left. Most children who have been brought up in a stable, loving family will continue to depend, from time to time, on the help and guidance of their parents for many years after they have left home. The Society feels it should provide exactly the same support and, through its Aftercare team, it does.

Whilst registered children's homes play a large part in the Society's work, and it remains one of the few voluntary organisations which continue to do this difficult and demanding work, its main aim of **'helping, educating and caring for children and young people who are suffering from the lack of a stable family upbringing or other social or educational disadvantage and enabling them to take their place in society as happy and responsible citizens'** is achieved in a wide variety of ways. As well as education and adventure training, at the Arethusa Venture Centre and onboard the *Arethusa* Ketch, it has four homes in London providing bedsitters and support for young people, who are leaving care or who have become homeless. Esher House continues to give a safe and caring family home to young girls and their babies who

Construction of the new Climbing Wall at the Arethusa Venture Centre. Part of a major redevelopment which will be completed in 1997 at a total cost of about £1.5 million

have no other means of support. Since the Society's foundation, it has cared for and prepared for adult life upwards of 60,000 children and young people. It has helped them to hold their

Teamwork aboard the **Arethusa** *Ketch*

own in competition with others from all walks of life. For over 150 years, from 1843 to the present day, the Shaftesbury Homes and Arethusa has been in the forefront of action and concern. Methods have changed enormously but the need is as real as ever. In the words of the present Director:

".. we provide homes, a sense of belonging and purpose to many thousands of children and young people who have had a disastrous start in life. They have usually been discarded by family, foster parents, friends and society and they tend to view their existence with deep resentment and their future with despair. They are often very damaged by their upbringing and sometimes quite seriously psychologically disturbed. This all too frequently manifests itself in an attitude of aggression, a distrust of adults and a loss of confidence in their ability to survive in what they see as an unjust world.

Our whole task is to rescue these youngsters and set them on the road to a worthwhile, fulfilling and enjoyable life. We do this in many ways because we believe that each individual has his or her own special needs. Growing up

Captain Neil Baird-Murray, CBE, RN, Director of the Shaftesbury Homes and Arethusa since 1989, greeting the Queen Mother at the Society's Thanksgiving Service, 1993

Her Majesty Queen Elizabeth, The Queen Mother, with The Countess Mountbatten of Burma, the Society's President, and Mr Henry Staveley-Hill, the Society's Chairman of Trustees, at a Thanksgiving Service to celebrate 150 years of caring for disadvantaged children and young people

through adolescence is difficult enough for anyone. But for those who have no family to support them, who have lost their confidence and self-esteem and have no real sense of belonging, it is a tough and lonely experience and many will view their future with deep despair.

Our fundamental aim is to pick up the pieces of these shattered beginnings and instil the self-confidence, self-discipline and courage which will enable our young people to tackle the challenges of independent living with spirit and determination."

Today the Society employs over a hundred and thirty staff, providing for the needs of those young people living in its homes and residential accommodation and all those who pass through the Venture Centre or sail in the *Arethusa*. Current economic conditions place severe restraints on both individuals and corporate bodies in their desire to support charitable causes. Nevertheless, the support is still there and regular subscribers, many of them old boys and girls, provide it willingly and generously. Without loyal financial support, through donations and bequests, the Society could not have survived. Without the commitment of William Williams, the influence of the seventh Earl of Shaftesbury and the many generations of volunteers serving as Council and Committee members and acting as its honorary officers, it could not have prospered.

In 150 years, so much has changed, and yet so much has remained the same. The small school in the Rookery of St. Giles has gone, the refuges, the large institutions, the rigidly

Her Majesty the Queen with HRH The Duke of Edinburgh and the Society's President, Lady Mountbatten, at a Mansion House reception to mark the Society's 150th Anniversary

defined job training, all have gone long since. Yet William Williams' spirit lives on unchanged.

From the walls of the Head Office at Rectory Grove, in Clapham, faces from the Society's past look down at life today. William Williams is there, with his clear gaze. Lord Shaftesbury is there, his face etched with lines through concern for the poverty, ignorance and deprivation of so many children needing the Society's care. Patrons past and present are there together with kindly Alf Fennings, the Society's great financial benefactor; Sir Francis Clayton, whose life was devoted to children and many others who have served faithfully. They all would surely be proud of what is happening now and would encourage the Society's staff in their work and plans for the future.

Arethusa Old Boys continue to meet each year for a Reunion at the Arethusa Venture Centre

BLACKBURN, Barbara **Noble Lord**: the Life of the 7th Earl of Shaftesbury
(Home, London, 1949)

BREADY, J. Wesley **Lord Shaftesbury and Social-Industrial Progress**
(George Allen & Unwin, 1926)

CLARK, E. A. G. **The Ragged School Union and the Education of the London Poor
in the 19th Century**
(unpublished London University MA Dissertation, 1967)

CLINCH, George **Bloomsbury and St. Giles's Past and Present**
(Truslove, London, 1890)

FINLAYSON, Geoffrey B.A.M., **The Seventh Earl of Shaftesbury 1801-1885**
(Eyre Methuen, 1981)

HODDER, Edwin **The Life and Work of the Seventh Earl of Shaftesbury, K.G.**
3 Vols. (Cassell, 1887)

MONTAGUE, C.J. **Sixty Years in Waifdom and the Ragged School Movement in
English History** (Charles Murray & Co., London, 1904)

FOOTNOTES

All the footnotes refer to source material other than that held exclusively at the Society's Head Office in Clapham. Footnotes have not been supplied when the material quoted is taken from sources which originated from the Society and are now held at the Clapham Head Office. In the main these quotations are taken from:

* Printed Annual Reports (called at various times The Annual Report, The Annual Record, or The Record)
* Manuscript General Committee meeting minutes from 1852 onwards
* Minutes of various Sub-Committees
* Information taken from publications printed by the Society for their subscribers and supporters - e.g. The Log Book, Our Work, Share.
* Various personal letters, memos, and notes concerning the work of the Society. Other quoted material is taken from the reminiscences of former boys, girls and teachers at the homes. In this case, too, numbered notes have not been supplied.

TIME CHART OF THE MAIN EVENTS IN THE SOCIETY'S HISTORY

1843   William Williams and friends open St. Giles' Rookery Ragged School.

1852   Society's first 'Refuge' (ie Home) for homeless and destitute children opened on the corner of Broad Street and George Street, St. Giles.

1855   Boys from Refuge moved to separate Home in Arthur Street, St. Giles.

1858   William Williams appointed full-time paid Secretary of the Society. Building in Arthur Street given up and Refuge moved to Great Queen Street.

1860   Older girls at Broad Street Refuge move to Acton.

1866   St. Valentine's Night Supper for homeless boys. Inauguration of Society's first Training Ship, the *Chichester*. Refuge at Acton closed and girls move temporarily to Kilburn. Lord Shaftesbury becomes Society's Patron.

1867   Opening of Farm School at Bisley. Kilburn home closed, and girls move to Ealing House, Ealing.

1871   Newsboys' Home (later known as the Working Boys' Home) opens in Gray's Inn Road.

1872   Girls in Broad Street Refuge move to new Home at Sudbury Hall, Sudbury, near Harrow.

1873   Shaftesbury School for boys opens at Bisley.

1874   Society obtains a second ship, the *Arethusa*, through help of Baroness Burdett-Coutts. Lord Shaftesbury becomes Society's President.

1878   Fortescue House, Twickenham, opens as Home for boys. Old London Refuge given up and smaller one leased in Great Queen Street as reception home for children applying for admission.

1883   Society rents a house in Hamilton, Ontario, as a Reception Home for boys on their arrival as immigrants in Canada.

1885   Death of Lord Shaftesbury. Lord Jersey becomes President.

1887   The Prince of Wales (later to become Edward VII) lays foundation stone of new building at 164 Shaftesbury Avenue, to be used as Society's Head Office, Reception Home, and London Refuge for 100 boys. The Working Boys' Home moves to this address.

1888   Financial difficulties force closure of home in Canada.

1889   Training Ship *Chichester* sold. Purchase of a brigantine *Ballerina of Cowes* (renamed the *Chichester*).

1890   William Williams retires.

1892   Death of William Williams. Working Boys' Home renamed Fordham House.

1896   Opening of the Technical Home in Shaftesbury Avenue for boys of school leaving age.

1904   Incorporation of Society in accordance with the Companies Act of 1867.

1908   Shaftesbury House, Royston, opens as Home for young children.

1915   Death of Lord Jersey.

1917   Sale of brigantine *Chichester*.

1919   The two Bisley schools combined into one with Senior and Junior Departments in the old Farm School and Shaftesbury School buildings.

1920   Society renamed The Shaftesbury Homes and Arethusa Training Ship.

1928   Acquisition of the Newport Market Army Training School (later renamed Newport Market Army Bands School) at Darrick Wood, Kent.

1930   Ealing House and Sudbury Hall Homes for Girls closed and sold. Opening of Esher Place Home for Girls, Esher, Surrey.

1932   SV *Peking* purchased to replace the *Arethusa*.

1933   The *Peking,* renamed the *Arethusa*, becomes Society's Training Ship at new berth on the River Medway, at Lower Upnor, near Rochester, Kent.

1935   Acquisition of The National Society for the Protection of Young Girls (Princess Louise Home). Esher Place renamed "Esher Place (Princess Louise Home for Girls)".

1937   Fortescue House School transfers to larger premises in Twickenham. The Newport Market Army Bands School moves from Darrick Wood to this new building. Combined School is called Fortescue House (Newport Market Army Bands School).

1945   Fordham House relocated in Hampstead.

1947   164 Shaftesbury Avenue sold and offices leased back to the Society.

1948   Closure of Fordham House.

1952   Sale of Esher Place and Shaftesbury House, Royston. Esher House in East Molesey, Surrey, bought to accommodate 20 girls.

1958   Sale of Bisley School. Remaining boys from Bisley transferred to Fortescue House, Twickenham.

1972   Report by Peter F. Hunt & Associates Ltd. on the future working of the Society.

1973   Society's first Hostel opens at Putney.

1975   Sale of the *Arethusa* to the South Street Seaport Museum, New York. Sale of Fortescue House to Property Developers and the London Borough of Richmond. Establishment of the Arethusa Venture Centre at Lower Upnor and the *Arethusa* Ketch.

1993   The Society's 150th Anniversary Celebrations.

For a list of projects set up since the Hunt Report, please refer to Appendix H

PATRONS

1866   The 7th Earl of Shaftesbury, KG – until 1885

1910   HM King George V – until 1936
        HM Queen Mary – until 1952

1919   HRH Prince Edward, The Prince of Wales, later HM King Edward VIII – until 1936

1927   HRH The Princess Royal – until 1963
        HRH Prince Arthur, Duke of Connaught, KG – until 1940

1934   HRH Princess Louise, Duchess of Argyll – until 1937

1936   HM King George VI – until 1951

1942   HRH Prince George, Duke of Kent, KG – until 1942
        HRH Princess Marina, Duchess of Kent – until 1966

1963   HM Queen Elizabeth II
        HM Queen Elizabeth, The Queen Mother

PRESIDENTS

1843 – 1856   The Rev. and Hon. Montague Villiers, who became –

1856 - 1860   The Rt. Rev. and Hon. The Bishop of Carlisle, who became –

1860 - 1861   The Rt. Rev. and Rt. Hon. The Lord Bishop of Durham

1862 - 1873   The Rt. Rev. The Lord Bishop of Ripon

1874 - 1885   The 7th Earl of Shaftesbury, KG

1885 - 1915   The 7th Earl of Jersey, PC, KCMG

1919 - 1935   HRH Prince Edward, The Prince of Wales
                  (who later became HM King Edward VIII)

1936 - 1940   HRH Prince George, The Duke of Kent

1946 - 1952   Admiral of the Fleet, The Earl of Cork and Orrery GCB, GCVO

1952 - 1958   Lieutenant-General The Lord Freyberg, VC, GCMG, KCB, KBE, DSO

1959 - 1981   The Rt. Hon. The Earl of Ranfurly, KCMG

1982 to date   The Countess Mountbatten of Burma, CBE, CD, JP, DL

HONORARY CHAIRMEN

Unnamed in the Annual Reports until 1890

1890-1917   W. E. Hubbard

1918-1926   C. E. Malden

1926-1950   F. H. Clayton

1951-1957   P. G. L. Cameron

1958-1963   Commander R. P. Garnett, Royal Navy

1964-1971   Sir John Child, Bart., DL

1971-1973   H. de B. Staveley-Hill

1974-1991   Capt. C. M. Knight, MNI

1991 to date   H. D. d'A. Staveley-Hill

HONORARY VICE-CHAIRMEN

Unnamed in the Annual Reports until 1890

1890-1892	William Williams *
1892-1908	C. T. Ware
1909-1917	C. E. Malden MA
1918-1925	H. F. Clayton
1926-1947	The Rt. Hon. Lord Daryngton of Witley, PC
1948-1952	Major-General A. R. Chater, CB DSO OBE
1953-1956	Major-General V. H. B. Majendie CB DSO DL
1957-1958	Commander R. P. Garnett, Royal Navy
1958-1963	Sir John Child, Bart., DL
1964-1971	H. de B. Staveley-Hill
1971-1972	G. K. M. St.Aubyn
1973-1978	D. Marner
1978-1991	Mrs. C. S. Cleverly OBE
1991 to date	A. Zinopoulos

* received salary as Secretary

HONORARY TREASURERS

1843-1845	(Mr.) Bragg
1846-1850	H. Lloyd
1851-1853	R. Gurney
1854-1871	H. Malden
1872-1874	J. H. Fordham
1885-1917	W. E. Hubbard
1918-1925	C. E. Malden
1926-1950	F. H. Clayton
1951-1963	G. K. M. St.Aubyn
1964-1965	C. S. Barnett
1965-1972	G. K. M. St.Aubyn
1973-1982	D. Marner
1983-1990	H. D. d'A. Staveley-Hill
1991-1993	D. Marner
1994 to date	R.W. Walmsley

GENERAL SECRETARIES/DIRECTORS

1843-1846   John Morison

1847-1889   William Williams

1890-1903   H. Bristow Wallen

1904-1925   H. Bristow Wallen and H. Copeland

1926-1953   F. B. Pelly AFC

1954-1963   F. A. Thorp

1964-1971   Lieutenant-Commander A. D. England, Royal Navy

1971-1989   Major R. P. A. de Bernière-Smart

1989 to date   Captain N. C. Baird-Murray CBE, Royal Navy

PROJECTS FROM 1952 ONWARDS

ESHER HOUSE (PALACE ROAD, EAST MOLESEY)   1952 - 1968
A Children's Home taking referrals from Local Authority Children's Departments.

ESHER HOUSE (HANSLER GROVE, EAST MOLESEY)   1969 - 1975
A Children's Home taking referrals from Local Authority Children's Departments.

ESHER HOUSE (ARNISON ROAD, EAST MOLESEY)   1975 - present
A supported Hostel for vulnerable, young, single mothers.

FORTESCUE HOUSE (TWICKENHAM)   1975 - 1983
Part of the premises was retained as a Children's Home after the closure of the school. After it was sold, FORTESCUE HOUSE (HANWORTH) was bought and this was used, between 1975 and 1983, as a Children's Home.

THE *ARETHUSA* VENTURE CENTRE   1974 - present
Developed on the shore base at Lower Upnor, near Rochester, after the sale of the old *Arethusa* (*Peking*), as an activity, education and environmental studies Centre. Providing excellent facilities, including a recently built new climbing wall, and accommodation for groups of children, young people and individuals.

ARETHUSA KETCH   1975 - present
Since 1975, and a second ketch with the same name since 1982, providing challenging ocean going sailing for groups of disadvantaged children and young people.

PUTNEY ADOLESCENT HOSTEL   1979 - 1995
A Hostel providing residential care for young people and preparing them for independent living. The care provided was in two stages; the first was at 24 Dealtry Road, Putney. The second was at 26 Dealtry Road until 1990 when this was sold and replaced by 213 Wimbledon Park Road, Southfields, which remains as one of the Society's Adolescent Units. 24 Dealtry Road was closed in 1995 and replaced by Arabella House in Roehampton in 1996.

AFTERCARE AND HOUSING SERVICE   1979 - present
Initially set up to provide a third stage of support to young people once they had left the Putney Hostel and were living independently in the Community. Later the service was also provided to those who had left Esher House. Currently three social workers provide this service.

CENTREPOINT HOUSE   1976 - 1982
The property, at 14 Sinclair Road, Olympia, was purchased by the Society and used as
semi-independent accommodation for young homeless people moving out of the
Centrepoint Night Shelter. Run by Centrepoint, Soho, in association with the Society,
it was sold to the Threshold Housing Association and is still used by Centrepoint.

THE JOHN COLLET BARGE   1979 - 1984
A 70 foot motor barge, moored at Odessa Wharf on the river Thames, and used as a
floating school for children from Southwark Schools who were experiencing difficulties
in mainstream education. The goal, after a period of remedial work, was always for the
children to return to their school.

SIR ALAN HERBERT BARGE   1980 - 1985
A Thames sailing barge used to take groups coastal sailing and exploring around the
waters and estuaries of the East Coast. Children and young people from schools, clubs,
homes and those on court orders made regular use of this project.

MacANDREW HOUSE FAMILY CENTRE   1980 - 1987
A Centre providing guidance and support to families where young children were "at
risk" - helping vulnerable families to stay together. Families would attend 3 or 4 times
a week depending on their needs. The service provided was preventive in that it tried
to avoid children being taken into care.

88 WOLFINGTON ROAD, WEST NORWOOD   1983 - present
A shared house for vulnerable young people in which they can, with support, prepare
for successful independent living. Mainly used by the young single homeless. The House
is owned by the South London Family Housing Association and managed by the Society.

THE IPSWICH YOUTH JUSTICE CENTRE   1985 - 1995
Initially established by the Society, with government funding, as an alternative to
Custody Centre for Young Offenders. When government funding ceased in 1988 the
Society entered into a partnership with Suffolk County Council and developed it into
a Youth Justice Centre. The Centre is now managed by Suffolk County Council.

48/50 RITHERDON ROAD, TOOTING   1991 - present
These properties were bought by the Society to provide individual self contained bed-
sit accommodation to young people who are homeless or those leaving care. It offers
them a period of stability and the chance to develop their independent living skills.

NIGHTINGALE COTTAGE, FOREST HILL, LONDON   1992 - present
A cottage bequeathed to the Society and now providing accommodation for a small number of residents on the recommendation of the Aftercare Department.

IPSWICH YOUNG PERSONS SUPPORT TEAM   1992 - present
Set up by the Society, with government funding, to provide guidance and support to vulnerable young people in Ipswich and the surrounding towns. As well as providing individual support packages, it aims to extend the range of accommodation options for young people in the private, voluntary, and statutory sectors. The staff team also helps young people leaving care under an agreement with Suffolk County Council and manages a house in Ipswich and one in Felixstowe which provide accommodation and support to eight young people.

LONDON BOROUGH OF WANDSWORTH   1994 - present
Under a partnership arrangement, the management of residential homes for adolescents and children on behalf of the London Borough of Wandsworth. There are currently five homes in South West London and one in Crawley, West Sussex.

ARABELLA HOUSE, ROEHAMPTON   1996 - present
Purchased in 1996 to replace the Putney Adolescent Hostel. An independent registered home for adolescents accepting referrals from a variety of Local Authorities.

ARETHUSA SAILING PROJECT   1996 - present
Located in Chatham Dockyard, an RYA registered sailing school and a valuable extension to the work of the Arethusa Venture Centre.

A concert party at Bisley School in 1948. Casting was always something of a problem for this all-boys school and, for this particular sketch, the acting talent of these four young boys was severely tested. The little 'girl' on the right is Paul Bolas. After Bisley School and a career in the Royal Navy, where he became a Commander, he was appointed as the Society's Finance Director in 1992.

Mary Ann Davis Jane Dennott Ann Reynolds Amy Emma Gabe Elizabeth Lighton Lydia Davis Elizabeth Maria Cheevar Sarah Amelia Carter Eliza Clements Hannah Tupt

The Secretary reported that Jeremiah Sullivan and William Gibbs left the Refuge on the January for Liverpool to embark on board the ship for Queensland the passage money being paid by Mrs Chesnell

The following sums for Salaries being due were ordered to be paid viz

	£	s	d
Mr Wood	77	18	8
Mrs Edmond	9	19	
Miss Dickson	15	5	4
Miss Gurney	8	19	
Miss Wood	1	13	4
Mr Warren	3	6	8
Mr Harvey	8	2	6
Mrs Golding	4	7	-

Beastly
BATH

Beastly BATH

Irreverent quotes about Bath from its greatest visitors

Gideon Kibblewhite & Kate McDonnell
Illustrated by Perry Harris

The History Press

First published 2014

The History Press
The Mill, Brimscombe Port
Stroud, Gloucestershire, GL5 2QG
www.thehistorypress.co.uk

British Library Cataloguing in Publication Data.
A catalogue record for this book is available from the British Library.

ISBN 978 0 7509 5968 1

Typesetting and origination by The History Press
Printed in India

Contents

THE AUTHORS

Introducing the Humble Authors of this Guide to the Complaints of Great Personages about the City of Bath and its Environs, Waters and People ...

Miss Kate McDonnell
Editor and Designer

Typesetter and artisan Miss Kate McDonnell arrived in Bath as a young Woman from The North. In Bath, she has grown in fame promoting the City to Visitors with her Picturesque Journals, Elaborate Maps and Badges with Amusing Slogans. After a Study of the Local Dialect, she now understands Bath to be "Gurt Lush".

Mr Gideon Kibblewhite
Writer and Compiler

Scandalous Scholar, Wit and Raconteur Mister Gideon Kibblewhite has been the Gossip of the Gin Palaces of Bath ever since his arrival in the City from darkest Wiltshire. It has been his Mission to devote his Life to the Study of Intrigue, Dandyism, Gambling and other Pursuits such as the City affords.

Mr Perry Harris
Illustrator

Famed Portrait and Landscape Cartoonist Mister Perry Harris studied under the Greats at Salisbury. He then packed his brushes and sought his fortune at Bath, where Fashionable Society patronised him. Mr. Harris, has since made his name producing artistic Works satirising the City's Folk, Events and Institutions.

INTRODUCTION

Who can ever be tired of Bath?

ath. Such a beautiful city. Famed throughout the world for being so lovely … the gushing hot waters, the magnificent Georgian architecture, the fantastic shopping – it all moved Jane Austen's Catherine Morland to declare excitedly, "Oh! Who can ever be tired of Bath?"

Well, the answer to that question is actually quite a lot of people down the centuries. And quite a lot of famous people too.

Though it has been a major tourist attraction for over 2,000 years, often during Bath's history its buildings, baths and people have left visitors distinctly underwhelmed – and sometimes appalled.

Even at the height of Bath's Georgian heyday, many people rode off from the city with hardly a single good word to say about it, having been variously jostled, insulted, swindled, stewed, frozen, married for money or simply bored to the brink of madness.

In this collection of beautifully jaundiced quotes, grumps from Tudor to modern times queue up to reveal why they simply couldn't bear the place …

THE CITY

Mean Streets ...

You might think that if there was anything about Bath that could be immune to criticism it would be its architecture. But no! Not a bit of it!

A few of the gripes that you will read about in this chapter predate the Georgian city – but even Palladian magnificence has failed to move some peevish visitors.

As for complaints about hills, overcrowded thoroughfares, constant building work, rubbish and a general, terrible stench ... well, it doesn't add up to a happy postcard!

11

She persisted in a very determined, though very silent disinclination for Bath; caught the first dim view of the extensive buildings, smoking in rain, without any wish of seeing them better.

Jane Austen, *Persuasion*, 1817

I hate Bath. There is a stupid sameness, notwithstanding the beauties of its buildings.

Benjamin Robert Haydon, *diary,* 1809

The town is entirely built of stone, but the streets narrow, uneven and unpleasant.

John Evelyn, *memoirs,* 1654

The small compass of the city has made the inhabitants crowd up the streets to an unseemly and inconvenient narrowness.

William Stukeley, *Itinerarium Curiosum,* 1724

They build upon the pinnacle of hills that only
to look up to breaks one's neck, and they build in
the deepest depths below, which only to look down
upon makes one giddy.

Fanny Burney, *letter,* 1791

Mountains are very good frames to a prospect, but
here they run against one's nose, nor can one stir out
of the town without clambering.

Horace Walpole, *letter,* 1766

Anne, though dreading the possible heats of
September in all the white glare of Bath, and grieving
to forego all the influence so sweet and so sad of the
autumnal months in the country, did not think that,
everything considered, she wished to remain.

Jane Austen, *Persuasion,* 1817

Park Street was very much like the perpendicular streets a man sees in a dream, which he cannot get up for the life of him.

Charles Dickens, *The Pickwick Papers,* 1836

In short, it is a delightful place enough, when you are in it, but a dreadful one to come at, down high hills, in some places like precipices … There are few pleasant walks out of the town, or even rides, without clambering much to Landsdown-hill, or that called Clarton-down.

William Stukeley, *Itinerarium Curiosum,* 1724

Very few people care to keep coaches here. And the hill up to Lansdown, particularly, is so steep that the late Queen Anne was extremely frightened in going up: her coachman stopping to give the horses breath, and the coach wanting a dragstaff, it ran back in spite of all the coachman's skill; the horses not being brought to strain the harness again, or pull together for a good while, and the coach putting the guards behind in great confusion: at last some of the servants, setting their heads and shoulders to the wheels, stopped them by mere force.

William Stukeley, *Itinerarium Curiosum,* 1724

They seem seldom to attempt levelling the ground for the sake of uniformity, but, very contentedly, when they have raised one house on the spot where it could stand most conveniently, they raise the next on the nearest and steepest acclivity, so precisely above it, that from the garret of one, you mount into the kitchen of the other.

Fanny Burney, *letter,* 1791

Nor can you make a visit from one street to another, without such an ascent, or such a declivity, that you must have the wheel of a carriage locked to go from neighbour to neighbour.

Fanny Burney, *letter,* 1791

Bath built of white stone, in trim streets, enclosed amid gnarled beautifully green and feathered hills, looked altogether princely, after these poor brick towns, — like an ancient decayed Prince, for it was smoke-soiled, dingy and lonely-looking…

Thomas Carlyle, *letter*, 1843

More like a prison than a place of diversion, scarce gives the company room to converse out of the smell of their own excrements, and where the very city itself may be said to stink like a general common-shore.

Daniel Defoe, *Tour Through the Whole Island of Great Britain*, 1724

The level of the city is risen to the top of the first walls, through the negligence of the magistracy, who, in this, and all other great towns, connive with the servants throwing dirt and ashes into the streets.

William Stukeley, *Itinerarium Curiosum*, 1724

The streets and public ways of the city were become like so many dunghills, slaughter-houses, and pig-sties; for soil of all sorts, and even carrion, was cast and laid in the streets, and the pigs turned out by day to feed and rout among it; butchers killed and dressed their cattle at their own doors; people washed every kind of thing they had to make clean at the common conduits in the open streets; and nothing was more common than small racks and mangers at almost every door for the baiting of horses.

John Wood, *Essay Towards a Description of Bath,* 2nd Edition, 1765

Their common sewer, which before stood in an ill place, stands now in no place, for they have not any at all.

Sir John Harington, *letter,* 1591

Our views on G. P. [Green Park] Buildings seem all at an end; the observation of the damps still remaining in the offices of a house which has been only vacated a week, with reports of discontented families and putrid fevers, has given the coup de grace. We have now nothing in view. When you arrive, we will at least have the pleasure of examining some of these putrefying houses again; they are so very desirable in size and situation, that there is some satisfaction in spending ten minutes within them.

Jane Austen, *letter,* 1801

It is plain that Bath has outgrown its beauty.

Robert Southey, *Letters From England,* 1808

Even the streets round the Pump Room [they] are pulling down for new edifices, and you can only drink from their choice stream by wading through their choice mud.

Fanny Burney, *letter,* 1791

The city is so filled with workmen, dust and lime, that you really want two pair of eyes to walk about in it – one for being put out, and the other to see with afterwards.

Fanny Burney, *letter,* 1791

Carried by mistake to a wrong party – which, I conclude, happens always, every house in every street being a facsimile of its neighbour.

James Beresford, *The Miseries of Human Life,* 1806

One sees new houses starting up in every outlet and every corner of Bath; contrived without judgment, executed without solidity, and stuck together with so little regard to plan and propriety, that the different lines of the new rows and buildings interfere with, and intersect one another in every different angle of conjunction. They look like the wreck of streets and squares disjointed by an earthquake.

Tobias Smollett, *The Expedition of Humphry Clinker,* 1771

Bath is extremely altered since I last visited it. Its circumference is perhaps trebled; its buildings are so unfinished, so spread, so everywhere beginning and nowhere ending, that it looks rather like a space of ground lately fixed upon for erecting a town, than a town itself, of so many years' duration.

Fanny Burney, *letter,* 1791

Goodbye to old Bath.
We who loved you are sorry
They've carted you off
by developer's lorry.

John Betjeman, *The Sack of Bath,* 1973

The cathedral, or abbey, at Bath is glaring and crowded with modern tablet-monuments.

Horace Walpole, *letter,* 1766

The cathedral church is small but well lighted. There are abundance of little monuments in it of people who come there for their health, but meet with their death.

John Macky, *A Journey Through England,* 1722

These walls, adorned with monument and bust,
Show how Bath waters serve to lay the dust.

Dr Henry Harington, *epigram, his own, on his tomb in Bath Abbey,* 1727-1816

No ancient iconoclast, or modern Calvinist, could have looked on the outside of the abbey church with more horror than the image of Jacob's Ladder, with all its angels, presented to my infant eye.

Sir Walter Scott, *memoir,* 1808

The abbey-church is a venerable pile, and has many monuments in it. But the principal front is almost blasphemously decorated, if it may be call'd decorated, with the figures of God the Father, and saints and angels, the work of superstition.

William Stukeley, *Itinerarium Curiosum*, 1724

Here a good organ; but a vain, pragmatical fellow preached a ridiculous, affected sermon, that made me angry.

Samuel Pepys, *diary*, 1668

It must be owned, indeed, that here, in Milsom Street, we have a precarious and scanty supply from the hill; which is collected in an open basin in the Circus, liable to be defiled with dead dogs, cats, rats, and every species of nastiness, which the rascally populace may throw into it, from mere wantonness and brutality.

Tobias Smollett, *The Expedition of Humphry Clinker,* 1771

Bath is like a Frenchman's shirt: the ruffle is very fine but the body is very coarse.

Charles Dibdin, *Musical Tour through England,* 1788

The nozzle of the Circus – bellows blowing you into the Crescent.

James Beresford, *The Miseries of Human Life,* 1806

A pretty bauble, contrived for show.

Tobias Smollett, on the Circus, *The Expedition of Humphry Clinker,* 1771

THE WATERS

Water, Water, Everywhere …

Bath's piping hot springs are the very reason for the city's existence, the reason the Romans founded Aquae Sulis some 2,000 years ago.

During that time, however, the bathing facilities haven't always been what you would call posh. Go back a couple of centuries and there were none of the "hot stones massages" and "Vichy rainforest showers" you can get at today's modern spa. Oh no!

Read on for grumbles about freezing rumps, foul reeks, clinging scum, floating dandruff, leprous frolicking, dodgy doctors, steamy nakedness, hurled dogs and much more …

As for the colour of the water of all the baths, it is most like to deep blue, and reeks much after the manner of a seething pot, commonly yielding somewhat of a sulphurous taste, and very unpleasant savour.

John Leland, *Itinerary, c.* 1542

It's very hot and tastes like the water that boils eggs, has such a smell …

Celia Fiennes, *journal,* 1687

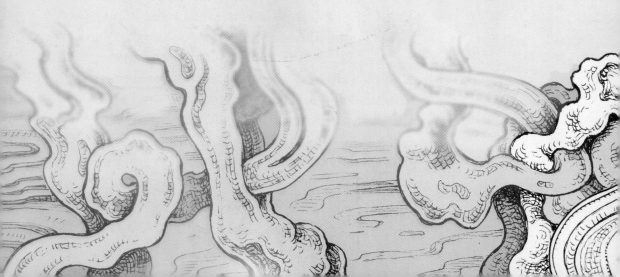

"Have you drank the waters, Mr. Weller?" inquired his companion, as they walked towards High Street.

"Once," replied Sam.

"What did you think of 'em, Sir?"

"I thought they was particklery unpleasant," replied Sam.

"Ah," said Mr. John Smauker, "you disliked the killibeate taste, perhaps?"

"I don't know much about that 'ere," said Sam. "I thought they'd a wery strong flavour o' warm flat irons."

Charles Dickens, *The Pickwick Papers*, 1836

I cannot but laugh to think of what a blessed pickle you are in at the Bath, where such crowds of you stew in so little a pipkin; where you broil upon the earth, parboil in the water, and breathe the composition of gunpowder.

Thomas Brown, *Collection of Miscellany Poems, Letters, etc.,* 1699

The baths I can compare to nothing but the boilers in Fleet Lane or Old Bedlam, for they have a reeking steam all the year.

Ned Ward, *A Step to the Bath, London Spy,* 1700

It is worthily called the Hot Bath, for at first coming into men think it would scald their flesh, and loose it from the bone.

William Harrison, *Description of England,* 1577

Strange to see, when women and men herein, that live all the season in these waters, that cannot but be parboiled, and look like the creatures of the bath!

Samuel Pepys, *diary,* 1668

Methinks it cannot be clean to go so many bodies together in the same water.

Samuel Pepys, *diary,* 1668

You cannot conceive what a number of ladies
Were washed in the water the same as our maid is.

Christopher Anstey, *The New Bath Guide,* 1766

So while little Tabby was washing her rump
The ladies kept drinking it out of the pump.

Christopher Anstey, *The New Bath Guide,* 1766

Some may be apprehensive of being tainted
with infectious distempers; or disgusted with the
nauseating appearances of the filth, which, being
washed from the bodies of the patients, is left
sticking to the sides of the place.

Tobias Smollett, *Essay on the External Use of Water*, 1752

If they go in while this scum is on it gives
them the Bath mantle, as they call it,
makes them break out into heat and pimples.

Celia Fiennes, *journal*, 1687

When I was at these baths with a certain man diseased with gout, I went into them myself with my patient, and brought forth slime, mud, bones and stones which altogether smelled evidently of brimstone.

William Turner, *A Book of the Natures & Properties of the Baths of England*, 1562

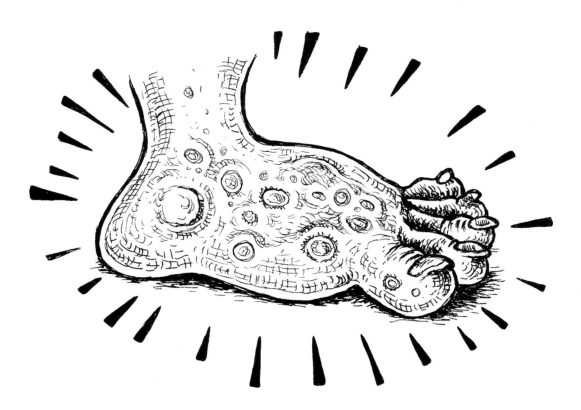

Diseased persons of all ages, sexes, and conditions are promiscuously admitted into an open bath which affords little or no shelter from the inclemencies of the weather.

Tobias Smollett, *Essay on the External Use of Water,* 1752

Like cells for the dead; and when I surveyed them they seemed more fit to fill the bathers with the horrors of death than to raise their ideas of the efficacy of the hot waters.

John Wood, *Essay Towards a Description of Bath,* 2nd Edition, 1765

This bath is much frequented of people diseased with leprosy, pox, scabies and great aches.

John Leland, on the Cross Bath, *Itinerary, c.* 1542

Upon inquiry, I find that the old Roman baths of this quarter were found covered by an old burying ground belonging to the Abbey; through which, in all probability, the water drains in its passage; so that as we drink the decoction of the living bodies at the Pump-room, we swallow the strainings of rotten bones and carcasses at the private bath – I vow to God, the very idea turns my stomach!

Tobias Smollett, *The Expedition of Humphry Clinker,* 1771

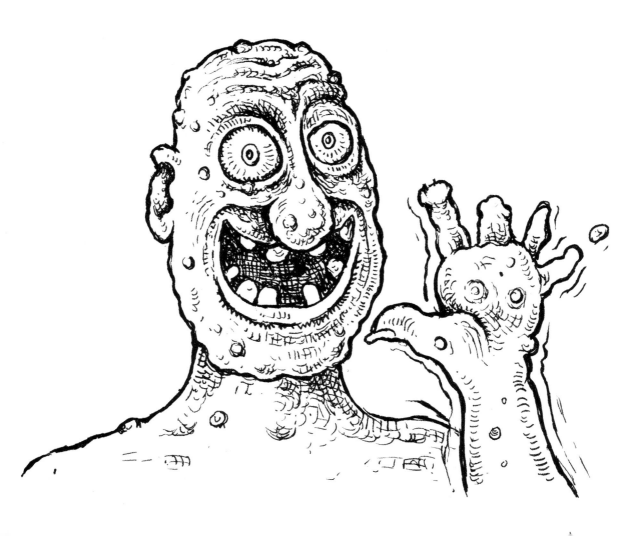

The first object that saluted my eye, was a child full of scrophulous ulcers, carried in the arms of one of the guides, under the very noses of the bathers. I was so shocked at the sight that I retired immediately with indignation and disgust. Suppose the matter of those ulcers, floating on the water, comes in contact with my skin, when the pores are all open, I would ask you what must be the consequence? Good Heaven, the very thought makes my blood run cold!

Tobias Smollett, *The Expedition of Humphry Clinker,* 1771

There are also people in the bath who are ready with knives, scissors etc., to cut people's corns, warts and nails, to earn some money.

William Schellinks, *journal,* 1662

I am now as much afraid of drinking as of bathing; for after a long conversation with the Doctor about the construction of the pump and the cistern, it is very far from being clear with me that the patients in the Pump-room don't swallow the scourings of the bathers. I can't help suspecting that there is, or may be, some regurgitation from the bath into the cistern of the pump. In that case, what a delicate beverage is every day quaffed by the drinkers, medicated with the sweat and dirt, and dandruff, and the abominable discharges of various kinds, from twenty different diseased bodies, parboiling in the kettle below.

Tobias Smollett, *The Expedition of Humphry Clinker,* 1771

The baths were like so many bear-gardens, and modesty was entirely shut out of them; people of both sexes bathing by day and night naked; and dogs, cats, and pigs, even human creatures, were hurled over the rails into the water, while people were bathing in it.

John Wood, *Towards a Description of Bath*, 2nd Edition, 1765

Men and women bathing together, as they do at Bath, is an instance of barbarity not paralleled in any part of the world.

Samuel Johnson, quoted by James Boswell in *The Life of Samuel Johnson*, 1791

The king, looking into the baths, saw in them men wholly naked with every garment cast off. At which he was displeased, and went away quickly, abhorring such nudity as a great offence, and not unmindful of that sentence of Francis Petrarch "the nakedness of a beast is in men unpleasing, but the decency of raiment makes for modesty".

John Blacman, *Compilation of the Meekness & Good Life of King Henry VI, c. 1449*

A report has reached the ears of the bishop that the heavenly gift of warm and healing waters with which the city of Bath has been endowed from of old is turned into an abuse by the shamelessness and uncleanliness of the people of that city, insomuch that when any persons whether male or female go to the said waters to bathe and recover their health, and through modesty and shame try to cover their privy parts, the men with drawers and the women with smocks, they, the said people, by what they say is an established custom of the city, barbarously and shamelessly strip them of their said garments and reveal to them to the gaze of bystanders.

Thomas Bekynton, *letter,* 1449

Here is performed all the wanton dalliances imaginable: celebrated beauties, panting breasts, and curious shapes almost exposed to public view; languishing eyes, darting killing glances, tempting amorous postures, attended by soft music, enough to provoke a vestal to forbidden pleasure, captivate a saint, and charm a Jove.

Ned Ward, *A Step to the Bath, London Spy,* 1700

In one corner was an old fornicator hanging by the rings, loaded with a rotten humidity. Hard by him was a buxom dame, cleaning her nunquam satis from mercurial dregs, and the remains of Roman vitriol. Another, half cover'd with sear-cloth, had more sores than Lazarus, doing penance for the sins of her youth.

Ned Ward, *A Step to the Bath, London Spy,* 1700

The physicians were not more busy in destroying old bodies than the young fellows in producing new ones.

Richard Steele, *The Guardian*, 1713

They chiefly came to feel, and to be felt.

Sir John Harington, *Epigrams*, 1618

These waters have a wonderful influence on barren ladies, who often prove with child even in their husbands' absence.

John Macky, *A Journey Through England*, 1722

The dowager Duchess of Norfolk bathes, and being very tall she had like to have drowned a few woman in the Cross Bath, for she ordered it to be filled till it reached her chin, and so all those who were below her stature, as well as her rank, were forced to come out or drown.

Elizabeth Montagu, *letter,* 1740

The waters do not benefit me so much as at first; the pains in my stomach return almost every morning, but do not seem the least allied to the gout. This decrease of their virtue is not near so great a disappointment to me as you might imagine; for I am so childish as not to think health itself a compensation for passing my time very disagreeably.

Horace Walpole, *letter,* 1766

But what is surprising,
no Mortal e'er view'd

Any one of the Physical
Gentlemen stewed;

Since the Day that King Bladud
first found out the Bogs

And thought them so good
for himself and his Hogs,

Not one of the Faculty
ever has try'd

These excellent Waters to
cure his own Hide

Christopher Anstey, *The New Bath Guide,* 1766

After all, they are carried to their lodgings, while their pores are open to the effects of the bath, in paultry chairs made of slight cross bars of wood, fastened together with girth web, covered with bays, and, for the most part destitute of lining: these machines, by standing in the streets till called for, are often rendered so damp by the weather, that bathers cannot use them without imminent hazard of their lives.

Tobias Smollett, *Essay on the External Use of Water,* 1752

THE COMPANY

Hell is
Other People ...

William Makepeace Thackeray once said of Bath that "all history went and bathed and drank there".
Didn't they just!

Since Roman times the city has been a place of pilgrimage for the sick, and during the Georgian era it became – in nothing short of a social revolution – a spa where the nobility rubbed shoulders with people from other classes.

Which is all fine and dandy, but the trouble with life in a social melting pot is, well, everyone else.

Cue scoundrels, bores, fops and snobs and a host of other beastly types …

In Bath they live in fine houses and are poor;
and in Bristol in shabby ones and are rich.

Charles Dibdin, *Musical Tour Through England,* 1788

Such is the composition of what is called the
fashionable company at Bath; where a very
inconsiderable proportion of genteel people are lost
in a mob of impudent plebeians, who have neither
understanding nor judgment, nor the least idea of
propriety and decorum; and seem to enjoy nothing so
much as an opportunity of insulting their betters.

Tobias Smollett, *The Expedition of Humphry Clinker,* 1771

Every upstart of fortune, harnessed to the trappings of the mode, presents himself at Bath ... men of low birth and no breeding ... all of them hurry to Bath, because here, without any further qualification, they can mingle with the princes and nobles of the land. Even the wives and daughters of low tradesmen, who, like shovel-nosed sharks, prey upon the blubber of those uncouth whales of fortune, are infected with the same rage of displaying their importance; and the slightest indisposition serves them for a pretext to insist upon being conveyed to Bath, where they may hobble country-dances and coalitions among lordlings, squires, counsellors, and clergy.

Tobias Smollett, *The Expedition of Humphry Clinker,* 1771

There is a very great narrowness of spirit in most of the inhabitants at Bath.

William Stukeley, *Itinerarium Curiosum,* 1724

Everything that passes here is known on the walks, and the characters of persons.

John Macky, *A Journey Through England,* 1722

I wish your Grace would consider Bath water is not Helicon, and affords no inspiration; and that there is no place where someone stands in greater need of something to enliven the brain.

Elizabeth Montagu, *letter*, 1740

The great metropolis of that second class gentility with which watering places are chiefly populated.

Nathaniel Hawthorne, *Our Old Home*, 1863

Apropos of dissipation, this place I take to be the seat of it, from morning till night, breakfasting, dancing, gaming, sauntering, crowds of men and women looking busy for want of something to do.

Philip Dormer Stanhope, *letter,* 1770

The taverns do not much improve, for it is a place of universal sobriety. To be drunk at Bath is as scandalous as mad.

John Macky, *A Journey Through England,* 1722

Bath being full, the company, and the sixpences for tea, poured in, in shoals.

Charles Dickens, *The Pickwick Papers,* 1836

Bath is a sort of great monastery, inhabited by single people, particularly superannuated females. No trade, no manufactures, no occupations of any sort, except that of killing time, the most laborious of all. Half of the inhabitants do nothing, the other half supply them with nothings.

Louis Simond, *Journal of a Tour and Residence in Great Britain,* 1815

If it were theatre night, perhaps they met at the theatre; if it were assembly night, they met at the rooms; and if it were neither, they met the next day. A very pleasant routine, with perhaps a slight tinge of sameness.

Charles Dickens, *The Pickwick Papers,* 1836

MEMENTO MORI

BATH'S 'Dreadful Viſitation:

Bills of Mortality

For this Preſent Year:

Beginning the 27th of December 1664, and
ending the 19th of December following:

As alſo, The GENERAL or whole years BILL:

According to the Report made to the
KING'S Moſt Excellent Majeſty.

By the Company of Pariſh-Clerks of Bath.

Bath:
Printed and are to be ſold by D. Dixon living in Walcot diſtrict.
Printer to the ſaid Company 1665.

I should be glad to send you some news, but all the news of the place would be like the Bills of Mortality, palsy, four; gout, six; fever, one, &c. &c.

Elizabeth Montagu, *letter,* 1740

The place looks to me like a cemetery which the dead have succeeded in rising and taking. Having built streets of their old gravestones, they wander about scantily trying to "look alive". A dead failure.

Charles Dickens, *letter,* 1869

It is also the Canaan of Physicians; for it abounds with wealthy patients, many of whom will have any disease the doctor will be pleased to find out for them; but even Canaan may be overstocked, and, it seems, more of Death's advanced guard have assembled here than can find milk and honey.

Robert Southey, *Letters From England,* 1808

The morning after I arrived, I went to the Ladies' Coffee House, where I heard nothing but the rheumatism of the shoulder, the sciatica of the hip, and the gout of the toe. I began to fancy myself in the hospital or infirmary, I never saw such an assembly of disorders. I dare say Gay wrote his fable of the Court of Death from this place.

Elizabeth Montagu, *letter,* 1740

She was so amazingly tired, it was so odious to parade about the Pump Room.

Jane Austen, *Northanger Abbey,* 1817

Every creature in Bath, except himself, was to be seen in the room at different periods of the fashionable hours; crowds of people were every moment passing in and out, up the steps and down; people whom nobody cared about, and nobody wanted to see; and he only was absent.

Jane Austen, *Northanger Abbey,* 1817

There is another pump room, into which infirm ladies and gentlemen are wheeled, in such an astonishing variety of chairs and chaises, that any adventurous individual who goes in with the regular number of toes, is in imminent danger of coming out without them.

Charles Dickens, *The Pickwick Papers,* 1836

As soon as divine service was over, the Thorpes and Allens eagerly joined each other; and after staying long enough in the pump-room to discover that the crowd was insupportable, and that there was not a genteel face to be seen, which everybody discovers every Sunday throughout the season, they hastened away to the Crescent, to breathe the fresh air of better company.

Jane Austen, *Northanger Abbey,* 1817

Yesterday morning, at the Pump Room, I saw a broken-winded Wapping landlady squeeze through a circle of peers to salute her brandy-merchant, who stood by the window, propped upon crutches; and a paralytic attorney of Shoe-lane, in shuffling up to the bar, kicked the shins of the chancellor of England, while his lordship, in a cut bob, drank a glass of water at the pump.

Tobias Smollett, *The Expedition of Humphry Clinker,* 1771

Crowded like a Welsh fair.

Tobias Smollett, *The Expedition of Humphry Clinker,* 1771

All my comfort is, that I lodge close to the Cross Bath, by which means I avoid the Pump Room and all its works.

Horace Walpole, *letter,* 1766

Made my escape (if such it could be called) to a dress-ball – alias a public parade of finery, dullness, and etiquette.

James Beresford, *The Miseries of Human Life*, 1806

The season was full, the room crowded, and the two ladies squeezed in as well as they could. As for Mr Allen, he repaired directly to the card-room, and left them to enjoy a mob by themselves.

Jane Austen, *Northanger Abbey*, 1817

Seated on some of the back benches, where they had already taken up their positions for the evening, were diverse unmarried ladies past their grand climacteric, who, not dancing because there were no partners for them, and not playing cards lest they should be set down as irretrievably single, were in the favourable situation of being able to abuse everybody without reflecting on themselves. In short, they could abuse everybody, because everybody was there.

Charles Dickens, *The Pickwick Papers,* 1836

It was, indeed, a compound of villainous smells, in which the most violent stinks, and the most powerful perfumes, contended for the mastery. Imagine to yourself a high exalted essence of mingled odours, arising from putrid gums, imposthumated lungs, sour flatulencies, rank armpits, sweating feet, running sores and issues, plasters, ointments, and embrocations, hungry-water, spirit of lavender, assafoetida drops, musk, hartshorn, and sal volatile; besides a thousand frowzy steams, which I could not analyse. Such, O Dick! is the fragrant ether we breathe in the polite assemblies of Bath.

Tobias Smollett, *The Expedition of Humphry Clinker,* 1771

Two ladies of quality quarreled in the ballroom. The rest of the company took part, some on one side, some on the other; Beau Nash was gone, and they stood in no awe of his successor: they became outrageous, a real battle-royal took place, and the floor was strewn with caps, lappets, curls and cushions, diamond pins and pearls.

Robert Southey, *Letters From England,* 1808

I was pressed by a party of restless Misses, two or three times in the course of the night, to take "the grand tour" with them; when I had already seen ten times more than I liked, from my own (comparatively) quiet corner.

James Beresford, *The Miseries of Human Life,* 1806

The pump house was without any director, the chairmen permitted no gentlemen or ladies to walk home by night without insulting them.

Oliver Goldsmith, *The Life of Richard Nash,* 1762

In the heaviest storm that ever fell – gave up one chair to this Lady, because she was old; another to that, because she was young; a third to one man, because he was weak, and ought to have it; and a fourth to another man, because he was strong, and would have it.

James Beresford, *The Miseries of Human Life,* 1806

"Your profession is not an exciting one?"
I suggested to a veteran chairman.
He considered for some time
and replied: "No."

H. V. Morton, *In Search of England,* 1927

Five months of the year 'tis populous as London, the other seven as desolate as a wilderness.

Ned Ward, *A Step to the Bath, London Spy,* 1700

Not a soul is seen in this place, but a few broken-winded parsons, waddling like so many crows along the North Parade.

Tobias Smollett, *The Expedition of Humphry Clinker,* 1771

There certainly were a dreadful multitude of ugly women in Bath; and as for the men! they were infinitely worse. Such scarecrows as the streets were full of! It was evident how little the women were used to the sight of anything tolerable, by the effect which a man of decent appearance produced.

Jane Austen, *Persuasion*, 1817

The worst of Bath was, the number of its plain women. He did not mean to say that there were no pretty women, but the number of the plain was out of all proportion. He had frequently observed, as he walked, that one handsome face would be followed by thirty, or five and thirty frights; and once, as he had stood in a shop on Bond Street, he had counted eighty-seven women go by, one after another, without there being a tolerable face among them.

Jane Austen, *Persuasion,* 1817

I was not now at Redriff, where, if I had set myself tolerably up, some honest sea captain or other might have talked with me upon the honourable terms of matrimony; but I was at the Bath, where men find a mistress sometimes, but very rarely look for a wife.

Daniel Defoe, *Moll Flanders,* 1722

The recommendations of a public lodging and boarding-house – presenting, first, the wear and tear of your nerves from hearing "Mr. (such a one's) Servant!" bawled through your ears from the bottom of the stairs at every half-minute, from 7 in the morning till 12 at night; – 2. the outer door of the house at all times hospitably left wide open; – 3. the state of the stairs, incessantly trodden by the unscraped feet of half the town; – 4. the motley association, at the general dinner-table, of Irish captains, English gamesters, French prisoners, Scotch physicians, &c. &c.

James Beresford, *The Miseries of Human Life,* 1806

At the only inn I saw at Bath they were extravagantly dear and intolerably impudent.

Charles Dibdin, *Musical Tour Through England,* 1788

It is a fine place for gamblers, and for that species of men called fortune hunters, a race of swindlers of the worst kind, who are happily unknown in Spain. They make it their business to get a wife of fortune, having none themselves: age, ugliness, and even idiocy, being no objections.

Robert Southey, *Letters From England,* 1808

Lounging near the doors, and in remote corners, were various knots of silly young men, displaying various varieties of puppyism and stupidity; and happily thinking themselves the objects of general admiration.

Charles Dickens, *The Pickwick Papers,* 1836

Scandal must therefore have fixed her throne at Bath, preferable to any other part of the kingdom.

Oliver Goldsmith, *The Life of Richard Nash,* 1762

The Bath produces nothing new but intrigues, the reading of which will not become the gravity of a Commissioner of Accounts, and especially so modest a one as yourself.

William Savile, *letter,* 1693

I hear you have a mint at the Bath for scandal, as we have here for money.

Thomas Brown, *Collection of Miscellany Poems, Letters, etc.,* 1699

Can the Gospel have a place where Satan's throne is?

John Wesley, *journal,* 1767

Satan took it ill to be attacked in his headquarters, that Sodom of our land, Bath.

Charles Wesley, *journal,* 1741

By day, even on Sundays, and within a stone's throw of St. James's Church, dissolute women, half-dressed, would stand in groups, soliciting passers-by. At night, riots, fighting and piano playing disturbed the whole neighbourhood. Respectable people were ashamed to live in or pass through such a district …

Rev. W. J. Bolton, *pamphlet,* 1883

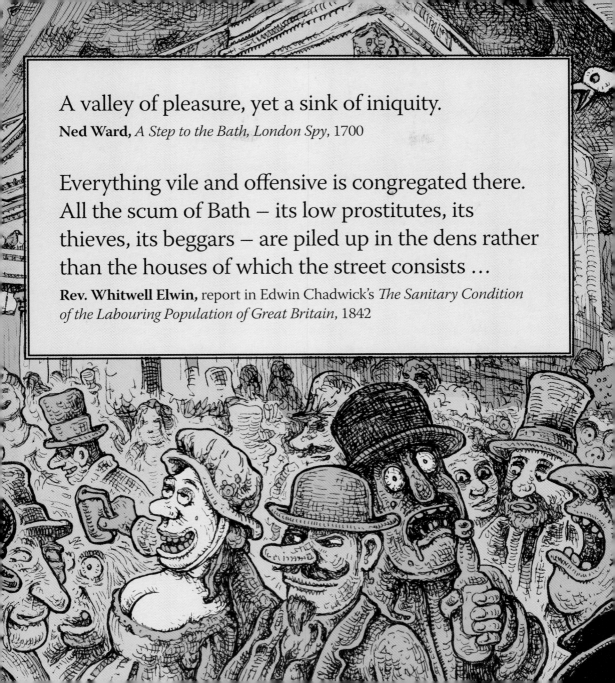

A valley of pleasure, yet a sink of iniquity.

Ned Ward, *A Step to the Bath, London Spy*, 1700

Everything vile and offensive is congregated there. All the scum of Bath – its low prostitutes, its thieves, its beggars – are piled up in the dens rather than the houses of which the street consists …

Rev. Whitwell Elwin, report in Edwin Chadwick's *The Sanitary Condition of the Labouring Population of Great Britain*, 1842

THE VERDICT

Goodbye and Good Riddance ...

The "holiday from hell" is no modern phenomenon. Indeed, some of our historic grumps had such a miserable time in Bath that they never forgave the city.

As you enjoy today's Bath, spare a thought for visitors of yore, who discovered a place whose streets were paved not with glistening gold but fetid brown; a city whose "legendary baths" – where people from your worst nightmares splashed – left you dirtier than you were to begin with.

A city that saw the hardiest of travellers leap thankfully into the next carriage home …

The sulphurous pit.

Alexander Pope, *letter,* 1739

This stewpan of idleness and insignificance.

Tobias Smollett, *The Expedition of Humphry Clinker,* 1771

I am sure you had time enough at Bath, for it has few amusements for the wise.

Elizabeth Montagu, *letter,* 1741

One of the most disagreeable places in the world.

Sydney Smith, *letter,* 1820

It will be two years tomorrow since we left Bath for Clifton, with what happy feelings of escape!

Jane Austen, *letter,* 1808

The grand Head Quarters of Misery

James Beresford, *The Miseries of Human Life,* 1806

The Bath is a place of gallantry enough; expensive, and full of snares.

Daniel Defoe, *Moll Flanders,* 1722

A city of the Romans and of the rationalist eighteenth century, with something of a valley of oblivion in between.

G. K. Chesterton, *Illustrated London News,* 1925

Bath is a disappointment – cold, monotonous, bald, poor, and dead.

Mary Russell Mitford, *letter,* 1843

Do you know, I get so immoderately sick of Bath; your brother and I were agreeing this morning that, though it is vastly well to be here for a few weeks, we would not live here for millions.

Jane Austen, *Northanger Abbey,* 1817

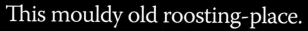

This mouldy old roosting-place.

Charles Dickens, *letter,* 1869

I never saw any place abroad that had more stinks and dirt in it than Bath.

Sarah, Duchess of Marlborough, *letter,* 1716

I hate the sight of the bygone assembly-rooms, and the Bath chairs trundling the dowagers about the streets.

Charles Dickens, *letter,* 1869

I think no place can be less agreeable; How d'ye do? is all one hears in the morning, and What is trumps? in the afternoon.

Elizabeth Montagu, *letter,* 1740

Its setting, in a bowl in the hills above the Avon River, is picturesque but soporific.

Jan Morris, *New York Times,* 1982

Great place to live – unless you live there.

Miles Kington, *The Independent,* 2005

Yes, thank you, I am quite well again; and if I had not a mind to continue so, I would not remain here a day longer, for I am tired to death of the place.

Horace Walpole, *letter,* 1766

A national hospital it may be; but one would imagine, that none but lunatics are admitted.

Tobias Smollett, *The Expedition of Humphry Clinker,* 1771

The Bath is sure of doing me some good, for I shall take great care of myself, for fear of being sent hither again.

Horace Walpole, *letter,* 1766

I like the place so little, that health itself could not draw me thither.

Alexander Pope, *letter,* 1739

The joy of leaving Bath produced half my cure, for I could not bear the place.

Horace Walpole, *letter,* 1766

Bath does not please me. After the great spectacle of the Abbey it seems to me incredibly dingy and wretched; and the infamous old men and youths carried in chairs and the mechanical carriages round the smoking baths horrify me, a horror not softened by the tender glances of certain old women clad in flounces supremely a la mode, who come and go eternally in this paradise of idlers and corpses.

William Beckford, *letter,* 1817

Anne disliked Bath, and did not think it agreed with her.

Jane Austen, *Persuasion,* 1817

They may say what they will, but
it does one ten times more good
to leave Bath than to go to it.

Horace Walpole, *letter,* 1766

Index

Visit our website and discover thousands of
other History Press books.

www.thehistorypress.co.uk